Business and Human Rights in Asia

James Gomez • Robin Ramcharan
Editors

Business and Human Rights in Asia

Duty of the State to Protect

palgrave
macmillan

Editors
James Gomez
Asia Centre
Bangkok, Thailand

Robin Ramcharan
Asia Centre
Bangkok, Thailand

ISBN 978-981-15-7272-2 ISBN 978-981-15-7273-9 (eBook)
https://doi.org/10.1007/978-981-15-7273-9

Cover illustration: © J Marshall - Tribaleye Images / Alamy Stock Photo

This Palgrave Macmillan imprint is published by the registered company Springer Nature Singapore Pte Ltd.
The registered company address is: 152 Beach Road, #21-01/04 Gateway East, Singapore 189721, Singapore

Preface

This book on Business and Human Rights (BHR) focuses on the duty of States in Asia to uphold international human rights standards in relation to business activities undertaken by business organisations in their jurisdictions so as to protect not only employees but also all stakeholders' value and supply chains. This book contributes to emerging analysis of BHR in Asia, which is seldom treated in the literature.

The focus on BHR is very timely in light of the unprecedented COVID-19 (coronavirus) global health pandemic that brought globalization to a halt. Governments worldwide struggled to provide health and financial support to their citizens as international trade and supply chains were disrupted which led to massive unemployment and hardships for workers, especially in the informal sector. National emergency measures to battle the virus contributed to this dire situation by limiting basic rights, such as freedom of assembly and of movement.

Asia has witnessed over recent years a surge in interest in BHR. International and domestic concern for the protection of fundamental human rights has led States to pay attention to BHR. This occurs as the region becomes increasingly interdependent, with trans-national corporations playing a greater role in domestic and international society through their business activities. Governments' commercial activities, notably military activities are also of concern. These concerns are rendered more acute in the context of the regression in democracy and rights across the region.

The purpose of the book, especially in the latter context, is to keep the spotlight on the duty of States to protect human rights and to hold business organisations accountable for existing commitments under international human rights law and domestic law. It examines international norms on BHR as well as regional policies and practices. While business organisations must 'respect' fundamental human rights, Governments have a duty to protect and to ensure that remedies are provided to victims. Authors offer critiques of BHR centred policies by states in the region. They also suggest avenues through which BHR can have a positive impact on advancing human rights in Asia.

Innovative topics are treated, such as the rights challenges amidst the construction of highly connected 'smart cities', the place of ethical consumption and the need for greater research in this area, and the development of human rights management systems within business organisations.

For this book on BHR, prior mapping took place through dedicated roundtable discussions, interactions with BHR experts and practitioners, participation in United Nations workshops on BHR and an international conference on BHR at Asia Centre in July 2018.

This book is the latest Asia Centre exploration of human rights protection in the region. The Centre will continue to explore protection challenges as it probes the human rights architecture and mechanisms in Southeast Asia and beyond.

Bangkok, Thailand

James Gomez
Robin Ramcharan

Acknowledgements

This book is part of Asia Centre's ongoing work aimed at responding to the changing global human rights landscape and its impact on the region. It involved ongoing conversations with academics, civil society activists, diplomats, professional staff in international non-governmental organizations, officials from the Association of Southeast Asian Nations, representatives from AICHR, NHRIs and the United Nations about the state of human rights protection in Southeast Asia.

The conversations centred around the responsibility of business entities for upholding human rights standards and the duty of governments to ensure that they do so. Collectively, the conversations identified a need not only for the business community to enhance their human rights policies and capacities throughout their operations and supply chains, but also for governments to adopt national policies that serve to uphold their existing commitments under international human rights law.

One way to explore this was to undertake a systematic analysis of the record of Asian governments on business and human rights. Hence the need for evidence-based research by scholars and practitioners to take stock of their track records as revealed in their national policies, reports by regional watch-dogs, submissions by civil society organisations and national reports in the Universal Periodic Review process of the United Nations Human Rights Council.

Thanks, therefore, are due to the authors who marshalled their experiences into these chapters and who were diligent in revising and editing their submissions within a short time frame. Their insights point towards the need to hold governments to honour the state's duty to protect and especially during periods of crisis such as the COVID-19 pandemic. The prolonged COVID-19 crisis has also had a negative impact on the advancement of the business and human rights agenda as Governments deploy emergency measures that negatively impact businesses operations and cause economic and social hardships.

Thanks are also in order to The Taiwan Foundation for Democracy for its generous support, to the team at Asia Centre: Yawee Butrkrawee for his assistance in the editorial work and Patcharee Rattanarong, for her administrative support. The Centre is appreciative of its short-term consultants, interns and volunteers who helped put together the BHR conference and the subsequent publication.

We are grateful to Palgrave Macmillan who came onboard for the publication and distribution of the international edition of the book and we look forward to working together to bring out a regional edition of the book for distribution.

We are pleased to bring out this publication at this critical juncture in regional and international affairs, when national human rights protection systems hold the key to the advancement of human rights and yet are being severely challenged by the evolving political forces in the region and beyond.

Contents

Notes on Contributors

Nukila Evanty is a legal researcher at research centre Faculty of Law, Jember University Indonesia, and visiting lecturer on human rights and social justice issues. Currently, Nukila is leading some organisations such as RIGHTS Asia, Women Working Group (WWG) and Amcolabora Institute-a think tank organisation. Graduated from Faculty of Law, Diponegoro University in Semarang, Indonesia; Faculty of Law, Groningen University in The Netherlands, and Faculty of Law, University of New South Wales in Australia.

Nurul Ghufron is a lecturer and Dean of Law Faculty of Jember State University, East Java Indonesia, Doctor of Law on criminal responsibility and human rights, resource person and trainer of regulations at government institutions and research institutes in Indonesia. He has published several books and journal in legal issues. He was appointed as the Commissioner of KPK (Corruption Eradication Commission) in 2019.

James Gomez is Regional Director, Asia Centre (Bangkok, Thailand and Johor Bahru, Malaysia)—a not-for-profit organisation that seeks to create human rights impact in the region. Dr.Gomez is a communications and human rights specialist having served in different academic and leadership roles in the last 25 years working for international NGOs, intergovernmental organizations, public and private universities, research institutes and think-tanks. He represents the Centre in media and public speaking engagements and builds relationships with key stakeholders around the world.

Emily Klukas is driven by a strong, personal commitment to community-driven collaborative solutions around human rights and stigmatized illnesses and identities. She currently provides consulting services working primarily with multi-national corporations and civil society organizations. Previously, she served as deputy director of research and evaluation supporting community-designed initiatives and co-directed a national capacity building program for AIDS service organizations. She completed her bachelor's degree in child psychology at the University of Minnesota, her master's degree in international community public health at New York University, and is a member of the Delta Omega Honorary Society for Public Health.

Min Zar Ni Lin is a Deputy Director of Research for Centre for Economic and Social Development (CESD), a Myanmar think tank focuses on research and advocacy. He holds a master's degree in economics from Chiang Mai University, Thailand and was a Fellow of the Sustainable Minerals Institute, the University of Queensland. He had worked as a Deputy National Coordinator at the Myanmar Extractive Industries Transparency Initiative National Coordination Office, to promote transparency and accountability in the extractive sector of Myanmar. His research interest is in the area of labour market, migration and natural resource governance.

Matthew Mullen is a researcher and international consultant specializing in business and human rights. Mullen recently concluded his tenure as Lecturer at the Institute of Human Rights and Peace Studies (IHRP), Mahidol University Thailand. Mullen is the founder of Article 30, a research and advising group dedicated to strengthening the human rights-base of the business and human rights field.

Hanh Nguyen is a researcher at the Mixed Migration Center—Danish Refugee Council. Previously, she was a researcher at the G7 and G20 Research Group in Canada and the Centre for Economic and Social Development in Myanmar, a policy consultant at the Global Green Growth Institute in Vietnam and a student consultant with the European Bank for Reconstruction and Development in Hungary. Her research incorporates both quantitative and qualitative approaches, with a strong emphasis on reflecting pressing development and policy issues. Hanh recently won the Decent Work prize of the ILO for the best research paper by an emerging scholar.

Samukelisiwe Ngwenya has background knowledge in labour migration, responsible supply chain in the garment and textile sector, global migration trends, and advocacy in gender inclusive policy making. Previously, she worked as the Research and Policy Coordinator for the Center for Economic and Social Development in Myanmar overseeing research portfolios on migration and development and the relationship between foreign direct investment and decent labour. She is proficient in bringing together research and policy advocacy in bridging existing gaps. Currently, she is a Masters candidate at the Yenching Academy of Peking University in Beijing, China. Her regional research focus is on Chinese investment in the garment and textile industry in East Africa and Southeast Asia.

Daniel Polomski is currently enrolled in the PhD in Human Rights and Peace Studies program at Mahidol University's Institute of Human Rights and Peace Studies. He has a background in Southeast Asian studies and human rights. His research focuses on BHR and mega-sporting events centering on the value chains of SMEs. He is currently involved in various research projects on human rights disclosure and ethical consumerism. As co-founder of Football Fans Asia—a local media production start-up—he develops football-related content for the sports community in Southeast Asia.

Iman Prihandono is Head of International Law Department at Faculty of Law Universitas Airlangga, Surabaya, Indonesia. He teaches Public International Law, and International Human Rights Law. Iman has extensively published articles on the area of business and human rights. Most recently, he published "Policy Paper on the Implementation of UNGPs in Indonesia", a project funded by the European Union, INFID, IGCN and Oxfam.

Robin Ramcharan is Executive Director, Asia Centre, Bangkok, Thailand. He specialises in human rights, intellectual property and security issues in Southeast Asia. Dr. Ramcharan is also Professor of International Relations at Mahidol University International College, Thailand with an extensive teaching and publications record. He has worked over the past two decades in the not-for-profit sector, international organisations, the private sector and in research institutes and think tanks. In Bangkok, Dr. Ramcharan represents the Centre in interaction with external partners and oversees the various research and publication projects.

Fajri Hayu Religi is a Researcher at the Institute for Responsible Business in Surabaya, Indonesia. She obtain her LL.B in International Law from the Faculty of Law Airlangga University.

Robert Sadleir is the Founder of the Initiative to Value Human Life: www.IVHL.org. He commenced his career with the United Nations in humanitarian operations in Ethiopia, Nepal, and Bosnia. A former head of sustainable infrastructure at Lloyd's Register in London, he has worked as a technical expert for British Standards to develop standards on sustainable communities and SMART cities for the International Standards Organisation (ISO).He has a Bachelor of Economics (University of Sydney), a Masters in International Relations (University of Geneva), and a Masters in Theological Studies (Harvard University). He completed the 'Peacekeeping, Staff, and Command Course' at the Lester B. Pearson Canadian International Peacekeeping Training Centre in Nova Scotia. He received the Humanitarian Overseas Service Medal from Australia for his work in the Balkans in the 1990s.

Socheata Sao is a law PhD candidate at Monash University, Australia, and a member of the Global Business and Human Rights Scholars Association. Her thesis explores avenue(s) for access to effective remedies for individuals and communities affected by arbitrary land takings in ASEAN. Socheata obtained her LL.M. in International Commercial Law (Distinction) from the University of Kent, United Kingdom. She used to work as a legal associate in a leading regional law firm in Phnom Penh and later as Deputy-Director of the English Language-Based Bachelor of Law Programme at the Royal University of Law and Economics where she obtained her LL.B.

Matthew Storey is the Director of the Office of the Victorian Aboriginal Heritage Council. Dr Storey is a lawyer who has practised in the areas of Indigenous land rights and mining for over twenty years. He has published widely in this field also. He has worked variously for Indigenous organisations and government and was formerly Associate Professor and Head of Law at Charles Darwin University (CDU) in the Northern Territory. He continues as a University Fellow at CDU and an Honorary Senior Fellow at the University of Melbourne Law School.

Saul Takahashi is Professor of Human Rights and Peace Studies at Osaka Jogakuin University. He has held positions in Amnesty International and in several UN organisations, and from 2014 to 2019 was the Japan Representative of the Business & Human Rights Resource Centre. Saul holds an LLM in international human rights law from the University of Essex and is the author of several books, including Civil and Political Rights in Japan: a Tribute to Sir Nigel Rodley (Routledge), Human Rights and Drug Control: the False Dichotomy (Hart Publishing) and Human Rights, Human Security, and State Security: the Intersection (Praeger Publishing, ed.).

Michael White is a human rights lawyer, advisor and advocate. He has a Masters in International Law and has worked in private practice, government organisations, international organisations and led human rights NGOs. Michael was the Senior Legal Adviser at the New Zealand Human Rights Commission for over a decade. He has advised business, government and international organisations on the scope and application of the UN Guiding Principles on Business and Human Rights. His current research interests include business and human rights, disability and accessibility issues, human rights in disasters and indigenous rights. He is an expert in the international human rights system and its mechanisms.

Jonathan Woodier A media and communications professional specializing in brand building and organizational transformation Jonathan is currently Group Head of Employee Communications for International Personal Finance PLC. Prior to joining IPF, Jonathan was a professor at the Department of Global Media and Communications Arts at Woosong University, South Korea. An Associate Fellow of the Strategic Communications Centre at King's College, London, and a member of the advisory board of the Asia Centre in Thailand, Jonathan was also the Primary Investigator on a research project funded by the Korean Government, "The Internet of Other People's Things: Dealing with the pathologies of a digital world". With a background in multi-platform journalism Jonathan has a proven track record of working with major brands, including Citibank and Santander, in Asia Pacific, EMEA and the Americas. Jonathan was awarded a PhD. in 2008, and the work was later published as a book, The Media and Political Change in Southeast Asia: Karaoke Culture and the Evolution of Personality Politics.

Andreas Zingerle is a media artist and researcher from Austria. He teaches at University of Bergen and worked in the past on art installations exploring creative misuse of technology and alternative ways of Human Computer Interaction. Since 2004 he has taken part in international conferences and exhibitions, among others Ars Electronica, ISEA, Siggraph, Japan Media Arts Festival, File, WRO Biennale. Together with Linda Kronman he started an artistic collaboration called 'KairUs'.

Abbreviations

AI	Artificial Intelligence
AICHR	ASEAN Intergovernmental Commission on Human Rights
AMS	ASEAN Member States
APF	Asia Pacific Forum
ARP	Accountability and Remedy Project
ASEAN	Association of Southeast Asian Nations
BHR/UNGPs	The United Nations Human Rights Council's Guiding Principles on Business and Human Rights
BKPM	Investment Coordinating Board (*Badan Koordinasi Penanaman Modal*)
BO	Beneficiary Owner
BPS	Central Bureau of Statistic (*Badan Pusat Statistik*)
CAO	Compliance Advisor Ombudsman
CCHR	Cambodian Centre for Human Rights
CCTV	Closed-circuit television
CESD	The Centre for Economic and Social Development, Myanmar
CLEC	Community Legal Education Centre
CLMV	Cambodia, Laos, Myanmar and Vietnam
CRCCF	Central Reinvestigation Committee for Confiscated Farmlands and Other Lands
CSO	Civil Society Organisations (CSOs)
DMU	District Mediation Units
ELC	Economic Land Concession
ERI	EarthRight International
ESG	Environmental and Social Governance
EU	European Union
FFP	Forest Peoples Programme

FIC	Farmland Investigation Commission
FIHRRST	Foundation for International Human Rights Reporting Standards
FPIC	Free, prior and informed consent
FTUB	The Federation of Trade Unions of Burma
GAD	General Administration Department
GAR	Golden Agri-Resources
GR	Government Regulation
HAGL	Hoàng Anh Gia Lai
HGU	Land Concession for Business Purposes (*Hak Guna Usaha*)
HRN	Human Rights Now
ICC	International Criminal Court
ICESCR	The International Covenant on Economic, Social and Cultural Rights
ICJ	International Commission of Jurists
ICT	Information and Communications Technology
IDI	Inclusive Development International
IDR	Indonesian Rupiah
IFC	International Finance Cooperation
IFEZ	Incheon Free Economic Zone
ILO	The International Labour Organization
IMG	Independent Mediation Group
IOM	International Organization for Migration
IoT	Internet of Things
ITUC	The International Trade Union Confederation
LIWG	Land Information Working Group
LUMCC	Land Utilization Management Central Committee
MCT	The South Korean Ministry of Construction and Transportation
MGMA	The Myanmar Garment Manufacturers Association
MIC	The South Korean Ministry of Information and Communication
MNC	Multinational Corporation
MR	Ministerial Regulation
MRLG	Mekong Region Land Governance
NALDR	National Authority for Land Conflict Resolution
NAP	National Action Plan
NCA	The South Korean National Computerization Agency
NGO	Non-governmental organisation
NGOF	NGO Forum on Cambodia
NHRC	National Human Rights Commission
NII	Korean National Information Infrastructure

NIS	Korean National Basic Information System
OECD	Organisation for Economic Cooperation and Development
OHCHR	Office of the United Nations High Commissioner for Human Rights
PR	Presidential Regulation
R.1, R.2	Respondent 1, Respondent 2, etc.
RFID	Radio frequency identification
ROK	Republic of Korea (South Korea)
RSPO	Roundtable on Sustainable Palm Oil
SCR	Supreme Court Regulation
SDGs	Sustainable Development Goals
SSB	Social Security Scheme
TNI	Transnational Institute
UN HRC	United Nations Human Rights Council
UN	United Nations
UNDP	United Nations Development Programme
UNGP	United Nations Guiding Principles on Business and Human Rights
USD	United States Dollar
VFV	Vacant, Fallow and Virgin
VMU	Village Mediation Units
VRG	Vietnam Rubber Group
YUE	Yangon University of Economics

List of Charts

List of Tables

CHAPTER 1

Introduction: Business and Human Rights Asia—Examining the Duty of the State to Protect

James Gomez and Robin Ramcharan

Introduction

This study of business and human rights (BHR) draws attention to the duty of States in Asia to uphold international human rights standards in relation to business activities undertaken by business organisations, including government-linked companies, in their jurisdictions. These standards are well defined in the United Nations (UN) Guiding Principles on Business and Human Rights (UNGPs), which were developed by Professor John Ruggie and adopted unanimously by the Human Rights Council in June 2011. The UNGPs, rooted in international human rights law, stipulate the duty of States to protect (Pillar 1), the responsibilities of business organisations (Pillar 2) and the duty to provide remedies for violations of rights (Pillar 3).

The focus on human rights dimensions of business activities, which moves away from voluntarist corporate social responsibility (CSR) rooted

J. Gomez (✉) • R. Ramcharan
Asia Centre, Bangkok, Thailand
e-mail: james@asiacentre.org; robin@asiacentre.org

J. Gomez, R. Ramcharan (eds.), *Business and Human Rights in Asia*,
https://doi.org/10.1007/978-981-15-7273-9_1

in the early years of the Cold War era (Spector 2008), was placed on the UN agenda due to the "growing reach and impact of business enterprises [which] have given rise to a debate about the roles and responsibilities of such actors with regard to human rights" (OHCHR 2019). The role of non-state, multinational corporations (MNCs) in international relations has been on the UN and academics' agendas since the early 1970s. During 1973, an Eminent Persons group met under the auspices of the UN Economic and Social Council to debate the role of MNCs. By then Nye noted some 200 giant multinational enterprises or large clusters operating in some 20 countries as well as projections that some 300 would dominate industrial production by the end of the twentieth century (Nye 1974). There are now thousands of enterprises operating globally and their impact on all aspects of human rights is well documented, including on the human rights of individuals and their communities. From an initial concentration on States, human rights activists turned their attention turned to the human rights dimensions of business corporations, well beyond corporate social responsibility and have moved on to consider, for example, the corporate responsibility to respect (RtR) human rights in light of jurisprudence to improve UNGP framework in relation to affiliates of parent companies or to the human rights responsibilities of State-owned enterprises (Mares 2010; Backer 2017). Concerns of BHR have extended to the environment, economic, cultural, and social rights, debt relief, and access to affordable medicines. This expansion of BHR has been fueled by the "discovery" of CSR by legal scholars in the past decade (Santoro 2015, p. 157).

Professor John Ruggie's UNGPs is at the forefront of international efforts to overcome the 'accountability gap' and reflects a convergence of understandings about the rights responsibilities of corporations. A variety of international mechanisms have addressed BHR, notbaly the Working Group on Business and Human Rights, Special Procedures of the Human Rights Council, the UN Global Compact (Nagafi-Nejad 2008), the Organisation for Economic Cooperation and Development (OECD) (2011), the Open-ended intergovernmental working group on transnational corporations and other business enterprises with respect to human rights[1] and the International Labour Organisation's (ILO) Tripartite

[1]The Open-ended group was created by Human Rights Council Resolution 26/9 of 2014, with the mandate to "to elaborate an international legally binding instrument to regulate, in international human rights law, the activities of transnational corporations and other business enterprises." OHCHR (2019), https://www.ohchr.org/EN/HRBodies/HRC/WGTransCorp/Pages/IGWGOnTNC.aspx

MNE Declaration) National Human Rights Institutions (NHRIs) also have a powerful role to play in advancing BHR and Haasz argues that, as domestic rights bodies, they are well placed to advance the UNGPs (Haász 2013). Ford has noted that the period "2015–25 will see fairly sustained pressure for the adoption of measures to narrow the 'governance gap' between corporate influence and accountability, including with regard to business respect for human rights" (Ford 2015).

Asia and Business and Human Rights

Asia's uptake of the UNGPs has been slow in contrast to other parts of the world but it has picked up steam in recent years, at least rhetorically. To give effect to the UNGPs 21 States around the world (19 in Europe and 2 in Latin America) had adopted NAPs at the time of writing while 23 (were in the process of developing NAPS) including Azerbaijan, Japan, Jordan, Malaysia, Mongolia, Myanmar, Thailand. The latter was portrayed 'progressively' as the current military dictatorship collaborated with the UN Working Group and announced the development of a NAP in 2018. Nine other States where a National Human Rights Institution (NHRI) or civil society has begun pushing for NAPs included India, Indonesia, Japan, Republic of Korea and The Philippines (OHCHR 2019).

The rhetorical uptake occurs amidst a regression in rights in Southeast Asia and a general discomfort with open discussion about human rights across the wider region. This is exacerbated by the COVID-19 health crisis that has led Southeast Asian countries to pass special temporary laws and formed committees to combat the virus. However, these laws hold the potential to suppress assemblies, freedom of expression, elections and meetings of parliaments (Gomez and Ramcharan 2020).

It is not surprising that this context is propitious for States to engage with the UNGPs, a soft approach to rights advancement, while sternly resisting harder legal commitments that they already hold or continue to resist under international human rights law. It is natural therefore that the spotlight be turned onto the duty of States in Asia under Pillar 1.

It is especially important to shine this spotlight amidst the COVID-19 global pandemic, which has disrupted international trade and supply chains resulting in the suspension of business operations and a dramatic rise in unemployment. The Government's duty to protect their citizens from health and economic hazards was severely tested. This situation will perdure post-COVID-19 crisis as businesses and national economies try to re-start. A serious economic downturn is expected by major international financial institutions such as the Asian Development Bank, the International Monetary Fund and the World Bank (Seawright 2019).

A Cross-Disciplinary Field

An emerging literature on BHR has led to lively academic debate on holding corporate (non-state) actors' responsible for violations of human rights is found across disciplines. Santoro has noted that BHR is a multidisciplinary and interdisciplinary academic field drawing from fields such as business ethics, law and the social sciences, and a social, economic and political justice movement involving governments and intergovernmental institutions, as well as indigenous peoples, nongovernmental organizations, and other civil society actors. BHR advocates seek, at a minimum, to hold businesses accountable for their own direct human rights violations and impacts along their entire value chains (Santoro 2015).

The richness, diversity and complexity of BHR is evident in the variety of themes that have emerged in BHR discussions. Martin and Bravo (2015) have noted that these include: what philosophies and norms are afoot in BHR; how can they be enforced and implemented; the role of hard law and soft law; the participation of multiple stakeholders and not only States in interpreting those norms and laws; the legal personality of corporate entities under international law versus their lack of international personality under international law (especially in light of the power disparities between powerful corporations and weak states); the credibility, legitimacy and impact of the UN BHR project; the adequacy of the international human rights construct (moral and legal); the scope of the relationship between business and human rights; the need to resort to domestic law to overcome shortcomings of international law; the role of the consumer in incentivizing good behaviour; the need to focus on all rights, not only civil and political; and the multidisciplinary nature of BHR as a project and as an academic enterprise. Broad surveys of BHR have been undertaken by Sullivan and Robinson who usefully survey dilemmas and solutions to bridging business and human rights (Sullivan and Robinson 2003; Cragg 2012; Martin and Bravo 2015).

The core BHR issues and controversies, notes Santoro (2015, p. 158) center around two sets of questions: (1) Fairness and justice—on what basis, if any, can business be said to owe moral duties regarding human rights? How extensive are the human rights duties of business in situations where business has no direct or indirect connection to human rights violations by states?; (2) Implementation, public policy, and law: How might voluntary codes of conduct and other self-regulatory mechanisms serve to bring business behavior into greater alignment with human rights duties? (See George 2018) What role should private law, state action, the United Nations, or treaties play in promoting business adherence to human rights norms? Can indicators help to monitor corporate human rights conduct? (de Felice 2015).

Ruggie's UNGPs have been met with criticisms notably on alleged lack of moral foundation. In this vein, it is useful to note Hsieh's argument against assigning human rights obligations to multinational enterprises (MNEs) based on "Status egalitarianism"—"the ideal that all members of society stand as moral equals in relation to one another and that the state has a duty to recognize and protect that equal standing, not only in terms of its dealings with citizens but also in their dealings with one another." He argues for other ways of holding corporations to account because "[t]o assign human rights obligations to MNEs and their managers..., involves attributing to them a certain status that is at odds with the position that MNEs occupy in society as private, profit-seeking entities" (Hsieh 2015, p. 219).

Karp, however, has noted a basic starting point when considering the application of human rights standards to business entities (Karp 2014). The protection of human rights is a fundamental value for the individual and for the interests of society as a whole. Fundamental human rights norms are in international treaties and have often been incorporated in constitutional norms in national legal orders. Corporations are asked to comply with these minimum standards, even if they do not have the same duties as States. International lawyers have debated the legal responsibility of corporations for human rights violations, which starts with a consideration of their legal personality.

Cernic argues that "corporations have obligations in relation to the human rights of individuals. Human rights constitute a normative minimum or normative floor which corporations have to observe" (Cernic 2013, p. 12). Indeed, it would not be appropriate or desirable to hold that corporations have a duty to guarantee fair trials, or the right to life, for example. At the same time, as businesses can affect nearly all internationally recognized rights, limiting their applicability may be problematic. Amidst legal, doctrinal debates about subjectivity and legal personality in international law, it has been suggested that corporations can bear international rights and obligations (Clapham 2006), which seems to suggest that corporations have obligations under international human rights law. Other commentators have suggested the same (See Ratner 2001; See also Buhmann 2017 and Kinley 2017). Scholars point to the International Court of Justice's (ICJ) *Reparations for Injuries Advisory Opinion* that

> the subjects of law in any legal system are not necessarily identical in their nature or in the extent of their rights, and their nature depends upon the needs of the community. Throughout its history, the development of international law has been influenced by the requirements of international life, and the progressive increase in the collective activities of States has already given rise to instances of action upon the international plane by certain entities which are not States. (ICJ 1949)

In this line of reasoning corporations also have a limited number of rights and obligations under international law and they might be held accountable for human rights violations. Legal commentators have begun to argue that even in relation to the tricky issue of legal personality, it is no longer tenable that corporations are not subjects of international law and that they do have human rights obligations (Jagers 2002; Bonfanti 2019).

The preceding debate testifies to the insufficiency of voluntarist CSR, which exhibits a diversity of approaches that coexist in silos (Deva and Bilchitz 2013; Walker-Said 2015; Baumann-Pauly and Nolan (2016). Pending an international treaty on BHR, the probability of which faces great scepticism from Thielbörger and Ackermann (2017), Bernaz has called for overcoming the accountability gap and, like Amao, argues for more emphasis on corporate human rights responsibilities at home, in States and host States which will allow for the strongest possible control of corporations (Bernaz 2017; Amao 2011). Cernic and Ho (2015) examine the complexities of enforcing human rights standards and holding businesses accountable for human rights impacts, which includes Ford's contention that "there is insufficient evidence behind claims that a general international law duty now exists on states to regulate the human rights impacts of corporate nationals abroad" (Ford 2015, p. 2). Holding business organisations to account, argues Woods, requires deploying the full panoply of human rights—civil and political and economic, social and cultural—especially in relation to the environment, "prioritizing the historically oppressed, marginalized, and most vulnerable people" and "elevating self-determination, the first norm specified in the two foundational human rights Covenants" which entails emphasizing strategies of participation and empowerment (Woods 2011). Through examination of national jurisdictions—UK and US—Lara et al. (2015) examine how lawyers and courts might deal with issues such as extraterritoriality in transnational litigation brought against companies for human rights abuses abroad (See also Krajewski 2018; Ryngaert 2018).

Regional analyses have merged recently. An analysis was undertaken on European approaches to tackling the responsibilities of business which examined the role of European and domestic legislations of member states (Bonfanti ed. 2019; Gatto 2011; Rubio and Yiannibas 2017). Mohan and Morel (2015) provide an overview of BHR in ASEAN. It includes perspectives on the role of the State, gender, children's rights, dam projects in Lao PDR, CSR in the palm oil industry, mining industry, human rights audits, remedies and the right to development.

The need for academic and policy scrutiny of BHR in Asia is evident in Iman Prihandono's account of the impact of foriegn direct investment in Indonesia. While contributing to overall economic growth, he notes that "the activities of transnational corporations have been a reason for a number of violent conflicts. Indeed, as foreign direct investment inflow increases, conflicts between transnational corporations and local communities in Indonesia intensify" (Prihandono 2013, p. 1). He argued for a strong human rights accountability mechanism for transnational corporations. Nguyen examines hydropower dam construction in Vietnam and found that "the people and community being displaced due to the construction of the dam have been facing a number of human rights concerns, including the violation of particular rights such as the right to livelihood/ food security, right to land, and the right to culture" (Nguyen 2016).

A solution proposed by Mohan, and discussed in Chap. 2 of this work, is the development of national action plans (NAPs) for the ASEAN region grounded in the Vienna Declaration and Programme for Action ("VDPA"[2] and premised on the UNGPs. He notes that given the onus of protection

[2] Article 71 of VDPA states that: "The World Conference on Human Rights recommends that each State consider the desirability of drawing up a national action plan identifying steps whereby that State would improve the promotion and protection of human rights."

that falls on Governments, "National and regional action plans in ASEAN should give due regard to issues that are underexplored in the global conversation about business and human rights, such as gender issues and concerns of emerging economies" (Mohan 2015). He called for a tailored, multi-stakeholder approach to developing NAPs, one that should be pursued through constructive engagement with business and might be titled "Responsible Business Conduct" as opposed to a NAP on "Business and Human Rights," given regional discomfort with the term "human rights" (Mohan 2015, p. 25). NAPs are not unique to the BHR context, but have been employed in other human rights areas.[3] Indonesia has adopted National Human Rights Action Plans.

The adoption of NAPS signals increasing recognition Governments must play a strong role in ensuring that corporations uphold their human rights responsibilities in the complex, modern world.

State Accountability in the Asia-Centred, Westphalia Order

As the centre of international politics and economics shifts to an Asia-centred and complex Westphalian Order, States still remain central actors amidst the rise of other entities, such as Transnational Corporations. In the period from Nye's reports to the UN in the early 1970s to Ruggie's UNGPs, 'complex interdependence' has intensified as the numbers and power of TNCs have increased dramatically (Keohane and Nye 2011). By 2006, the UN Conference on Trade and Development (UNCTAD) *Investment Brief* had noted 77,000 TNCs in the world, with preferred investment destinations including China, Hong Kong, Indonesia, Japan, Korea, Malaysia, Singapore and Taiwan. With the proliferation of multinational corporations in the world, it was noted a decade later that "currently multinational corporations are controlling more than ½ of international trade. Today, the number of parent TNCs is about 60 000, with about 500 000 branches being spread all over the world" (Kordos and Vojtovic 2016, p. 152). Particularly noteworthy is the presence of State-owned TNCs, which are active globally. UNCTAD's *World*

[3] Mohan notes The Philippines NAP on women, peace and security which implements the UN Security Council Resolutions 1325 and 1820 and Singapore's NAP on human trafficking which has led to the Anti-Human Trafficking Act, passed in Parliament in October 2014 (Mohan 2015, p. 26).

Investment Report for 2014, noted that "State-owned TNCs are FDI heavyweights". They were at least 550 State-owned TNCs from both developed and developing countries with over 15,000 foreign affiliates and foreign assets of over $2 trillion (UNCTAD 2014, p. viii). Their ability to affect rules of international and domestic society has been well noted as has their impact on the lives of people directly employed by them,[4] and within and across societies.

States, domestically and internationally, retain the primary responsibility for making and enforcing rules in this complex system, including ensuring compliance by non-state actors with international human rights norms. International relations theories on norms diffusion note a number of well-known ways that this has been achieved: through great powers (global or regional) seeking to spread such norms, through institutions (universal or regional) that hold their members accountable to rights-based behaviour and through socialization between actors in a society of states. Other such norm entrepreneurs are civil society organisations (CSOs), inclusive of think tanks like Asia Centre through its social impact initiatives.

The UNGPs on Business and Human Rights Guidelines[5] were developed at the United Nations and presented as a soft law tool for States to

[4] Apple, 66,000; Alphabet 69,953; Microsoft 114,000; Berkshire Hathaway, 360,000; Exxon Mobile, 73, 500; Amazon, 222,400; Facebook, 15,724; Johnson and Johnson 128,000; General Electric 333,000, China Mobile, 438,645. Alex Gray (2017) These are the world's 10 biggest corporate giants," World Economic Forum.

[5] See list on BHR Resource Centre Website: *Updated DIHR & ICAR toolkit on National Action Plans on business & human rights*, 2017; *Guidance on how to include human rights defenders in Natl. Action Plans on business & human rights*, ISHR & ICAR, Jun 2016; *Guidance on children's rights in Natl. Action Plans on business & human rights*, ICAR, DIHR & UNICEF, Nov 2015; *Guidance on National Action Plans on Business and Human Rights*, updated in Nov 2015, UN Working Group on Business and Human Rights; *DIHR & ICAR toolkit on National Action Plans on business & human rights*, Jul 2014; *10 Criteria for National Action Plans (NAPs) on Business and Human Rights*; *A Toolkit for the Development, Implementation, and Review of State Commitments to Business and Human Rights Frameworks*; UN Working Group on business & human rights: *Repository of State National Action Plans*; Centre for Applied Legal Studies (CALS), Wits University: *Centre for Applied Legal Studies & partner organizations to develop National Action Plan template to implement UN Guiding Principles*, 21 Nov 2013; Andreas Graf, swisspeace: "*Developing National Action Plans on Business and Human Rights*" [PDF], Apr 2013; Report on procedural aspects of developing national action plans on business & human rights in Netherlands, Norway, Spain & UK; European Group of National Human Rights Institutions: "*Implementing the UN Guiding Principles on Business and Human Rights: Discussion paper on national implementation plans for EU Member States*", Jun 2012. All available at: https://

sensitise business organisations on their human rights responsibilities, which States have the duty to uphold, and to cajole States into adopting enabling legislation known as NAPs. In the drafting of NAPs "the relevance of the UN guiding principles to the Asean Community is undeniable" (Nonthasoot 2017).

The duty of the State to protect human rights and regulate the behaviour of business organizations was the focal point of discussions at Asia Centre's International Conference on Business and Human Rights: Holding Governments Accountable (BHR Conference), in July 2018 in Bangkok. The focus on the duty of the State was deemed important by the conference participants as Asian countries increasingly consider the development of national action plans (NAPs) on BHR. Experts from around the world analysed the multifaceted linkages between business operations and international human rights norms but circled back to point to the duty of the State to protect. They highlighted policy and legislative challenges affecting the capacity of states to uphold such norms as stipulated in Pillar One of the UN Guiding Principles (UNGPs) on Business and Human Rights.

This qualitative study is the culmination of initial mapping of the BHR landscape in Asia through desk research, subsequent engagement with local stakeholders, followed by scholarly investigations by scholars and practitioners leading to an international conference, in which findings were analysed and debated.

Outline of Book and Chapters

The chapters in this volume, stemming from analysis conducted for Asia Centre's conference, are centred on the different ways that States in Asia have addressed their duties to address rights concerns in the BHR context. Indeed international human rights law prescribes to States the duty to respect, the duty to protect, and the duty to fulfil (SOURCE). Practitioners and scholars together undertook evidence-based research on this theme. The book focuses on Asia and the chapters together delve into key contemporary challenges—such as workers rights, women's rights, land grabbing, mining, forest depletion, indigenous peoples rights and remedies for violations—in a variety of countries (Australia, Cambodia, Indonesia,

www.business-humanrights.org/en/un-guiding-principles/implementation-tools-examples/implementation-by-governments/by-type-of-initiative/national-action-plans

Japan, Laos, the Philippines, Myanmar and Vietnam). Three innovative themes round off the work on BHR in the context of "smart cities" (notbaly in South Korea), on the relevance of ethical consumption in Southeast Asia and on the need to develop a preventive tool namely a human rights management system (HRMS) within a business enterprise.

In Chap. 2, Michael White examines critically a core challenge of the BHR agenda: the extent to which NAPs have had an impact on the realisation of rights. He also probes the appropriateness and accessibility of remedies where rights have been breached. He addresses the role of the state in Southeast Asia, where "[t]he "State-business nexus" is particularly important" as there is "a high degree of involvement of governments in business activities." He probes arenas where regulation and reform could be facilitated through NAPs: trade and investment agreements, the informal economy and conflict/post-conflict situations. White argues that NAPs hold the potential to embed culturally appropriate remedies frameworks—both judicial, non- judicial—into NAPs.

In Chap. 3, James Gomez and Robin Ramcharan survey the uptake in NAPs on Business and Human Rights in Asia and some policy challenges in elaborating NAPs. While NAPs are welcome in the BHR context, limitations and critiques based on existing action plans globally are outlined. A critical point for this work is that NAPs lack clarity on the roles and responsibilities of States and companies in relation to human rights violations. In addition, they note that NAPs should not provide a means for States to neglect their existing obligations under international law and that NAPs are not written in the same language of international human rights treaties, which would help to reconcile national plans with such law.

In Chap. 4, Nukila Evanty and Nurul Ghufron, while noting a regional trend in Southeast Asia of allegations of human rights violations by large scale corporate projects such as plantations, mining and other forms of extractive industries, they also note that state regulation, and national and regional mechanisms such as in ASEAN, are not strong enough to bring the enforce the responsibility of MNCs with regard to their human rights impacts. MNCs, they note, do not have expertise on human rights. They analyse this situation through using the case on forest and peatland fires across Sumatera Island and Kalimantan Island for several months over 2014–2015, to demonstrate the complexity of addressing responsibility given the involvement of multiple stakeholders from the local and national government, smallholder farmers, communities and multinational corporations (MNCs). They offer some pathways to remedy this situation.

In Chap. 5, Saul Takahashi examines human rights regulation of companies in Japan, which he argues is lacking. While the UNGPs are directed at States mostly, his analysis raises doubts about the willingness of the Japanese government to adhere to them. He notes a preference in Japan for non-binding standards and voluntary compliance. Despite laws and policies already adopted on business and human rights issues, he says they have been "little more than statements of intent, providing for non-binding targets, statements of principles and lacking penalties for non-compliance. He dissects the problem through case studies on karoshi (death by overwork), the timber industry and women's rights in Japan.

In Chap. 6, Matthew Storey shows the operation of two key principles of the UNGPs in the context of the extractive (mining) industry and its interactions with Indigenous Peoples, with case studies from Australia and the Philippines. Principles 11 and 13 of the UN Guiding Principles on Business and Human Rights (the Guiding Principles) set out two key responsibilities of businesses: to avoid causing or contributing to adverse human rights impacts through their own activities and to prevent or mitigate human rights impacts that are directly linked to their operations. He exposes the dilemma faced by mining corporations faced with potentially competing rights-based obligations. On the one hand mining corporations, particularly those operating in developing nations must accept the sovereignty of the host state and the latter's right to develop its natural resources. However, mining operations will frequently involve the interaction of some of the world's largest corporations with Indigenous peoples rights, notably Indigenous Peoples' right to Free Prior and Informed Consent (FPIC) in respect to the development of natural resources within their traditional lands. Storey explores the competing obligations of mining corporations to assist a state with the development of its natural resources on the one hand while respecting Indigenous Peoples' right to demand consent to such development. He suggests that the dilemma faced by mining corporations arises only when the state actor in question has not fully accepted its own human rights obligations.

Chapter 7, by Hanh Nguyen, Min Zar Ni Lin and Samukelisiwe Ngwenya, looks at government policy on minimum wage in Myanmar and its impact on precarious workers. A minimum wage has been acknowledged, in both literature and practice, as an important tool to redistribute wealth between different income groups, thus giving protection to the most vulnerable segment of labour in the society. It is generally recognized that besides employers, it is the duty of the state to have overall responsibility for upholding the rights of workers, especially precarious workers who are often exposed to the highest risk of employment insecurity. This chapter examines the motives of Myanmar's government for enforcing the minimum wage law in late 2015 and the effects of this policy on precarious workers in garment and food processing factories. Their research finds that the proportion of precarious workers in the survey reduced from 33.5 per cent to 7.4 per cent after the minimum wage enforcement.

In Chap. 8, the theme of remedies for violations of human rights by corporations, an emerging theme in the literature, is explored. Iman Prihandono and Fajri Hayu Religi, note the Indonesian government's commitment to implement UNGPs at the G20 Meeting in 2017. They show, however, that despite its role at international level in promoting UNGPS, the implementation of UNGPs at national level remains very slow. In 2017, the Indonesian Human Rights Commission took the initiative to launch the NAP on Business and Human Rights. Unfortunately, this NAP is difficult to be implemented because it does not come from the government. Nevertheless, they cite recent positive initiatives taken by the government and the Courts which may help to curb human rights violations by companies. Two instruments may help victims of corporate human rights abuse to seek remedies: The Supreme Court Regulation (SCR) 13/2016 on Procedures in Handling of Corporate Crime and the President Regulation (PR) 13/2018 on the Disclosure of Corporate Beneficiary Owner. They find that although the SCR 13/2016 may open the way to bring criminal cases against corporations, it remains difficult for the victims to obtain remedies. Likewise, despite the obligation for companies to disclose their beneficial ownerships under the PR 13/2018, the procedure to obtain information on beneficiary owners remains burdensome. They propose a revision to the SCR 13/2016.The prosecutor should be given authority to put restitution for the victims of corporate abuse in its indictment. Likewise, they propose revisions to the Indonesian corporate law to include an obligation for companies to disclose a beneficial owner, and to impose a sanction on companies which fail to comply.

In Chap. 9, Socheata Sao explores remedies in relation to land rights in the agri-business sector in Southeast Asia. Accusations of business-related human rights abuses, particularly in relation to land, are rampant in the Association of Southeast Asian Nations (ASEAN), especially in Cambodia, Laos, Myanmar and Vietnam (CLMV). In response, she notes that there have been continuous efforts by ASEAN Member States (AMS) through regulatory reforms and various attempts over the last several years by relevant stakeholders within ASEAN, including businesses, to address the problems and foster responsible business conduct. These attempts, while providing some relief, are not yet adequate in remediating the wrongs perpetrated upon the people and communities who are adversely affected by business-related human rights violations, including land rights abuses. In the meantime, there remains a region-wide lacuna in access to remedy for victims to seek justice and redress.

An original Chap. 10 by Jonathan Woodier and Andreas Zingerle examines the management and sustainability of urban areas which they argue is one of the most critical challenges our society faces today. The massive implementation of networked sensors and Internet of Things infrastructure in hyper-connected urban environments, pave the way to 'smarter cities'. State city planners and commercial organizations promise improved living standards, optimizing efficiency, sustainable development, Eco-friendliness and personal security in a 4th generation of smart cities, where "Imagination Becomes Reality". They argue that in a highly-urbanised future 'smart' living will test the UN Guiding Principles on Business and Human Rights as never before, as the business and the state collide with the citizen in the new electronic polis, sometimes in collusion, but all too often in a mutually agreed hand-off of governance and responsibilities. Decoding the visions of ongoing smart city initiatives in East Asia shows what concerns and consequences the citizens may face in the near future, the importance of informal socio-economic activities, citizen agency and the emerging inadequacy of the normative principles of human rights.

In Chap. 11, Daniel Polomski, Emily Klukas and Matthew Mullen turn the spotlight onto the consumer. They ask: Could ethical consumption be a catalyst for the human rights agenda in Southeast Asia? They argue for the pursuit of an empirical understanding of ethical consumption in Southeast Asia through the lens of an ecological systems framework. They posit the need to understand how consumers fit into the business ecosystem. An ecological approach attempts to account for the collective interactions between personality, culture, capabilities, community, institutions, legislation, legitimacy, markets, the media, civil society, regional bodies and international bodies. Operationally, this means that when designing and conducting research, studies should account for interacting levels of the business ecosystem: the individual, microsystem, mesosystem, exosystem, macrosystem and chronosystem. It is not necessary for ethical consumption as a strategy in the region to follow the path of the West. Rather, through a mix of empirical research that tests locally-relevant hypotheses and strategies within the reality of the ecosystems of the regions, a unique approach may arise to facilitate and support ethical consumption, ultimately advancing human rights.

Finally, in an innovative Chap. 12 by Robert Sadlier argues that in order to achieve the goals of Pillar 1, it is necessary to develop a human rights management system (HRMS) within business organisations. He argues that an HRMS would reduce reliance on the State and government institutions in enforcing human rights, which is premised on the inability of States to fulfill their duties under human rights law. This is partly due to the all too close relationships between Governments and companies in Asia, where state-directed capitalism prevails. Developing an HRMS, he asserts, begins by asking "How do companies value a human life?"

Conclusion

A concluding Chap. 13 reiterates major findings and explores further avenues for research on the duty of governments to protect human rights by making sure that business entities uphold their human rights responsibilities and are pursued for any violations. This is especially pertinent amidst the COVID-19 crisis and the difficult aftermath.

Overall, the authors in this book examine the role of States in Asia in advancing the BHR agenda and in so doing, upholding human rights standards. While TNCs have their role to play, Governments remain central to protection. This book examines the multi-faceted norms, policies and practices on BHR, that impact on human rights protection.

References

AICHR (2014) *ASEAN Baseline Study on Corporate Social Responsibility and Human Rights*. Jakarta AICHR. Avialable at https://aichr.org/wp-content/uploads/2019/01/AICHRs_Thematic_Study_on_CSR_and_Human_Rights_in_ASEAN.pdf

Alex Gray (2017) "These are the world's 10 biggest corporate giants," Geneva: World Economic Forum. Available at https://www.weforum.org/agenda/2017/01/worlds-biggest-corporate-giants/

Backer, Larry (2017) "The Human Rights Obligations of State-Owned Enterprises: Emerging Conceptual Structures and Principles in National and International Law and Policy," Vanderbilt Journal of Transnational Law, Vol. 50, No. 4, pp. 827–888.

Baumann-Pauly, Dorothée, Justine Nolan (2016). Business and Human Rights: From Principles to Practice 1st Edition. Routledge.

Bernaz, Nadia (2017) *Business and Human Rights: History, Law and Policy*—Bridging the Accountability Gap (Human Rights and International Law) 1st Edition. London and New York: Routledge.

Blecher Lara, Nancy Kaymar Stafford, Gretchen C. Bellamy (Eds) (2015) Corporate Responsibility for Human Rights Impacts: New Expectations and Paradigms Paperback. American Bar Association.

Bonfanti, Angelica (2019) Business and Human Rights in Europe: International Law Challenges. Routledge.

Buhmann, Karin (2017) *Changing Sustainability Norms through Communication Processes: The Emergence of the Business and Human Rights Regime as Transnational Law*, Cheltenham, Edward Elgar Publishers

Clapham, Andrew (2006) Human Rights Obligations of Non-State Actors. Oxford University Press

Cragg, Wesley (2012) Business and Human Rights. Edward Elgar Publishing.

de Felice, Damiano (2015) "Business and Human Rights Indicators to Measure the Corporate Responsibility to Respect: Challenges and Opportunities," *Human Rights Quarterly*, Vol. 37 (2015), pp. 511–555.

Deva, Surya and Bilchitz, David (2013) Human Rights Obligations of Business: Beyond the Corporate Responsibility to Respect. Cambridge University Press.

Ford, Jolyon (2015) Business and Human Rights Bridging the Governance Gap. Chatham House for the Royal Institute of International Affairs.

Gatto, Alexandra (2011) Multinational Enterprises and Human Rights: Obligations Under EU Law and International Law. Edward Elgar

Gomez, James and Ramcharan, Robin (2020) "Coronavirus and Democracy in Southeast Asia." Bangkok Post, 1 April Available: https://www.bangkokpost.com/opinion/opinion/1890655/coronavirus-and-democracy-in-southeast-asia

Haász, Veronika (2013) "The Role of National Human Rights Institutions in the Implementation of the UN Guiding Principles," Human Rights Review, Vol. 14, pp. 165–187

Hsieh, Nien-he (2015) Should Business Have Human Rights Obligations? Journal of Human Rights. Vol, 14, pp. 218–236

International Court of Justice (1949) Advisory Opinion of April 11, 1949 on Reparation For Injuries Suffered In The Service Of The United Nations, *Reports Of Judgments, Advisory Opinions And Orders*. Available at https://www.icj-cij.org/files/case-related/4/004-19490411-ADV-01-00-EN.pdf

Jagers, Nicola (2002) Corporate Human Rights Obligations: in Search of Accountability. Antwerpen, Oxford, New York: Intersentia.

Jernej Letnar Cernic (2013) "Corporations and Human Rights: Towards Binding International Legal Obligations," in *Business and Human Rights*, Manoj Kumar Sinha (Ed.), New Delhi: Sage.

Černič, Letnar and Ho, Tara Van (Editors) (2015). Human Rights and Business: Direct Corporate Accountability for Human Rights. Wolf Legal Publishers

Karp, David (2014) Responsibility for Human Rights: Transnational Corporations in Imperfect States. Cambridge University Press.

Krajewski, M. (2018) The State Duty To Protect Against Human Rights Violations Through Transnational Business Activities, Deakin Law Review, Vol. 23, pp. 13–39

Keohane, Robert O. and Nye, Joseph S. Jr (2011) Power and Interdependence. Longmann

Kinley, David. (Ed.) (2017) *Human Rights and Corporations.* Milton Park and New York, Routledge.

Mahdev Mohan and Cynthia Morel (2015) Business and Human Rights in Southeast Asia: Risk and the Regulatory Turn. Routledge.

Marcel Kordos and Sergej Vojtovic "Transnational corporations in the global world economic environment," Procedia—Social and Behavioral Sciences 230 (2016) 150–158

Mares, Radu (2010), "A Gap In The Corporate Responsibility To Respect Human Rights," Monash University Law Review (Vol 36, No 3), 51.

Martin, Jena and Bravo, Karen E. (2015) The Business and Human Rights Landscape: Moving Forward, Looking Back. Cambridge University Press.

Mohan, Mahadev (2015) "Corporate Accountability in Southeast Asia: National Action Plans for Responsible Business Conduct under International Law," Vill JEAIL 1, pp. 9–28.

Nagafi-Nejad, Tagi (2008). *The UN and Trans National Corporations: From Code of Conduct to Global Compact.* University of Indiana Press.

Nguyen, Thi Thanh Hai (2016) "Business and Human Rights in Viet Nam The Human Rights Implication of Involuntary Resettlements for Hydro Power Dams," Asia-pacific Journal on Human Rights And The Law Vol. 17 pp. 42–53

Nonthasoot, Seree (2017) "Thai action plan a step to rights protection by business," Bangkok Post, 28 January 2018. https://www.bangkokpost.com/opinion/opinion/1188481/thai-action-plan-a-step-to-rights-protection-by-business.

Nye Jr., Joseph (1974) "Multinational Corporations in World Politics," Foreign Affairs, Vol. 53, No. 1 (Oct., 1974), pp. 153–175

OECD (2011) OECD Guidelines for Multinational Enterprises, OECD Publishing. http://dx.doi.org/10.1787/9789264115415-en

OHCHR (2019) State national action plans on Business and Human Rights. Available at https://www.ohchr.org/EN/Issues/Business/Pages/NationalActionPlans.aspx

Olufemi Amao (2011) Corporate Social Responsibility, Human Rights and the Law: Multinational Corporations in Developing Countries (Routledge Research in Corporate Law) 1st Edition

Prihandono, Iman (2013) "Transnational Corporations and Human Rights Violations in Indonesia," Australian Journal of Asian Law, 2013, Vol 14 No 1, pp. 1–23

Ratner, Stephen (2001) "Corporations and Human Rights: A theory of Legal Responsibility," *Yale Law Journal*, Vol 111, pp. 443–545.

Rubio, Juan José Álvarez, Katerina Yiannibas (2017). Human Rights in Business: Removal of Barriers to Access to Justice in the European Union. Routledge.

Ryngaert, Cedric (2018) "Accountability of Multinational Corporations for Human Rights Abuses," Utrecht Law Review, Volume 14, Issue 2, 2018, pp. 1–5

Santoro, Michael (2015) "Business and Human Rights in Historical Perspective," Journal of Human Rights, V. 14, pp. 15–161

Seawright, Amy (2019) The Economic Toll of Covid-19 on Southeast Asia: Recession Looms as Growth Prospects Dim, Centre for Strategic and International Studies, 14 April. Available: https://www.csis.org/analysis/economic-toll-covid-19-southeast-asia-recession-looms-growth-prospects-dim

Spector, Bert (2008) "Business Responsibilities in a Divided World": The Cold War Roots of the Corporate Social Responsibility Movement, Enterprise & Society, Volume 9, Number 2, June 2008, pp. 314–336

Sullivan, Rory and Robinson, Mary (Eds.) (2003) Business and Human Rights Dilemmas and Solutions. London: Routledge.

Thielbörger, Pierre and Tobias Ackermann (2017), "A Treaty on Enforcing Human Rights Against Business: Closing the Loophole or Getting Stuck in a Loop?" Indiana Journal of Global Legal Studies Vol. 24 #1 (Winter 2017), pp. 43–79

UNCTAD (2014) World Investment Report. Geneva, UNCTAD

Walker-Said, Charlotte, John D. Kelly (Editors) (2015) Corporate Social Responsibility?: Human Rights in the New Global Economy 1st Edition

Woods, Jeanne (2011) "A Human Rights Framework For Corporate Accountability," ILSA Journal of International & Comparative Law, Vol. 17:2 pp. 322–334

PART I

Norms and Policy

CHAPTER 2

Does the Slipper Fit? National Action Plans on Business and Human Rights in South East Asia

Michael White

Introduction

To date, 21 countries have produced a National Action Plan (NAP) on Business and Human Rights, and NAP processes have been initiated by governments in another 23 countries. The Danish Institute for Human Rights has also noted that non-State actors are pushing for NAPs in at least 15 additional countries.[1] It is abundantly clear that NAPs are increasingly seen as the best mechanism for States to fulfil their existing human rights obligations under pillar 1 of the UNGPs. What is less clear however is the extent to which these NAPs have had an impact on the realisation of rights and equally importantly the appropriateness and accessibility of remedies where rights have been breached.

[1] The Danish Institute for Human Rights (2018) National Action Plans on Business and Human Rights.

M. White (✉)
Wellington, New Zealand
e-mail: james@asiacentre.co.th

J. Gomez, R. Ramcharan (eds.), *Business and Human Rights in Asia*,
https://doi.org/10.1007/978-981-15-7273-9_2

Some academics have suggested that most NAPs have failed to date in relation to both process and content. In relation to process, most NAPs have failed to:

1. conduct comprehensive baseline assessments to inform the NAP content; and
2. facilitate the participation and consultation of key stakeholders, including individuals historically discriminated against; Lesbian, Gay, Bisexual, Transgender, and Intersex (LGBTI) people; women; children; and afro-descendants.[2]

NAPs generally do not present new policy or legislative commitments. They often merely summarise existing State commitments. The issue of remedy has also not been dealt with in a meaningful way in the majority of NAPs to date.

As more States continue to undertake NAPs processes, it is crucial that they address these important concerns.

The Emergence of NAPS on Business and Human Rights

Despite the current popularity of NAPs to fulfil international obligations in the business and human rights sphere, it should be remembered that the concept of NAPs did not emerge from the corporate responsibility movement. Rather the concept dates back to at least 1993 and the Vienna Declaration and Programme of Action. The Vienna Declaration and Programme of Action encouraged States to adopt action plans to reinforce the promotion and protection of human rights generally.[3] Such human rights NAPs have been promulgated in various forms around the world since this time but have been largely ineffective in improving the realisation of rights. The reasons for this are not addressed and analysed in this chapter. However, it is important to note that as States continue to develop NAPs in the business and human rights spheres lessons should be learnt from the implementation of broader human rights NAPs over the years.

[2] See for example Assessment of existing NAPs on Business and Human Rights, Accountability Roundtable (2017).

[3] World Conference on Human Rights, "Vienna Declaration and Programme of Action', A/RES/48/121 (20 December 1993), para 71.

In the business and human rights sphere, the call to develop NAPs first appeared in 2011. In its Communication 681 the European Union urged States to adopt NAPs to implement the UNGPs.[4] This Communication has been criticised by some as it focused on corporate responsibility, a concept which was progressively being understood as being different and separate to the business and human rights dialogue. Nevertheless the Communication was clearly the catalyst for the development of NAPs around the globe.

Initially the focus on NAPs remained Eurocentric. In 2012 the Council of the European Union set a timeline for States to develop their implementation strategies and plans.[5] Interestingly by the deadline only the United Kingdom and the Netherlands had published their respective action plans. Thankfully this number has dramatically increased and at the time of writing 17 NAPs have been developed, representing around half EU member states.

The momentum at a regional level, although glacial at the beginning, had an impact at the global level. In its 2012 report to the Human Rights Council, the UN Working Group on Business and Human Rights expressed its support for the development of NAPs.[6] Subsequently its 2014 report to the General Assembly was focused on analysing NAPs and distilling their constitutive elements.[7] In its assessments the Working Group noted that:[8]

> *[t]he fundamental purpose of a national action plan is to prevent and strengthen protection against human rights abuses by business enterprises through an inclusive process of identifying needs and gaps and practical and actionable policy measures and goals....*
>
> *States take stock of what they are already doing to implement the Guiding Principles and identify gaps which require further policy action to implement the Guiding Principles.*

[4] European Commission, 'A Renewed EU Strategy 2011–14 for Corporate Social Responsibility', COM/2011/681/FINAL (25 October 2011), para 4.8.2.

[5] Council of the European Union, 'EU Strategic Framework and Action Plan on Human Rights and Democracy', Doc 11855/12 (25 June 2012), para 25(c).

[6] Human Rights Council, 'Report of the Working Group on the Issue of Human Rights and Transnational Corporations and Other Business Enterprises', A/HRC/20/29 (10 April 2012), para 68.

[7] General Assembly, 'Report of the Working Group on the Issue of Human Rights and Transnational Corporations and Other Business Enterprises', A/69/263 (5 August 2014).

[8] Ibid.

Since this time the development of NAPs has extended at a slow but steady pace to other regions of the world.

NAPS in Southeast Asia

To date the update of NAPs by South East Asian governments has been underwhelming. In stark contrast to the interest of civil society and national human rights institutions, government commitments have been largely invisible until recently. This presents a significant barrier to achieving the purpose of NAPs—the development of a global Governance system that can avert corporate human rights violations.

In April 2013, Human Rights Resource Centre—an Indonesian based NGO—commenced a baseline study on business and human rights for ASEAN countries. Subsequently in 2014 the ASEAN Intergovernmental Commission on Human Rights (AICHR) commissioned its own baseline study. In 2015 the Human Rights Commission of Malaysia (SUHAKAM) launched a "Strategic Framework for a National Action Plan". This was welcomed by the government at the time.[9] However, it took the government 5 years to commit to developing a NAP. On 24 June 2019 the Minister of Laws, YB Liew, formally announced a cabinet decision to launch a process to develop a business and human rights NAP.[10] As noted in the introduction processes are now underway at various stages in Indonesia, Malaysia, Philippines and Thailand.

There are many challenges for South East Asian governments to adopt NAPS. Lack of capacity and budget are two key obstacles. Global South states are also subject to continual scrutiny and reporting pressure by the global community—most recently through the Sustainable Development Goals (SDGs). Furthermore there remains strong resistance from the corporate sector as they consider NAPs in the region will reduce competitiveness.[11]

[9] Rakyat Post (2015) http://www.therakyatpost.com/news/2015/03/24/national-action-plan-on-business-and-human-rights-to-be-drafted/

[10] Globalnaps.org (2019) https://globalnaps.org/country/malaysia/

[11] Martens, Jens and Seitz, Karolin (2016) *The Struggle for a UN Treaty: Towards Global Regulation on Human Rights and Business*, Rosa Luxemburg Stiftung and Global Policy Forum, p. 12.

Scope of NAPs in the Region

There appears to be a consensus that NAPs need to address the implementation of business and human rights norms beyond the scope of the UNGPs. The Danish Institute for Human Rights considers that NAPs should be aligned with new constitutional provisions in each country, which in some cases are remarkably progressive and entail a possible status of companies as duty bearers.[12] Civil Society organisations equally strongly advocate for NAPs that impose new regulations on business. It is felt that NAPs that do not impose new government regulations on business—failing to make the second pillar of the UNGPs mandatory:[13]

> *reinforc[e] the idea that the companies do not have obligations, only moral responsibilities of secondary character, derived from social expectations of protection and respect for Human Rights.*

The "State-business nexus" is particularly important in the South East Asian context, where there is a high degree of involvement of governments in business activities. This can create uncertainty about where government action ends and business activity begins.[14] This complexity reinforces the need for NAPs to include commitments to develop new laws, policies, and regulations that send clear signals to business on how to conduct their activities. Transparency and accountability of the state in these environments is equally important and should be incorporated in NAPs.

Possible Areas for Inclusion in South East Asian NAPs

Taking into account the political, economic and social environment in South East Asia there three key areas can be distilled where regulation and reform could be facilitated through NAPs:

[12] ICAR-DIHR Toolkit, p. 74.

[13] HOMA Center for Business and Human Rights, *National Action Plans on Human Rights and Business: Inputs for The Brazilian Reality Part I: General Perspectives on the National Action Plans on Business and Human Rights*, p. 7, http://homacdhe.com/wp-content/uploads/2016/02/General-Perspective-on-the-National-Action-Plans-on-Business-and-Human-Rights.pdf

[14] Supra note 12, p. 79.

Trade and Investment Agreements

Investment and trade has increased dramatically in the region over the past decades and continues to surge at unprecedented levels in some ASEAN states. Governments see this as an important opportunity to improve economic and social wellbeing. Governments have reduced regulatory barriers and entered into a number of bilateral agreements. However some of the investment continues to cause harm and it remains difficult to inject human rights into the conversation.

Few investment treaties consider human rights, and arbitral tribunals designed to protect investors have proved reluctant to consider human rights arguments.[15] The concept of human rights in this context must be broad and include concepts such as poverty and environmental displacement. Embedding human rights protections into investment promotion and regulation is a "key dimension for States to consider when implementing their duty to protect."[16] Yet the European NAPs published to date have only partially addressed it. There is an opportunity for South East Asian states to lead the way in this regard.

The Informal Economy

According to the World Bank the informal sector accounts for about half of total non-agricultural employment in East Asia, and up to 80% in other parts of ASIA. Despite their significant contribution to a country's GDP, estimated at 20–65 percent, without the social protections of the formal sector informal sector workers are marginalised. Poverty especially impacts women workers. The 2016 Asia Regional Working Group Report on Business and Human Rights report recognized the informal sector as "a considerable, systemic challenge" to achieving wide uptake of the Guiding

[15] Lorenzo Cotula, "Rethinking Investment Treaties to Advance Human Rights," IIED, Traidcraft, and Trade Justice Movement, September 2016, p. 1. http://pubs.iied.org/pdfs/17376IIED.pdf (accessed 7 Oct 2016). For a contrary opinion—that sustainable development and "responsible business conduct" is increasingly being considered in trade agreements—see, Kathryn Gordon, Joachim Pohl, Marie Bourchard, *Investment Treaty Law, Sustainable Development and Responsible Business Conduct: A fact-finding survey* (OECD Working Papers on International Investment 2014/01) at p. 9, available at: http://www.oecd.org/investment/investment-policy/WP-2014_01.pdf

[16] Andrea Saldarriaga and Andrea Shemberg, "Implementing the State Duty to Protect Human Rights in Investment Policy," *The Business and Human Rights Review*, Issue 4, Summer 2016, p. 33.

Principles.[17] There remains in this regard a lack of clarity about how to link human rights breaches of companies with initiatives to overcome inequality.

Ignoring the informal sector in business and human rights NAPs needs to change if they are going to be relevant and effective in the region.

Conflict/Post-Conflict Situations

Business and human rights in conflict and post-conflict situations is an important consideration for Naps. Guiding Principle 7 requires states to ensure that business enterprises operating in conflict-affected areas are not involved with human rights abuses. It also requires businesses to pay particular attention to both gender-based and sexual violence. Guiding Principle 23 introduces the concept of enhanced due diligence. Businesses operating in high risk zones—including conflict zones—must exercise enhanced due diligence, and should consider whether to remain or leave the country, acknowledging recognize that since the human rights regime cannot be expected to function as intended in these circumstances.

In addition to ceasing operations that may fuel conflict, companies (particularly foreign multi-nationals) should have a responsibility to provide support to the community to avoid what is often referred to as the conflict trap. The conflict trap is the concept that conflict breeds conflict by:

(a) polarising populations and building up the organisational capacity for future warfare;
(b) undermining democratic institutions; and
(c) exacerbating the conditions that favour insurgency by increasing poverty, causing capital flight and destabilising neighbouring countries.

Placing a positive obligation on companies could be seen as going beyond the UNGPs and the do not harm concept. However, in the alternative it could be argued that by providing support businesses are operating as collaborators in realising human rights and preventing harm.[18]

[17] Report of the Working Group on the issue of human rights and transnational corporations and other business enterprises on the Asia Forum on Business and Human Rights," p. 10.

[18] David Bilchitz, "A Chasm between "Is" and "Ought"? A Critique of the Normative Foundations of the SRSG's Framework and the Guiding Principles" in Surya Deva and

Accountability of corporate entities in post conflict environments also presents challenges due to a lack of mandate, resources and political will. NAPs could address this by requiring that businesses themselves undertake human rights due diligence—that they investigate and report on their past human rights impacts.[19]

Access to Remedy

Providing access to remedy is a key component of the UNGPs. The UNGPs call on states to take steps to ensure that when abuses occur within their territory or jurisdiction, those affected have access to an effective remedy. Assessing the availability and effectiveness of domestic mechanisms—including non-judicial—providing remedy is a useful exercise for governments to create a baseline upon which to ensure access to remedy. The National Contact Points (NCPs) established under the OECD Guidelines are one of the few existing non-judicial mechanisms providing access to remedy for cases of alleged non-observance of the OECD Guidelines, and by corollary the UNGPs. For this reason they have been incorporated into relevant States' NAPs, albeit in a vague manner. For example, countries such as Finland, France, Germany, Italy and Spain committed in their NAPs to strengthen their NCP.

NCPs are not relevant to the South East Asian situation at this stage. However, NAPs present a unique opportunity to review domestic mechanism and embed bespoke culturally appropriate remedies frameworks—both judicial, non-judicial—into NAPs. It may also in some situations be appropriate to regulate operational level grievance mechanisms. These frameworks must themselves be human rights compliant. In other words they must be accessible, affordable and provide efficient and appropriate reconciliation.

David Bilchitz, eds., *Human Rights Obligations of Business: Beyond the Corporate Responsibility to Respect?* New York: Cambridge University Press, 2013. p. 137.

[19] This idea is put forth by Sabine Michalowski of University of Essex, who specializes in corporations and transitional justice. See: https://business-humanrights.org/en/business-and-human-rights-in-transition-from-conflict-to-peace

Implementation and Monitoring

NAPs should take stock of existing governmental actions relevant to the UNGPs and introduce new actions to be implemented. To support implementation of these actions, actions must be attributed to an agency or agencies and given a specific and achievable timeframe. Communicating clear actions to be taken enhances the transparency of the NAP and the accountability of the government.

Some governments plan to monitor NAPs by consulting stakeholders. The United Kingdom NAP provides for regular stakeholder consultations to monitor implementation of the NAP and has established a dedicated email address to facilitate ongoing input from interested parties By contrast, in line with the Guidance of the UN Working Group on Business and Human Rights, the French NAP is to be monitored by an independent entity, the existing National Commission on Human Rights which will release regular reports on the implementation of the NAP. Whilst this type of monitoring is important, it fails to provide a robust framework to assess the effectiveness of NAPs in improving the realisation of rights. Linked to the SDGs, South East Asia countries could individually or collectively develop a set of indicators (in consultation with civil society) to measure the impact of NAPs on the human rights situation. Assessment against these indicators could be informed by consultation, complaint data, judicial proceedings and prosecutions and company due diligence reporting.

Setting timeframes for revisions can also be a useful tool to ensure continued relevance in a rapidly changing environment.

An Asian Solution; A Regional Approach?

Acknowledging the challenges set out above and the slow pace with which things are moving in South East Asia, some have suggested that a regional action plan (RAP) would be a more achievable and culturally appropriate step. Reasons for this suggestion are that:

(a) it may be easier to persuade governments concerned that a RAP would not compromise their competitiveness vis a vis their neighbours;

(b) a RAP may be necessary to address cross border issues, such as human trafficking and "land grabbing,' which have become prevalent in Southeast Asia;
(c) a RAP will help prevent a race to the bottom.
(d) a RAP could provide regional harmonization of standards, while addressing shared problems of weak governance, a lack of transparency, and the need to empower civil society; and
(e) a RAP is aligned with the objectives the ASEAN Economic Community (AEC) Blueprint 2025. According to the Asian Development Bank, which led the drafting of the blueprint, within ASEAN states:[20]

Proper combination[s] of domestic reforms and initiatives for closer integration that complement and reinforce one another are needed to promote the region's equitable and inclusive development, strengthen its macroeconomic stability, and protect the environment.

NAPs could then be developed at a domestic level to make the required regulatory, legislative and policy reforms to implement the RAP.

Recent Developments: The Thai NAP

During its second Universal Periodic Review in May 2016, the Royal Thai Government received a recommendation from Sweden to develop, enact, and implement a NAP on business and human rights. The Thai government accepted this recommendation.

The Thai government established a comprehensive process to develop the NAP under the leadership of the Rights and Liberties Protection Department of the Ministry of Justice. A NAP National Committee[21] has the mandate to draft the NAP and oversee its implementation.

The government has adopted a robust process to the development of the NAP with extensive consultation domestically, regionally and internationally. A National Baseline Assessment (NBA) was also undertaken by

[20] *ASEAN 2030, Towards a Borderless Community* at p. xxi; available at: http://www.adbi.org/book/2014/07/18/6357.asean.2030.borderless.economic.community/

[21] Chaired by the Director-General of the Rights and Liberties Protection Department, Ministry of Justice, and comprising representatives of other Government ministries as well as the National Human Rights Commission of Thailand.

the Thai Business and Human Rights Network to inform the development of the NAP. The NBA development process involved four sub-regional dialogues organised. The participation and inclusion of the most at-risk and marginalized communities in the context of business and human rights was cornerstone to these interactions. Indigenous peoples, environmental human rights defenders, migrant workers, formal and informal labour workers, LGBTI activities, persons living with HIV/AIDS, sex workers, persons with disabilities and the elderly were actively engaged in the process.

In 2018, the United Nations Working Group on Business and Human Rights completed a 10 day mission to Thailand. They engaged in an open dialogue with various stakeholders including government, civil society organisations and business on current initiatives, opportunities and challenges to implement the UNGPs. Despite the consultations that had been undertaken, from a process perspective the Working Group considered more still needed to be done. It noted that further efforts would be needed to ensure an inclusive process, for example by making information about the NAP process available on the Ministry's website, an open call for input and comments, and engagement with a wider group of civil society and business actors.

In addition, the Working Group recommended that the NAP place special attention on:

(a) access to remedy;
(b) gender; and
(c) links with the SDGs.

In February 2019, the Thailand government circulated a final draft NAP for consultation. The key focus areas of the NAP are:

(a) labour;
(b) land, environment and natural resources;
(c) human rights defenders; and
(d) cross border investment and multi-national enterprises.

Whilst it is good to see these focus areas (particularly cross border investment), the draft Thai NAP suffers from many of the same content issues of its predecessors from other countries. It fails to deal with remedy in any meaningful way—it does not adequately include state-based non-judicial grievance redress mechanisms; customary laws and practices of affected communities; and barriers to accessing remedy. Similarly in many areas it does not provide concrete forward looking steps and an implementation/monitoring framework. It does not have legally binding mandatory provisions to hold business to account. It does not appropriately address the state business nexus and fails to incorporate key elements specific to the South East Asian context such as the informal economy and post conflict/conflict situations. It will be interesting to see whether a Eurocentric model (with its identified issues for achieving impact) without being adapted to the specific South East Asian context and culture will deliver meaningful change.

Conclusion

It is uncontested that states have a duty to protect against human rights abuses by corporations and ensure access to remedy in cases of corporate harm is. Many have convincingly argued that a well-crafted binding instrument is needed to support that norm, to make mandatory corporate respect for human rights, and to clarify the state duty to take legislative and administrative measures to control, regulate, investigate and prosecute actions by corporations that violate human rights both within and outside their territories. Despite the start of a treaty process—or even because of it—a NAP remains an important part of the human rights framework.

However there is good reason to be skeptical as to whether NAPs in their current form are appropriate to substantively improve the human rights situation in South East Asia. As more NAPs are developed in the region it is important to increase focus on content and ensure that a NAP is responsive to the situation on the ground, includes the involvement of a broad range of stakeholders (including affected communities), is culturally appropriate and contains bold, forward looking commitments in areas that are pertinent to the South East Asian region and its economic, social and political context.

References

ASEAN. *ASEAN 2030, Towards a Borderless Community* at p. xxi; available at: http://www.adbi.org/book/2014/07/18/6357.asean.2030.borderless.economic.community/

Assessment of existing NAPs on Business and Human Rights, Accountability Roundtable (2017), A/HRC/32/45/Add.2.

Bilchitz, David (2013) "A Chasm between "Is" and "Ought"? A Critique of the Normative Foundations of the SRSG's Framework and the Guiding Principles" in Surya Deva and David Bilchitz, eds., *Human Rights Obligations of Business: Beyond the Corporate Responsibility to Respect?* New York: Cambridge University Press, 2013. p. 137.

Cotula, Lorenzo (2016) "Rethinking Investment Treaties to Advance Human Rights," IIED, Traidcraft, and Trade Justice Movement, September 2016, p. 1. http://pubs.iied.org/pdfs/17376IIED.pdf

Council of the European Union, 'EU Strategic Framework and Action Plan on Human Rights and Democracy', Doc 11855/12 (25 June 2012), para 25(c).

European Commission, 'A Renewed EU Strategy 2011–14 for Corporate Social Responsibility', COM/2011/681/ FINAL (25 October 2011), para 4.8.2.

General Assembly, 'Report of the Working Group on the Issue of Human Rights and Transnational Corporations and Other Business Enterprises', A/69/263 (5 August 2014).

Gordon, Kathryn, Pohl, Joachim, Bourchard, Marie (2014) *Investment Treaty Law, Sustainable Development and Responsible Business Conduct: A fact-finding survey* (OECD Working Papers on International Investment 2014/01) at p. 9, available at: http://www.oecd.org/investment/investment-policy/WP-2014_01.pdf

HOMA Centre for Business and Human Rights, *National Action Plans on Human Rights and Business: Inputs for The Brazilian Reality Part I: General Perspectives on the National Action Plans on Business and Human Rights*, p. 7, http://homacdhe.com/wp-content/uploads/2016/02/General-Perspective-on-the-National-Action-Plans-on-Business-and-Human-Rights.pdf

The Rakyat Post (2015) National Action Plan on Business and Human Rights to be drafted, 24 March. Available at http://www.therakyatpost.com/news/2015/03/24/national-action-plan-on-business-and-human-rights-to-be-drafted/

Globalnaps.org (2019) National Action Plans on Business and Human Rights (2019), Malaysia. Available at https://globalnaps.org/country/malaysia/

Human Rights Council, 'Report of the Working Group on the Issue of Human Rights and Transnational Corporations and Other Business Enterprises', A/HRC/20/29 (10 April 2012), para 68.

International Corporate Accountability Roundtable and Danish Institute for Human Rights (2017) National Action Plans on Business and Human Rights Toolkit, 2017 Edition. Available at: https://icar.squarespace.com/publications/2017/12/21/national-action-plans-naps-toolkit-2017-edition.

Martens, Jens and Seitz, Karolin (2016) *The Struggle for a UN Treaty: Towards Global Regulation on Human Rights and Business*, Rosa Luxemburg Stiftung and Global Policy Forum, August 2016, p. 12.

National Action Plans on Business and Human Rights, The Danish Institute for Human Rights (2018).

United Nations (2016) Report of the Working Group on the issue of human rights and transnational corporations and other business enterprises on the Asia Forum on Business and Human Rights. UN General Assembly, October, Doc. A/HRC/32/45/Add.2.

Saldarriaga, Andrea and Shemberg, Andrea (2016) "Implementing the State Duty to Protect Human Rights in Investment Policy," *The Business and Human Rights Review*, Issue 4, Summer 2016, p. 33.

World Conference on Human Rights (1993), "Vienna Declaration and Programme of Action', A/RES/48/121 (20 December 1993), para 71

CHAPTER 3

National Action Plans on Business and Human Rights: Norms, Procedures and Pitfalls

James Gomez and Robin Ramcharan

Introduction

The uptake in Asia on developing NAPs on BHR was noted in the Introduction. Significant processes are under way in with Indonesia, Malaysia, Philippines Thailand, which are developing National Action Plans on BHR. Southeast Asia in particular is particularly active amidst serious human rights regression across the region. As governmental action on NAPs increase in Asia the UNGPs constitute both a normative and procedural guide to the elaboration of these policy tools. This chapter, after a brief overview of the UNGPs, outlines the normative contribution of NAPs on BHR in a complex international system, the procedural elements that guide the elaboration of NAPs and their pitfalls in light of experiences in non-Asian jurisdictions. The central role of the State in driving the process of elaborating NAPs is emphasized.

J. Gomez (✉) • R. Ramcharan
Asia Centre, Bangkok, Thailand
e-mail: james@asiacentre.org; robin@asiacentre.org

J. Gomez, R. Ramcharan (eds.), *Business and Human Rights in Asia*,
https://doi.org/10.1007/978-981-15-7273-9_3

The UNGPS: Basic Structure

The UNGPs, adopted by the Human Rights Council in 2011, sought to clarify the roles of governments and companies as they addressed human rights impacts of business enterprises. They are grounded in three principles:

1. States' existing obligations to respect, protect and fulfil human rights and fundamental freedoms;
2. The role of business enterprises as specialized organs of society performing specialized functions, required to comply with all applicable laws and to respect human rights;
3. The need for rights and obligations to be matched to appropriate and effective remedies when breached (OHCHR 2011, p. 1).

Their implementation is to be achieved through relevant policies, legislation and regulations, through progressive policies and practices from corporations and through providing remedies for victims of business-linked human rights abuses.The UNWG defined a NAP as an "evolving policy strategy developed by a State to protect against adverse human rights impacts by business enterprises in conformity with the UN Guiding Principles on Business and Human Rights (UNGPs)."

A NAP, which is preventive in nature and is a vital tool suggested by the UNGPs to implement the 'Protect, Respect and Remedy' framework. The UNWG emphasized that for a effective NAP to be effective it needed to be founded on the UNGPs:

> As an instrument to implement the UNGPs, NAPs need to adequately reflect a State's duties under international human rights law to protect against adverse corporate human rights impacts and provide effective access to remedy. A NAP further needs to promote business respect for human rights including through due diligence processes. Moreover, NAPs must be underpinned by the core human rights principles of non-discrimination and equality. (UNWG 2014, p. ii)

In addition, NAPs ought to be context-specific and address the country's actual and potential adverse corporate human rights impacts, to be developed in inclusive and transparent processes and to be regularly be reviewed and updated (UNWG 2014, p. ii).

States were exhorted to use the UNGPs as a foundational reference, conduct capacity building on the UNGPs among government entities, to identify gaps in State and business performances based on the UNGPs and to take the UNGPs as the guiding instrument when identifying and deciding upon adequate measures to address protection gaps

From CSRS To UNGPS

The UNGPs build on the CSR initiative that emerged in the1990s in an increasingly complex international system, with TNCs operating large value chains across spaces, with less and less commitment to value-upholding behaviour on behalf of national communities. Nike and Shell became CSR leaders at that time and two distinct UN-based initiatives emerged in 1999: the drafting of the 'Norms on the Responsibilities of Transnational Corporations and Other Business Enterprises with Regard to Human Rights' and the UN Global Compact. They were developed independently, and at the outset with limited awareness of one another (Ruggie 2013, p. 7). The former sought to impose human rights obligations on business entities but met a cool reception in the former Commission on Human Rights in 2004, perhaps because it did not clearly delimit the responsibilities of business entities. The Global Compact followed Secretary General Kofi Annan's speech at Davos (drafted by Ruggie) in 1999, in which he argued that

> The spread of markets outpaces the ability of societies and their political systems to adjust to them, let alone to guide the course they take. History teaches us that such an imbalance between the economic, social and political realms can never be sustained for very long...The industrialized countries learned that lesson in their bitter and costly encounter with the Great Depression...Our challenge today is to devise a similar compact on the global scale, to underpin the new global economy. (Quoted in Ruggie 2017, p. 9; Annan 1999)

Annan urged corporations at Davos to not wait for their countries to adopt laws but instead, "You can uphold human rights and decent labor and environmental standards directly, by your own conduct of your own business." (ibid.) Reflecting a 'social constructivist approach', Ruggie and his team at the UN designed the Global Compact "as a norms-based learning forum and engagement mechanism, which we saw as a necessary complement to other approaches, including business initiatives and law-making" (Ruggie 2017, p. 10). It sought to socialise business entities in a variety of ways—conducting learning forums and identifying best practices; generating public/private partnerships around the UN "people and planet" agenda; serving as an incubator for innovative initiatives across different business sectors that are then spun off, such as the Principles for Responsible Investment with nearly 1,700 signatory institutions from over 50 countries, representing $62 trillion under management; and establishing national GC networks, including in emerging market countries such as Brazil, China and India, as well as in developing countries. By 2017, the GC was the world's largest corporate responsibility initiative (it now prefers the term "sustainability"), with more than 12,000 institutional participants—including companies, civil society and workers organizations, investor groups, business schools, local networks, and even cities—from 170 countries (Ruggie 2017, p. 10).

Following the failure of the above-mentioned norms, the UNGPs would eventually be developed as a result of Ruggie's well known work on BHR. The UNGPs "reaffirm that business enterprises must comply with all applicable laws. Beyond legal compliance, they also stipulate that enterprises have the responsibility to respect human rights, irrespective of a state's willingness or ability to enforce the law" (Ruggie 2017, p. 13). The UNGPs *were drafted with* the hope that "they would trigger an iterative process of interaction… producing cumulative change over time." Such a 'reflexive' prescribed "a framework of institutionalized procedures and organizational norms" within which " entities that are targeted for regulation…acquire the capacity needed to more effectively address their social and environmental externalities. And the framework itself is subject to adjustment based on experiential feedback" (Ruggie 2017, p. 1). In a world where multilateral rule-making is increasingly difficult, national jurisdictions have a necessary and complementary role to play in upholding international human rights law and guiding business entities in that direction via NAPs and other legislative and policy tools. The European Union, for example, requested in 2011 that all member states adopt a NAP and the UNWG has recommended that all states do the same (European Union 2011).

Normative Contribution of the UNGPS And NAPS

NAPs are guided by the UNGPs, which constitute not a legal tool but a normative tool that was adopted by a Resolution of the Human Rights Council, though they build on existing human rights obligations and state practice. Ruggie has noted that the UNGPs, to date, "constituted the only official guidance the Council and its predecessor, the Commission on Human Rights, have issued for states and business enterprises on their respective obligations in relation to business and human rights" (Ruggie 2017, p. 1). This normative approach, Ruggie argued, was the consequence of several factors affecting governance in a complex international system:

- An increasingly complex world that has conformed to his predictions of an embedded liberalism[1] leading to an international economy in which " the multinational enterprise is the standard mode of organizing economic activities across countries (Ruggie 2017, p. 2).
- The fragmentation of international rule making (also referred to as the fragmentation of international law) in which rule or law-making by States through multilateral instruments has diminished as a result of three factors: (a) the emergence of a multipolar world in which new powers render coalition building and consensus seeking more difficult; (b) the rise of "networked governance: essentially

[1] Embedded liberalism, developed in his early theoretical work on international relations, is summarised as follows: "after World War II the commitment to international liberalization was institutionally coupled with norms and practices protecting national social communities. Governments played a key role in enacting and sustaining it: on the one side, re-establishing a multilateral monetary and trade regime and progressively removing barriers to trade; and, on the other side, providing domestic social investments and safety nets, while moderating the volatility of cross-border transaction flows by, for example requiring capital controls to prevent destabilizing flows of "hot money," and allowing for temporary safeguards against sudden surges in imports. Reconciling these two competing policy objectives—open international markets and domestic economic and social stability—required delicate national and international balancing acts, which took different forms in different countries: social democracy, the social market economy, and the New Deal state. In the industrialized world, this grand bargain formed the basis of one of the longest and most equitable periods of economic expansion in history" Ruggie (2017, p. 2). See John Gerard Ruggie, 'International Regimes, Transactions and Change: Embedded Liberalism in the Postwar Economic Order' (1982) *International Organization* 379.

self-constituting transnational public or private governance arrangements, focused on specific problems”,[2]

- The sheer substantive complexity of global issues, coupled with the extensive interest diversity across and even within states that many exhibit (Ruggie 2017, p. 6)

The Duty of States

The UNGPs did not create new international law obligations, nor did they limit or undermine any legal obligations a State may have undertaken or be subject to under international law with regard to human rights. With regard to the duty of states the Guidelines stipulate that:

1. States must protect against human rights abuse within their territory and/or jurisdiction by third parties, including business enterprises. This requires taking appropriate steps to prevent, investigate, punish and redress such abuse through effective policies, legislation, regulations and adjudication.
2. States should set out clearly the expectation that all business enterprises domiciled in their territory and/or jurisdiction respect human rights throughout their operations.
3. In meeting their duty to protect, States should: (a) Enforce laws that are aimed at, or have the effect of, requiring business enterprises to respect human rights, and periodically to assess the adequacy of such laws and address any gaps; (b) Ensure that other laws and policies governing the creation and ongoing operation of business enterprises, such as corporate law, do not constrain but enable business respect for human rights; (c) Provide effective guidance to business enterprises on how to respect human rights throughout their operations; (d) Encourage, and where appropriate require, business enterprises to communicate how they address their human rights impacts.
4. States should take additional steps to protect against human rights abuses by business enterprises that are owned or controlled by the State, or that receive substantial support and services from State

[2] Such as the Basel Committee on Banking Supervision, Financial Action Task Force, Financial Stability Board, International Accounting Standards Board, and Proliferation Security Initiative (Ruggie 2017, p. 5).

agencies such as export credit agencies and official investment insurance or guarantee agencies, including, where appropriate, by requiring human rights due diligence.

5. States should exercise adequate oversight in order to meet their international human rights obligations when they contract with, or legislate for, business enterprises to provide services that may impact upon the enjoyment of human rights.
6. States should promote respect for human rights by business enterprises with which they conduct commercial transactions.
7. Because the risk of gross human rights abuses is heightened in conflict affected areas, States should help ensure that business enterprises operating in those contexts are not involved with such abuses, including by: (a) Engaging at the earliest stage possible with business enterprises to help them identify, prevent and mitigate the human rights-related risks of their activities and business relationships; 9 (b) Providing adequate assistance to business enterprises to assess and address the heightened risks of abuses, paying special attention to both gender-based and sexual violence; (c) Denying access to public support and services for a business enterprise that is involved with gross human rights abuses and refuses to cooperate in addressing the situation; (d) Ensuring that their current policies, legislation, regulations and enforcement measures are effective in addressing the risk of business involvement in gross human rights abuses.
8. States should ensure that governmental departments, agencies and other State-based institutions that shape business practices are aware of and observe the State's human rights obligations when fulfilling their respective mandates, including by providing them with relevant information, training and support.
9. States should maintain adequate domestic policy space to meet their human rights obligations when pursuing business-related policy objectives with other States or business enterprises, for instance through investment treaties or contracts.
10. States, when acting as members of multilateral institutions that deal with business-related issues, should: (a) Seek to ensure that those institutions neither restrain the ability of their member States to meet their duty to protect nor hinder business enterprises from respecting human rights; (b) Encourage those institutions, within their respective mandates and capacities, to promote business

respect for human rights and, where requested, to help States meet their duty to protect against human rights abuse by business enterprises, including through technical assistance, capacity-building and awareness-raising; (c) Draw on these Guiding Principles to promote shared understanding and advance international cooperation in the management of business and human rights challenges.

In the commentaries on each of these, the following key observations were made:

1. The State duty to protect is a standard of conduct. States may breach their international human rights law obligations where such abuse can be attributed to them, or where they fail to take appropriate steps to prevent, investigate, punish and redress private actors' abuse.
2. At present States are not generally required under international human rights law to regulate the extraterritorial activities of businesses domiciled in their 4 territory and/or jurisdiction.
3. States should not assume that businesses invariably prefer, or benefit from, State inaction, and they should consider a smart mix of measures—national and international, mandatory and voluntary—to foster business respect for human rights. The failure to enforce existing laws that directly or indirectly regulate business respect for human rights is often a significant legal gap in State practice.
4. States individually are the primary duty-bearers under international human rights law, and collectively they are the trustees of the international human rights regime. Where a business enterprise is controlled by the State or where its acts can be attributed otherwise to the State, an abuse of human rights by the business enterprise may entail a violation of the State's own international law obligations. The closer a business enterprise is to the State, or the more it relies on statutory authority or taxpayer support, the stronger the State's policy rationale becomes for ensuring that the enterprise respects human rights
5. States do not relinquish their international human rights law obligations when they privatize the delivery of services that may impact upon the enjoyment of human rights.
6. Where transnational corporations are involved, their "home" States therefore have roles to play in assisting both those corporations and host States to ensure that businesses are not involved with human

rights abuse, while neighboring States can provide important additional support.

7. To achieve the appropriate balance amidst different societal needs,, States need to take a broad approach to managing the business and human rights agenda, aimed at ensuring both vertical and horizontal domestic policy coherence.
8. States should ensure that they retain adequate policy and regulatory ability to protect human rights under the terms of economic agreements with other States or with business enterprises, while providing the necessary investor protection.
9. Greater policy coherence is also needed at the international level, including where States participate in multilateral institutions that deal with business related issues, such as international trade and financial institutions. States retain their international human rights law obligations when they participate in such institutions.

The UNGPs were to be implemented in a non-discriminatory manner, with particular attention to the rights and needs of, as well as the challenges faced by, individuals from groups or populations that may be at heightened risk of becoming vulnerable or marginalized, and with due regard to the different risks that may be faced by women and men.

NAPS Development: Procedural Aspects

In the process of drafting of NAPs "the relevance of the UN guiding principles to the Asean Community is undeniable" (Nonthasoot 2017). In their paper on procedural aspects of elaborating NAPS across ASEAN, Benjamin and Sta.Maria have noted that Indonesia, Malaysia, the Philippines and Thailand have publicly committed to ensuring their plans are consistent with the UNGPs. Myanmar has also committed to the same, even though its process is lagging behind (Benjamin and Sta. Maria 2018, p. 4). They highlighted four critical procedural aspects applicable to NAP development in Southeast Asia: (1) Seeking a formal commitment from government to engage in the NAP process and designating leadership, (2) creating a format of cross-department collaboration with government, (3) establishing platforms of engagement and consultations with various stakeholders and providing resources for the process and (4) arriving at agreements on what do with the outcome of consultations.

On point one, in Indonesia it was KOMNAS Ham that recommended the development of a NAP on BHR given that the National Human Rights Action Plan 2014–2019 did not reflect the UNGPs. Komnas HAm, supported by civil society, launched a NAP in June 2017 with scant support from Government. By November 2017, the Government indicated that it would develop national guidelines by 2018, with the Ministry of Economic Affairs leading the initiative. In Malaysia, government action emerged after SUHAKAM released a study on BYR in 2010, though progress has stalled. Governmental action has been spurred by the PHRC, backed by CSOs. Work is stalled. In Thailand, the Rights and LIberties Protection Department of the Ministry of Justice is mandated to implement recommendations received in the second UPR.

On point two, cross departmental collaboration, Benjamin and Sta. Maria have noed "weak or non-existent collaboration" (p. 10) with the exception of Thailand, which created a national committee to work on the NAP. An implementation MOU involved the NHR Committee, the Ministry of Justice, the Ministry of Foreign Affairs, Ministry of Commerce, Federation of Thai Industries, the Thai Bankers association, the Thai Chamber of Commerce and the Global Computing Network of Thailand. A Thai CSOs Coalition for the UPR is collaborating in the process. Elsewhere, collaboration is weak perhaps due to concerns of departmental jurisdictions over human rights and the "optimistic belief" that a NAP, once adopted by the highest authority, may be readily implemented. How this might be achieved is not clear in Indonesia, for example, where regional governments have local autonomy. Failing an agreement national authorities or KOMNAS Ham would have difficulty with implementation.

On point three, platforms of engagement with stakeholders, Thailand and Indonesia established such platforms. The Thai National Committee and the CSO coalition were noted, though it remains unclear at the time of writing the degree to which the latter and the business sector is able to affect the final text of the NAP. In Indonesia Komnas HAM, ELSAM and the Business and human Rights Working Group (BHWG) collaborating on ensuring consultations, notably between CSOs and the private sector.

On point four, the credibility of NAPs is tied to stakeholder participation and input. In the Thai process, stakeholders were informed that baseline studies carried out by the Thai CSO coalition, notably in marginalized communities, would be considered in developing policies and recommendations for the NAP.

The credibility and effectiveness of NAPs, note Benjamin and Sta. Maria, depends on several key aspects for the State were noted in their analysis: (1) the commitment of the highest-ranking state officials, (2) State allocation of resources (technical and financial, (3) State-defined leadership structure to coordinate across ministries; (4) Engagement of the executive branch of government, (5) State bureaucracies engaging with their respective neworks to inform the process, and (6) a State led process of drafting a terms of reference for the process, the priority issues, for implementation and for eventual claims by victims (pp. 17–18).

As states pursue this process, they must also take into consideration the experiences of other jurisdictions, which point to significant pitfalls.

Positive Uptake of NAPS, with Pitfalls

NAPs on business and human rights, as noted earlier, have enjoyed an uptake in practice globally and rhetorically across Asia, especially in Southeast Asia as ASEAN Regional Economic Community featuring increased regional trade and investment. Moreover, the 2030 Agenda for Sustainable Development in September 2015 recognised the role of business organisations as drivers for economic growth and infrastructure, which are necessary components for achieving the Sustainable Development Goals (SDGs), and at the same time, called on businesses to act in accordance with the UNGPs. *Australia, Bangladesh, Japan, India, Malaysia, Nepal and the Philippines are discussing NAPs, while civil society have pushed for instruments in Myanmar and South Korea* (BHR Resource Centre 2018). Thailand has taken the lead and adopted a NAP in December 2019.

Thailand *stepped out in front of fellow-ASEAN members in 2018, then under military dictatorship*. Nonthasoot has noted that it accepted a Swedish recommendation in the second cycle of the Universal Periodic Review (UPR) of the Human Rights Council (HRC) to develop and enact a NAP. Homegrown efforts were apparently already underway, led by Thailand's National Human Rights Commission (NHRC) following allegations of overseas human rights violations by Thai companies. The NHRC had submitted to the cabinet a proposal for the government to ensure observance of human rights by Thai corporations, including in their overseas investment (Nonthasoot 2017). Thailand adopted a NAP in December 2019, having made a commitment to do so in collaboration with the UN Working Group on BHR (OHCHR 2018).

The overall objectives of NAPs, note Augenstein, Dawson And Thielbörger, are to: take stock of existing state measures that contribute to the implementation of the UNGPs; identify gaps in states' legal and policy framework that require further action; and outline strategies to close protection gaps and to otherwise prevent and redress corporate-related human rights abuse (Augenstein et al. 2018, p. 4). These objectives are not properly served by existing NAPs.

While NAPs are welcome in the BHR context, limitations and critiques based on existing action plans globally are noteworthy. First, NAPs should not provide a means for States to neglect their existing obligations under international law. This was the key message of Dr. Seree Nonthasoot, Thailand's former representative to the ASEAN Intergovernmental Commission on Human Rights (AICHR) at Asia Centre's International Conference on Business and Human Rights: Holding Governments Accountable (BHR Conference) in July 2018 that (Asia Centre 2018). The UNGPs did not create any new duty but amalgamated existing human rights precepts underpinned by the the recognition of the roles of businesses in human rights protection (Nonthasoot 2017).

Second, NAPs are not written in the same language of international human rights treaties, which would help to reconcile national plans with such law. A recent report by the The Sao Paolo Law School and UK Embassy in Brazil, noted that the use of traditional human rights language "is a key element for the effectiveness of the human rights and business agenda, since it makes it possible to establish a common ground between the demands of the affected peoples, which commonly use the human rights grammar, and the actions taken by States and by companies" (Brazil Embassy UK, Sao Paolo, c. 2016). The absence of human rights language runs the risk of NAPs being used as mere political tools and not as human rights tools.

Third, existing NAPS across the world display a lack of clarity on the roles and responsibilities of States and companies in relation to human rights violations. In addition there tended to be a confusion between business responsibility to respect human rights with corporate social responsibility, which are voluntary actions taken by companies (Sao Paulo Law School, c. 2016). The ASEAN Intergovernmental Commission on Human Rights' first study on CSR noted that STates had to move beyond CSR and to address human rights based responsibilities (Thomas and Chandra 2014).

Fourth, the consequence of a lack of clarity of the roles and responsibilities of States and companies, is the difficulty in monitoring the implementation of the NAP. Indicators should be incorporated in the NAPs to guide the adoption of further policies and practices for the implementation of the UN Guiding Principles (Augenstein et al. 2018, p. 7; Sao Paolo Law School, c. 2016)

Fifth, transparency and participation during the elaboration of the NAP as well as the provision of clear instruments to implement and to monitor the implementation are conditions for achieving this expectation. The Sao Paolo Law School report noted that "a NAP elaborated without proper consultation does not consider the views and demands of all stakeholders and, therefore, may not relate to the human rights reality of the country. Furthermore, "a NAP which does not have legitimacy amongst relevant stakeholders faces the risk of not being implemented" (Sao Paolo Law School, c. 2016). Although a "zero daft"[3] had been circulated for commentary by June 2018, the consultation and drafting process in Thailand has faced some criticism for being top heavy, with limited consultation with community organisations (Manushya 2018). The European Network of National Human Rights Institutions (ENNHRI) has offered biting criticism of procedural and substantive shortcomings in the development of EU member state NAPs: It noted that NAP processes in some Member States were "neither participatory nor transparent", that stakeholders were involved "weakly or not at all", and that civil society organizations in particular frequently lacked "even basic information or opportunities to engage in dialogue with government representatives."

Sixth, early NAPs in the UK, 'Denmark, the Netherlands, Finland, and Sweden, suffered from a failure to conduct baseline studies, which is necessary to address the specific problems faced in each jurisdiction (ICARR and ECCJ 2015). Mohan (2015) noted the need for addressing specific contexts.

Sixth, NAPs did not sufficiently explore regulatory options—proper regulatory mix—to ensure adequate human rights protections nor the issue of access to remedy. Action plans tended to focus on 'awareness raising', 'research', 'other voluntary measures'. There was little focus on supporting the development to regulatory actions (ICARR and ECCJ 2015, p. 4). Effective implementation requires that the three pillars—Protect, Respect, Remedy—be treated as complementary, but many NAPs treated

[3] See Ministry of Justice of Thailand (2018) 'Zero Draft' (National Action Plan on Business and Human Rights—NAP), Available at http://www.rlpd.go.th/rlpd-new/2017-06-14-08-39-27/8810-2018-06-21-08-59-56 and https://drive.google.com/file/d/1Cz6NdFePbz_uDDiE17wOGRaAAqihConZ/view

them "unevenly, with little attention given in particular to remediation (Pillar 3)" (Augenstein et al. 2018, p. 10).

Finally, NAPs tended to be backward looking and not forward looking. Such NAPs pointed to past actions as opposed to identifying future actions (ENNHRI 2015, p. 6; ICARR and ECCJ 2015, p. 4). ENNHRI noted in its 2015 report that EU Member States' published NAPs had by then mostly describe historical actions, and lacked specific commitments capable of demonstrably improving UNGPs implementation at national level (ENNHRI 2015, p. 2).

Conclusion

Given these serious critiques of NAPs in countries that are progressive on the human rights front, it is therefore necessary to keep the focus on Asian Government's actions, duties and responsibilities as BHR in Asia advances through NAPs and other regulatory and policy frameworks. These critiques of NAPs also point to the need to identify complementar ways in which to advance BHR, elements of which are explored in this work.

References

Annan, Kofi, "United Nations, Secretary-General Proposes Global Compact on Human Rights, Labour, Environment in Address to World Economic Forum in Davos (1999) Press Release SG/SM/6881, http://www.un.org/press/en/1999/19990201.sgsm6881.html,

Augenstein, Daniel, Dawson, Mark and Thielborger, Pierre (2018) The UNGPs in the European Union: The Open Coordination of Business and Human Rights? Business and Human Rights Journal, 3 (2018), pp. 1–22.

BHR Resource Centre (2018). National Action Plans.

Benjamin, Golda and Sta. Maria, Bobbie (2018) "National Action Plans on Business and Human Rights in ASEAN: Observations and REcommendations on the Procedural Aspects of NAP Development," paper presented to International Conference on Business and Human Rights: Holding Governments Accountable," Asia Centre, Bangkok, 12–13 July 2018.

Brazil Embassy UK, Sao Paolo (c. 2016) Preliminary Essay on National Action Plans on Business And Human Rights and Recommendations to Brazil. Available at: https://direitosp.fgv.br/sites/direitosp.fgv.br/files/arquivos/gdhee_embaixada_do_uk_no_brasil_paper_en.pdf

European Network of National Human Rights Institutions (ENNHRI) (2015), 'Recommendations for the next EU Strategy on CSR' (April 2015), 2, https://business-humanrights.org/sites/default/files/documents/EU%20CSR%20Communication%20ENNHRI%20Final%20Apr%202015%20(2).pdf

European Union (2011) "A renewed EU strategy 2011–14 for Corporate Social Responsibility," Communication from the Commission to the European Parliament, The Concil, The European Economic and Social Comittee and the Commtitee of the Regions. Brussels, 25 October, COM(2011) 681.

International Corporate Accountability Roundtable (ICAR) and European Coalition for Corporate Justice (ECCJ) (2015) Assessments of existing National Action Plans on Business and Human Rights. ICARR, ECCJ.

Manushya (2018) "Thailand: Call on the Government to be Sincere and Transparent in the Drafting Process of the National Action Plan on Business & Human Rights with Respect to the Process and Content," Statement of the Thai Business & Human Rights Network on the National Action Plan of Business and Human Rights 23 August 2018, Bangkok.

Mohan, Mahdev (2015) "Corporate Accountability in Southeast Asia: National Action Plans for Responsible Business Conduct under International Law," Journal of East Asian International Law, Vol 3, No. 1, pp. 9–28.

Nonthasoot, Seree (2017) "Thai action plan a step to rights protection by business," Bangkok Post, 28 January 2018 https://www.bangkokpost.com/opinion/opinion/1188481/thai-action-plan-a-step-to-rights-protection-by-business.

Office of the High Commissioner for Human Rights (OHCHR) (2011) *Guiding Principles on Business and Human Rights*. United Nations. Available at https://www.ohchr.org/documents/publications/Guidingprinciples Businesshr_eN.pdf

OHCHR (2018) Statement at the end of visit to Thailand by the United Nations Working Group on Business and Human Rights, 4 April. https://www.ohchr.org/EN/NewsEvents/Pages/DisplayNews.aspx?NewsID=22915&LangID=E

Ruggie, John (2013) Just Business: Multinational Corporations and Human Rights. New York: W.W. Norton & Co.

Ruggie, John (2017) The Social Construction of the UN Guiding Principles on Business and Human Rights. Corporate Responsibility Initiative, Harvard Kennedy School, Working Paper No. 67, June.

Sao Paulo Public Law School and British Embassy in Brazil (2016) Preliminary Essay on National Action Plans on Business and Human Rights and Recommendations to Brazil. Available at: https://direitosp.fgv.br/sites/direitosp.fgv.br/files/arquivos/gdhee_embaixada_do_uk_no_brasil_paper_en.pdf.

Thomas, Thomas & Chandra, Alexander (2014) AICHR Thematic Study on CSR and Human Rights in ASEAN.

UN Working Group on Business and Human Rights (UNWG) (2014) Guidance on National Action Plans on Business and Human Rights. December. Available at https://www.ohchr.org/documents/issues/business/unwg_%20napguidance.pdf

PART II

Contemporary Issues in Asia

CHAPTER 4

Multinational Corporations and Human Rights in Indonesia: The Need for Improvement in Legislation

Nukila Evanty and Nurul Ghufron

Introduction

There is a regional trend in Southeast Asia regions of allegations of human rights violations by large scale corporate projects such as plantations, mining and other forms of extractive industries. While human rights concerns feature across all the activities of business organisation, the spotlight is especially on business operations that affect natural resources and the environment. Their devastating impact on Indonesia is well documented: deforestation by palm oil producing companies that contribute majorly to climate change, the destruction of prime rainforests, the dis-posession of Indigenous of their lands, the poisoning waterways, the construction of dams and so on. People suffer the consequence of environmental

N. Evanty (✉)
Jakarta, Indonesia

N. Ghufron
Kabupaten Jember, Indonesia

J. Gomez, R. Ramcharan (eds.), *Business and Human Rights in Asia*,
https://doi.org/10.1007/978-981-15-7273-9_4

degradation and pollution from these projects, adversely affecting their health and culture.

While solutions to these problems must involve multiple-stakeholders, this chapter emphasises the critical role of the Indonesian Government, whose responses have hitherto been weak, in providing a regulatory framework that can hold businesses accountable. This is vital given that regional mechanisms to address such problems are weak or non-existent (Howland 2007). Following the general trend noted in the Introduction to this work, in Indonesia initial emphasis on Corporate Social Responsibility regulation has proven insufficient to deter rights violations. The Government has moved on to considering legislation on the human rights responsibilities of corporations.

Academic literature on corporate social responsibility regulations in Indonesia, has made several points: the voluntarist versus mandatory nature of CSR regulation (Fajar 2018; Maris 2015), the ineffectiveness of the regulation due to imprecise definitions (Waagstein 2011), the minimal impact in curbing corporate rights violations the regulation (Fajar 2018; White et al. 2018), the minimal impact on sensitizing such corporations to fully disclose rights dimensions to their operations (Cahaya and Hervina 2019) and a tendency of corporations to "de-couple" from ascendant international rights dicousrse (Bartley and Egels-Zandén 2016) Treatment of the human rights dimensions of corporate behaviour is nascent. Prihandono (2013), for example, examined various cases of multinationals violating human rights across Indonesia and noted the improved human rights framework in Indonesia after General Suharto's departure. He writes:

> This transformation brought major change to the national legal framework, aimed at strengthening the promotion and protection of human rights. Despite some limitation…continuing law reform in Indonesia has also resulted in significant changes in the way corporations conduct their business and their attitude to human rights.

In assessing Indonesia's legal instruments that regulate the conduct of TNCs towards human rights, he borrows UNGPs as an assessment framework, a fundamental principle of which is that the laws regulating business conduct should not prevent, but enable, firms to respect human rights (Prihandono 2013, p. 6). He examines a number of laws include the Indonesian Constitution, Indonesian Human Rights Law, International Human Rights law that has been incorporated into domestic law, corporate regulation that has mandatory CSR requirements, regulations on industrial relations, land acquisition regulations, criminal and civil liability law and institutional mechanisms such as the human rights court, industrial courts and civil society. Two noteworthy insights are: (1) The urgent need for an independent, accountable and effective judiciary "because other legal enforcement mechanisms do not seem to work effectively in preventing human rights violations by TNCs." (p. 18) and "the other measure that should be considered by the Indonesian government is entry into bilateral cooperation with the home country governments of TNCs to regulate TNC conduct regarding human rights." (p. 18).

This chapter seeks to contribute to this emerging discussion. In this qualitative study, the co-authors undertake a brief overview of the problem of corporation' violations of human rights, followed by a discussion on multinational Corporations and human rights accountability, which outlines human rights accountability that can be carried out by the State where the MNCs operate and by the State of origin of MNCs. It then looks at the implementation under the UN Guiding Principle on business human rights in a country's business policy that can be implemented by government and civil society effectively. Thereafter, it explains the case mechanism on holding governments accountable, the broad lesson, and the procedure and steps taken by National Commission on Human Rights and Indonesian government have taken. Finally it makes some recommendations for improvement.

A Brief Overview of the Problem

During his visit to Indonesia in February 2018, former UN High Commissioner for Human Rights, Zeid Raad al Hussein, informed the press that:

> Civil society actors have told us how, from the islands of Sumatra to Papua, mining and logging by large corporations have been a source of serious human rights violations against farmers, workers and indigenous communities. By and large, these projects are approved and implemented without meaningful consultation with the local communities. Land grabbing, environmental degradation, contamination of water supplies and resulting health hazards have ensued. Having lost control over their natural resources to corporations that wield enormous power, people spoke to me about their great frustration. There is a clear need for inclusive dialogue and consultation

> and such projects must not be undertaken without the free, fair and informed consent of the affected communities. Civil society estimates suggest that some 200 land rights and environmental defenders were facing criminal charges as of August last year.

In this connection, he appealed to the Government "to ensure the protection of human rights defenders, in particular those advocating on land and environmental issues" (OHCHR 2018).

The High Commissioner's appeal highlighted a dire situation in Indonesia in relation to the abusive exploitation by corporations of natural and environmental resources. A case in point is the forest and peatland fires across Sumatera Island and Kalimantan Island that raged for several months over 2014–2015 and claimed millions of hectares of forest and peatland and ten of thousand of lives including to the most vulnerable, indigenous peoples. In addition, health impacts were felt in neighboring Malaysia and Singapore (Cifor report 2017).

Indonesia's forest fires and haze crisis in 2014–2015 have been described by many international society as an environmental disaster. Large parts of the Indonesia forests and peatland area have burned out of control since August 2015, impacting the health, education and livelihoods of millions of Indonesians particularly Indigenous peoples living in the areas with the worst burning, moreover the toxic smoke spread across the country, reaching as far as neighboring Malaysia and Singapore. Transboundary haze pollution because of forest and peatland fires is considered one of the most serious environmental problems in Southeast Asia.

The devastating impact of foreign mining companies in West Papua is also well documented (Taylor 2011a, b, c; Muchlinski 2015) as is the activities of BP and ExxonMobil in the same area (McKenna 2015). A Court case against Exxon Mobil was accepted by US Courts in 2008, for alleged violations of human rights in Aceh. The plaintiff victims alleged that Exxon Mobil contracted Indonesian security forces to provide security for its operations and thereby aided and abetted human rights violations committed by the Indonesian security forces (ICTJ c.2009, p. 11).

The preceding have resulted resulted in accusations of a new "corporate colonialism", especially as corporations seize lands of indigenous peoples (Vidal 2013). However, they have note been addressed in human rights terms.

Malaysia and Singapore have sought to address the transboundary haze hazard through different means. Whereas Malaysia chose to pursue its haze grievances through diplomatic channels,Singapore decided to enact a law, the Transboundary Haze Pollution Act after observing the city-state's experience.[1]

Singapore sued the Indonesian plantation company deemed responsible for the burning of forests and peatland causing haze pollution that endangers the health of Singapore's population. Singapore sued five Indonesian companies which are Rimba Hutani Mas, Sebangun Bumi Andalas Wood Industries, Bumi Sriwijaya Sentosa and Wachyuni Mandira, in September 25, 2015 including a multinational corporation, Asia Pulp and Paper (APP) was proven to have burned the forest which triggered the haze pollution based on the evidence collected by the National Environment Agency in Singapore.[2]

According to Singapore's Transboundary Pollution Act of 2014,[3] then Singapore may impose a fine of SGD 100,000 to local companies or mul-

[1] Available at https://www.businesstimes.com.sg/government-economy/malaysia-prefers-to-use-diplomacy-to-fight-haze-causing-fires

[2] Available at https://www.cnnindonesia.com/internasional/20150926093725-106-81046/singapura-sebut-empat-perusahaan-indonesia-pemicu-. APP is the pulp and paper susbidiary of the Sinar Mas Group, and is one of the largest pulp and paper corporates in the world. The Sinar Mas Group was established in 1962 by Eka Tjipta Widjaja. It is an Indonesian conglomerate with activities in the pulp and paper, food, palm oil, and finance sectors. APP's first paper mill, Tjiwi Kimia, started production in 1978. This was followed by the 1986 acquisition of the pulp and paper producer Indah Kiat. The APP Group produces more than 19 million tons of pulp and paper annually, and operates in China and Indonesia.

[3] Transboundary Pollution Act 2014 (No. of 2014) states that Criminal Liability for haze pollution in Singapore: (1) An entity shall be guilty of an offence, and shall be liable on conviction to a fine not exceeding $300,000, if (a) the entity (i) engages in conduct (whether in or outside Singapore) which causes or contributes to any haze pollution in Singapore; or (ii) authorises or condones (whether in or outside Singapore) any conduct (whether in or outside Singapore) which causes or contributes to any haze pollution in Singapore; and Civil Liability for haze pollution in Singapore (1) It shall be a duty of an entity to ensure that (a) it does not engage in conduct (whether in or outside Singapore) which causes or contributes to any haze pollution in Singapore; and (b) it does not authorise or condone (whether in or outside Singapore) any conduct (whether in or outside Singapore) which causes or contributes to any haze pollution in Singapore.Where any entity engages in conduct that is in breach of any duty (...) other incidents applicable to actions for breach of statutory duty, that is actionable conduct at the suit of any person in Singapore who, in consequence of that breach; (a) sustains any personal injury, contracts any disease, sustains any mental or physical incapacity or dies; (b) sustains any physical damage to property; or (c) sustains any economic loss, including a loss of profits. A cause of action for any actionable conduct (...) shall be actionable in Singapore, whether or not that conduct is also actionable in the foreign jurisdiction where that conduct occurred.

tinational corporations that contribute to harmful haze pollution for the health of the population. From some research findings including an NGO, Friends of the Earth in 2016 stated that the company and multinational corporations are contributed on those forest and peatland fires, also some private banks and other EU countries were also contributed in providing financial services to the palm oil plantation sector. Another factor is lack of supervision over burning to clear the land for other development purposes such as for growing agricultural crops like plantation trees such as oil palm, rubber, or pulpwood, lack of legal enforcement including having weak judicial systems, lack of capacity on the part of concerned authorities, lack of awareness and adequate information, limited resources on human resources, the lack of political will to handle the problem, and the associated businesses and individual profit motives including corruption practices at the expense of environmental and social costs (Apichai 2015).

However, recent trends in addressing transboundary environmental harm show that States prefer to adopt and implement a prevention and cooperation regime and less emphasize on human rights accountability, particularly in Southeast Asia. The ASEAN agreement on Transboundary Haze Pollution (AATHP) which came into force in 2003, which 20 January 2015 thus completing the ratification process of this agreement by all 10 ASEAN member countries. One major shortcoming of the AAHTP is that there is no sanction clause for failure to meet the stipulated obligations. Then an agreement in principle to develop a Roadmap on ASEAN Cooperation towards Transboundary Haze Pollution Control with Mean of Implementation to achieve a vision of a hazefree ASEAN by 2020.

Recent trend also shows that environmental defenders who are at the forefront of community struggles thus face myriad threats from outright assassination, threats, harassment, illegal arrest, detention, also to discourage them to continue their advocacy (Bautista and Yang 2018) Indonesian courts, for example, have also currently used various obscure and draconian laws to prosecute environmental defenders, including at least 157 individuals in 2017.

In this context of human rights violations and regional tensions over the haze and other abuses by corporations, the UN High Commissioner urged the Government and corporations involved in the extraction of natural resources, plantations and large scale fisheries, comply with the UN Guiding Principles on Business and Human Rights in order to bring greater accountability by corporations by corporations (UN 2011).

Multinational Corporations and Human Rights Accountability

Multinational Corporations (MNCs) are non state actors that have an important role in the development of the Indonesian and the world economy. The role of MNCs in international capital flows has grown substantively in recent years through Foreign Direct Investment (FDI), especially to developing countries because it has been recognized as an important driver of development (Hussein 2009). MNCs are heavily involved in Indonesia's Palm Oil Sector, which accounted for US$18 billion in revenue in 2017. Therefore the role of MNCs in the development of global and national politics can not be avoided. Nevertheless, while they have a beneficial impact on overall development,—through creating jobs, technological transformation and economic income—they can leave a devastating impact on the environment and contribute to human rights abuses, addressed previously.

It is instructive for present purposes to recall a few salient points about MNCS, for the purposes of this paper. Multinational corporations (MNCs) are corporate entities that perform economic activities in two or more States, that have legal status both in the home state of the MNCs and in a host state in which the MNC is running its business which is established either by individuals or groups (UN ECOSOC 2003). MNCs are large industrial companies with extensive business networks or branches and subsidiaries which are scattered throughout home and host countries (Lalnumawia 2009). The two main characteristics of MNCs are large size and the fact that they have a parent company centrally controlling their worldwide activities, most of which are found in the Canada, France, Germany, the United Kingdom and the United States of America (Lalnumawia 2009). In addition, a corporation is a company, identified as such by the law, and owning municipal legal personality. Hence an MNC, is one that operates in multiple jurisdictions (Kogut 2001). The State in which the corporation is incorporated is its "home State", and the nation in which it conducts its activities is the "host State" or "territorial State". However, to determine the nationality of a corporation is quite difficult. In some case, nationality is determined by reference to the home state or place of incorporation. But nationality can also be determined by reference to the principal place of business or the seat, or to the nationality of the controlling interest (Muchlinski 2015).

International law and international human rights law standards may be incorporated into national law that regulates individual and corporate activity, through direct integration of international standards into national law or through ratification followed by an enabling act (See Mueller 2013). Hence a national law would establish a new penalties or offence for individuals or corporations that engage in conduct in contravention of relevant UN covenants with strict liability for corporations.

In addition to that, the international actors that have responsibility under International law are those that have extra territorial capacity, which are; (1) Multinational Corporations; and (2) other business enterprises (UN General Assembly 2014), inclusive of several business entities, which are companies in transnational corporations, contractors, sub-contractors, suppliers, licensors or distributors, corporations, partnerships, or other legal companies operating in the international as well as at national level including their officers, managers, members of corporate boards or directors and other executives and persons working for them (Alvarez 2010, p. 8).

Recent development in various international fora is the increasing participation of corporations and many non-state actors. They have contributed in the making of international law including the making of international trade and investment law through investor state adjudication (Alvarez 2010, p. 9).

Holding Governments Accountable; a Lesson Learned

According to Indonesian law, a corporation is a legal subject which means it is an artificial person a 'form of a human being' who can have legal rights and obligations. However the difference is that a corporation cannot be imprisoned or criminalized. Hence the judge may impose a penalty on the corporation or the management of corporation either alternatively or cumulatively. Therefore the principal punishment that can be imposed on the corporation is a fine. Whereas the additional criminal sanction imposed on the corporation shall be in accordance with other laws and regulations, notably Supreme Court Regulation No. 13 of 2016 on Criminal Procedures, hence for criminal case committed by corporations.

In addition to that the Indonesian Criminal Code does not recognize corporate criminal liability. The draft version of the Criminal Code 2015,[4] provided for regulation of corporate criminal liability in which the board of corporation and or corporation may be held liable when engaging in criminal offenses. However, the draft Criminal Code does not provide the scope of corporate responsibility for human rights violations *per se*, so that when corporations commit human rights violations, the mechanisms of human rights accountability can not be imposed on the corporation.

Multinational corporations conducting their activities within the territory of Indonesia must adhere to Law No. 25 Year 2007 on Capital Investment. The law provides that "companies in foreign investment are required in the form of *limited liability corporate* under Indonesian law and domiciled within the territory of the Republic of Indonesia, unless otherwise provided by law". Furthermore, the Law states that "In an investment, a corporate must be based on the principles of: (a) legal certainty, (b) openness, (c) accountability, (d) equal treatment and no distinction of national origin, (e) fair efficiency, (f) sustainable environmental concerns, i) independence, and j) balance of progress and national economic unity.

Furthermore, Law No. 40 of 2007 concerning Limited Liability Companies has explained that any Multinational Corporations which will conduct its business activities in Indonesia shall refer to the provisions of Article 5 point (1) which reads: "the corporate has the name and place of domicile within the territory of the Republic of Indonesia as determined in the articles of association". Then multinational corporations engaged in forestry industries and plantation have a social and environmental responsibility in the area of their business or concession area, including if the business is conducted in a local community furthermore the corporate should take more responsibility to the most marginalized community or indigenous peoples. The responsibilities of this corporate are, among others, as stipulated in Article 74 of Law No. 40 of 2007 regarding a Limited Company which states: (1) The corporate carries out its business activities in the field or related to natural resources shall carry out the Social and Environmental Responsibility; (2) Hence, social and environmental responsibility shall be the obligations of the corporate which should be allocated the budget and calculated as the corporate's expenses which its

[4] http://dpr.go.id/dokakd/dokumen/K3-26-2ea83388ece0ae0d13b3977bebb049c1.pdf

performance shall be carried out with due consideration of "proper" and "fairness". (3) A corporate that does not perform its obligations will be sanctioned in accordance with the provisions of laws and regulations.

Then, the national regulation on environmental protection in Law No.32 of 2009 has anticipated every form of activities either individual or corporate that conduct their activities directly or indirectly related to the problem of environmental pollution. In Article 1 point (14) explains that environmental pollution is environmental damage due to human activities and other ways that exceeded the established environmental quality standards. In Law no. 32 of 2007, article 76 states that sanctions are administrative in nature relating to violations of environmental permits. Hence administrative sanctions consist of: a. written warning; b. government coercion; c. freezing of environmental permits; or d. revocation of environmental permits.

From the explanation of some policies and regulations above therefore the national regulations still lack provisions that can sanction the impact of corporate burning of the forest and peatland that cause environmental pollution and harm the local communities, including indigenous peoples who are living in the forests and peatlands areas. National law is needed to be strengthen in order to empower the oversight function of government to monitor forest and forestry management in the region, including to empower the role of local governments to endorse the laws and ensure the safety of local communities including indigenous peoples.

Moreover, civil society organizations and the corporate's supervisory commission needs to provide the data on the adverse impacts of the corporate's activities to the local community and to provide sustainable empowerment activities for community directly affected by forestry business activities and are entitled to:

(a) obtain appropriate compensation for any damages in the operation of forestry activities;
(b) file a lawsuit in the court against the damages resulting from the corporate violating the terms and agrement;
(c) Under the supervision and guidance of the government due to the impacts of forest and peatland fires of indigenous peoples, therefore it is necessary to develop new instruments to protect the rights of indigenous peoples in their land, among others by requiring MNCs which already operated and based on concession licenses from the central government should rehabilitate on the environ-

mental damaged and to pay health compensation for local community.

In this situation, where national laws seem insufficient and regional mechanisms are weak or non-existent, can international standards help?

Indonesia and the UN Guiding Principle on Business and Human Rights

Indonesia, spurred on by its National Human Rights Institution (KOMNAS Ham) has begun to engage with the UNGPs developed by the Special Representative of the Secretary General on the issue of human rights and transnational corporations and other business enterprises (SRSG) to operationalise the UN 'Protect, Respect and Remedy' Framework (See Kinley and Chambers 2006). However, the advancement of UNGPs face several impeding factors in Indonesia, unlike in other parts of the world where a variety of responses have been noted. The SRSG pointed out, the UNGPs endorsement marked 'the end of the beginning: by establishing a common global platform for action, on which cumulative progress can be built (ibid.)

States around the world have responded variously: the application of national measures with extraterritorial implications, requirements on "parent" corporates to report on the global operations of the entire enterprise, adhering to multilateral soft-law instruments such as the Guidelines for Multinational Enterprises of the Organisation for Economic Co-operation and Development (OECD), performance standards required by institutions that support overseas investments and direct extraterritorial legislation and enforcement. The latter includes criminal regimes that allow for prosecutions based on the nationality of the perpetrator no matter where the offence occurs. Furthermore various factors may contribute to the perceived and actual reasonableness of States' actions, for example whether they are grounded in multilateral agreement.

It is encouraging that, as reported by the Business and Human Rights Resource Centre (BHRC), in 2011 that 73% of governments referred to the UN Guiding Principle as international standards in their responses, sometimes they particularly citing on how their actions relate to State duty to protect human rights, as stipulated by Guiding Principles, however, at least 18% of respondents of government particularly stated that they have not taken action on business and human rights since since the UN Guiding Principles adopted. It is said by the report that 60 percent of government do not communicate anywhere else on their actions on business and human rights (Business & Human Rights Resource Centre 2015, p. 6).

In Indonesia, the implementation of the UNGPs' in the broader sense have been led by the National Human Rights Institutions (Komnas HAM) and Indonesia also the first country in Southeast Asia to launch the NAP (National Plan of Action) Business and Human Rights. This NAP on Business and Human Rights was regulated under Komnas HAM Regulation No. 1 Year 2017 on Ratification of the National Plan of Action on Business and Human Rights, State News No. 856.[5] This is not surprising as Indonesia and other Southeast Asia NHRIs were already engaging actively in this topic at the stage of the UNGPs' development and were undertaking numerous efforts as follow-up to the UNGPs' endorsement (See Government of Indonesia, 2007, 2009, 2014; Franciscans Interntional, 2016; Human Rights Committee 2004).

The UN Guideline mentioned that the corporation as a business entity, is positioned as the subject who has responsibility for the process and the impact of its business activities in the community. These principles are supported by a number of corporates, including civil society organizations, trade unions, and other stakeholder groups. According to UN Guiding Principles on Human Rights that business enterprises including MNCs have the responsibility to respect human rights which requires that they:

(a) Avoid causing or contributing to adverse human rights impacts through their own activities, and address such impacts when they occur;
(b) Seek to prevent or mitigate adverse human rights impacts that are directly linked to their operations, products or services by their business relationships, even if they have not contributed to those impacts (Faracik 2017, p. 14).

[5] http://elsam.or.id/2017/06/komnas-ham-lauches-national-action-plan-on-business-and-human-rights/

Moreover, the responsibility of MNCs applies to respect human rights regardless of MNCs size, sector, operational context, ownership and structure. Nevertheless, the scale and complexity of the means through which MNCs meet that responsibility may vary according to these factors and with the severity of the enterprise's adverse human rights impacts (Faracik 2017, p. 15).

In order to meet their responsibility to respect human rights, hence MNCs should have in place policies and processes appropriate to their size and circumstances, including: (a) a policy commitment to meet their responsibility to respect human rights; (b) a human rights due diligence process to identify, prevent, mitigate and account for how they address their impacts on human rights; (c) processes to enable the remediation of any adverse human rights impacts they cause or to which they contribute (Faracik 2017, pp. 15–16).

Despite this movement towards a NAP, there are various factors impeding factors that affect the Indonesian Government's ability to take action on Business and Human Rights, according to the responses provided in the individual states' responses to the Business & Human Rights Resource Centre questionnaire administered in 2015 (BHRC 2015). These are summarised in Table 4.1 below.

Table 4.1 Factors impeding the UNGPs in Indonesia

No	*Factors*	*Categories*
1.	Lack of understanding or awareness of business and human rights in governance	The most significant factor
2.	Challenges of coordinating across government departments	Significant factor
3.	Lack of resources for enforcement, monitoring and prosecution	The most significant factor
4.	Opposition by economic interest groups or business associations	Significant factor
5.	Opposition or lack of consensus within government	Significant factor
6.	Other opposition by influential people or group outside government	The most significant
7.	Political limitations imposed by foreign governments or multilateral institutions	Significant factor
8.	Lack of capacity and capability of government	Significant factor

Source: Business & Human Rights Resource Centre (2015), *Government Action Platform, Individual country responses to the BHHRC survey 2015*, all responses are available at https://businesshumanrights.org/en/government-action-platform

Conclusion

Universal human rights laws were developed to protect the dignity of the human being and to provide redress and remedies for behaviour that violates their dignity and rights. However the recent policy and legislation in some Southeast Asia Countries are not sufficient to protect individuals from powerful international non-State actors, namely MNCs. Therefore, there is a need to provide and enforce human rights mechanisms and to regulate human rights accountability for MNCs from mere norms such as the UN Guiding Principle on Business and Human Rights to become a norm of binding legal force.

The National Action Plan (NAP) in Indonesia, which seeks to regulate the legal obligation for ministries, government institutions, and local governments in accordance with the scope of their authority needs to be further regulated through Presidential decree, given the complex linkages between business and human rights linkages. Carefully crafted legislation is needed to provide more operational power that will advance human rights law. Furthermore, federal law and local law must be drafted so that there is no gap that allows for loopholes at the local level.

States' territorial responsibility has proven to be insufficient for human rights protection since new forms of globalized political, economic and financial relations have emerged. Hence the entire international community has an obligation to ensure that human rights are protected, and must ensure that the States directly or indirectly involved in violations are made accountable. In the case of MNCs' wrongful behaviour, whether on transboundary haze pollution or on health in the city and local community, this should be linked to a concurrent responsibility between the home and host States, depending on the situation. International law has already accepted regulatory frameworks for some types of corporate misconduct, such as the ones punishing and preventing environmental harm and corruption.

The government must encourage MNCs to create proper remedies, compensation and enforcement mechanisms. In the process of achieving a comprehensive and complete international law for the protection of human rights equally, each social actor must work together in the promotion of corporate accountability and incorporation international human rights law in national legal systems. Indonesia and all States should guarantee protection to rights holders who have been violated by MNCs.

References

Alvarez, José (2010) "Are Corporations "Subjects" of International Law?, available at http://www.law.nyu.edu/sites/default/files/ECM_PRO_069097.pdf

Apichai, Sunchindah, ERIA Discussion Paper Series, "Transboundary Haze Pollution Problem in Southeast Asia: Reframing ASEAN's Response", December 2015, ERIA-DP-2015-82, pp. 4–5

Bartley, Tim and Egels-Zandén, Niklas (2016) "Beyond decoupling: unions and the leveraging of corporate social responsibility in Indonesia," *Socio-Economic Review*, Volume 14, Issue 2, April 2016, Pages 231–255.

Bautista Jr., Clemente and Paul Christian Yang (ed) (2018), In peril: Southeast Asia's environment and its defenders (Part 1 of 2) available at http://bulatlat.com/main/2018/07/10/peril-southeast-asias-environment-defenders-part-1-2/, 10 July

Business & Human Rights Resource Centre (BHRC) (2015), *Government Action Platform, Individual country responses to the BHHRC survey 2015*, all responses are available at https://businesshumanrights.org/en/government-action-platform.

Business & Human Rights Resource Centre (2015) Action on Business and Human Rights; Where are we know, key finding from our action platform, Business and Human Rights Resource Centre, p. 5, available at https://www.business-humanrights.org/sites/default/files/Action_Platform_Final.pdf

Cahaya, Fitra Roman and Hervina, Rizka (2019) "Do human rights issues matter? An empirical analysis of Indonesian companies' reporting", Social Responsibility Journal, Vol. 15 Issue: 2, pp. 226–243.

Center for International Forestry Research (CIFOR) (2017) Annual Report 2017. CGIAR Research Program on Forests, Trees and Agroforestry. Available at: https://www.cifor.org/publications/pdf_files/AReports/CRP/ARCRP2017.pdf

Fajar, Mukti (2018) Vol: 21 Issue: 3 "Corporate Social Responsibility in Indonesia: Regulation and Implementation Issues," Journal of Legal, Ethical and Regulatory Issues (Univ of Yogyakarata). Vol: 21 Issue: 3, https://www.abacademies.org/articles/corporate-social-responsibility-in-indonesia-regulation-and-implementation-issues-7240.html

Faracik, Beata (2017) "Implementation of the UN Guiding Principles on Business and Human Rights", Directorate General for External Policies, Policy Department, European Parliament 2017, Poland.

Franciscans International (2016) *Human Rights Situation in Indonesia Specific focus on Human Rights in West Papua*. Submission to the UPR REview of Indonesia, April/May 2017.

Government of Indonesia, Law No.4 Tahun 2009 on Mining

Government of Indonesia, Law No.25 Tahun 2007 on Capital Investment

Government of Indonesia, Law No.40 Tahun 2007 on Limited Company
Government of Indonesia, Law No.32 Tahun 2009 on Environmental Protection.
Government of Indonesia, Law No.23 tahun 2014 on Local Government
Howland, Todd (2007) "The Multi-State Responsibility for Extraterritorial Violations of Economic, Social and Cultural Rights". Denver Journal of International Law and Policy, Vol. 35: 3/4, pp. 389–411.
Hussein, Muawya A. (2009) Impacts of Foreign Direct Investment on Economic Growth in the Gulf Cooperation Council (GCC) Countries. [online] Available at http://www.bizresearchpapers.com/27.Mua.pdf. Accessed 21 August 2011.
International Center for Transitional Justice (ICTJ, c.2009?) A Matter of Complicity? Exxon Mobil on Trial for its Role in Human Rights Violations in Aceh. https://drive.google.com/drive/folders/1v49ioz30WW8QEILEEGKuijibYEHspJT9
Kinley, David and Chambers, Rachel (2006) The Un Human Rights Norms for Corporations: The Private Implications of Public International Law. Sydney Law School Research Paper No. 07/06; Human Rights Law Review, Vol. 2. Available at SSRN: https://ssrn.com/abstract=944153
Kogut, B. (2001) "Multinational Corporations" in Neil J Smelser and Paul B Baltes (eds) International Encyclopedia of the Social & Behavioural Sciences (Pergamon, Oxford, 2001)
Maris, Armand (c.2015) Compulsory CSR: Indonesia takes a tough stance but clarity on definitions is lacking,IPRA, 2015. https://www.ipra.org/news/itle/compulsory-csr-indonesia-takes-a-tough-stance-but-clarity-on-definitions-is-lacking/
McKenna, Kylie (2015) BP, security and human rights in West Papua, New Mandala, 04 SEP, 2015, https://www.newmandala.org/bp-security-and-human-rights-in-west-papua/
Muchlinski, P. (2015) "Operationalising the UN Business and Human Rights Framework: The Corporate Responsibility to Respect Human Rights and Due Diligence," In: Lundan S. (eds) Transnational Corporations and Transnational Governance. Palgrave Macmillan, London.
Müller, Amrei (2013) "Relationship between national and international law", Public International Law, University of Oslo, available at https://www.uio.no/studier/emner/jus/jus/JUS5540/h13/undervisningsmateriale/nat-int-law_14oct2013.pdf
Office of the UN High Commissioner for Human Rights (2018) High Commissioner for Human Rights, Zeid Raad Al Hussein, https://www.ohchr.org/EN/NewsEvents/Pages/DisplayNews.aspx?NewsID=22637&LangID=E
Prihandono, Iman, Transnational Corporations and Human Rights Violations in Indonesia (July 22, 2013). Australian Journal of Asian Law, Vol. 14, No. 1, Article 5, 2013. Available at SSRN: https://ssrn.com/abstract=2296748

Taylor, Naj (2011a), "The blacklisting of Rio Tinto," *Al Jazeera*, 19 October https://www.aljazeera.com/indepth/opinion/2011/08/2011823133628702154.html

Taylor, Naj (2011b), "West Papua: A history of exploitation," Al Jazeera, 19 October. https://www.aljazeera.com/indepth/opinion/2011/08/201182814172453998.html

Taylor, Naj (2011c) Mining companies funded Indonesian abuses," *Al Jazeera*, 19 October, https://www.aljazeera.com/indepth/opinion/2011/08/2011828142858857222.html

UN Human Rights Committee (2004), General Comment No. 31 (80) Nature of the General Legal Obligation Imposed on States Parties to the Covenant, 5/26/2004.CCPR/C/21/Rev.1/Add.13

United Nations, International Covenant on Civil and Political Rights (ICCPR), 1966

United Nations International Covenant on Economic, Social and Cultural Rights (ICESCR), 1966

United Nations (2011), Guiding Principles on Business and Human Rights, Implementing the United Nations, Protect, Respect and Remedy Framework, United Nations Human Rights, Office of the High Commissioners, Geneva 2011

United Nations, Economic and Social Council (2003), Commission on Human Rights, Sub-Commission on the Promotion and Protection of Human Rights, Norms on the responsibilities of transnational corporations and other business enterprises with regard to human rights, E/CN.4/Sub.2/2003/12/Rev.2, 26 August

United Nations General Assembly (2014), Human Rights Council, Twenty-sixth session, Agenda item 3, Promotion and protection of all human rights, civil, political, economic, social and cultural rights, including the right to development, Resolution adopted by the Human Rights Council, 26/9 Elaboration of an international legally binding instrument, A/HRC/RES/26/9, 14 July 2014

Vidal, John (2013) The Guardian, "Indonesia is seeing a new corporate colonialism" 25 May. https://www.theguardian.com/world/2013/may/25/indonesia-new-corporate-colonialism

Waagstein, Patricia Rinwigati (2011) "The Mandatory Corporate Social Responsibility in "Indonesia: Problems and Implications," *Journal of Business Ethics*, Vol. 98, No. 3 (February 2011), pp. 455–466.

White, Nigel D., Footer, Mary E., Senior, Kerry, Dorp, Mark van, Kiezebrin, Vincent Puraka, Y. Wasi Gede, Fajri Anzas, Ayudya (2018) *Blurring Public and Private Security in Indonesia: Corporate Interests and Human Rights in a Fragile Environment*. https://link.springer.com/article/10.1007/s40802-018-0107-8

CHAPTER 5

All Carrots and No Stick: Human Rights Regulation of Companies in Japan

Saul Takahashi

Introduction

Though often thought of as a document aimed only at companies, the majority of provisions in the UN Guiding Principles on Business and Human Rights (UNGPs) are in fact directed at states, as the bearer of obligations under international law and the entity that can, so it is envisioned, both require and enable companies to improve practices having implications for human rights. The first foundational principle of the UNGPs, for example, states that states should take 'appropriate steps to prevent, investigate, punish and redress [human rights] abuse through effective policies, legislation, regulations and adjudication', with the second stating that states must 'set out clearly the expectation that all business enterprises domiciled in their territory and/or jurisdiction respect human rights throughout their operations.' Performing these duties includes, inter alia, '[enforcing] laws that are aimed at, or have the effect

S. Takahashi (✉)
Osaka, Japan
e-mail: james@asiacentre.co.th

J. Gomez, R. Ramcharan (eds.), *Business and Human Rights in Asia*,
https://doi.org/10.1007/978-981-15-7273-9_5

of, requiring business enterprises to respect human rights' (Office of the High Commissioner for Human Rights 2011: 3, 4).

As with most provisions of international law, how exactly the above provisions are implemented varies from country to country. Many countries have adopted legislation requiring companies to fulfill certain specified standards in human rights related areas, with penalties for companies that do not comply. Japan, however, has generally preferred a different approach, based largely on non binding standards and voluntary compliance. Laws and policies related to business and human rights issues have been adopted in Japan, but many of them have been little more than statements of intent, containing non binding targets and statements of principles, and lacking penalties for non compliance. Certification schemes and other incentives are often made to act as carrots for companies to perform well—however, sticks are lacking against companies that fail to live up to the required standard.

Presumably there are a multitude of factors that give rise to this situation. Unquestionably, the immense power of big business in Japan, in particular the mighty Keidanren, the Japanese Business Federation, is one. Besides lobbying politicians on issues of concern, Keidanren co-ordinates the hefty donations of Japanese companies to political parties,[1] ensuring a stable stream of funds for parties that promote pro business policies (mainly the Liberal Democratic Party, which has been in power more or less constantly since 1955). Keidanren's policy demands go far beyond deregulation and other issues directly related to the operation of businesses—for example, it has been a leading advocate for reductions in the welfare budget, raising the rate of value added tax, and increases in military spending.[2]

Trade unions are weak in Japan. The unionization rate, 55 percent in the late 1940s, currently stands at 17 percent, partially due to the exponential increase in contract employment (and the exclusion of contract employees by many unions) in recent years. Equally (or even more) relevant is the fact that the overwhelming majority of unions in Japan are

[1] Japanese law allows for corporations to make donations to political parties, and, indirectly, to particular candidates.

[2] Keidanren's influence on human rights and other social issues has of course not been only negative. In 2017, Keidanren adopted a revised Charter of Corporate Behaviour, which makes reference to the UNGPs and states that corporations should, inter alia, '[respect] the human rights of all persons.' The manual for implementation of the Charter, also published in 2017, devotes a chapter to human rights. (Keidanren 2017).

company unions, and therefore often reticent to take strong stances against management (Kosei Roudou-sho 2017a: 2, 8). The media is equally docile (Kaye 2017), and the capacity of human rights and other NGOs is extremely limited. Therefore, there is a general lack of social forces that might be expected to counter balance the influence of businesses in contributing to government policy. Many Japanese place more trust in companies more than other actors, including the government, politicians, the media, and NGOs (with NGOs scoring last) (Edelman 2017).

At the same time, it is worthy to note that there is a recurring theme within Japanese discourse that ties this preference for carrots over sticks to the notion that companies (and people) are naturally inclined towards good. According to this narrative, the 'foreign' (meaning Western) paradigm is based on the assumption that people are inherently bad. This paradigm necessarily results in binding legislation, formal checks and balances, and a generally legalistic approach, since compulsory rules are needed to make sure that people do not engage in prohibited activities. In contrast, the Japanese (or, depending on the context, the 'Asian') approach is presented as one that trusts in the inherent goodness of people. In this paradigm, all people require is a goal (set by the government in the role of a benevolent father figure) and a nudge in the right direction, and they will embark on the correct path. Even in the unusual circumstance that deviant actions are taken, they are surely the result only of honest mistakes or simple misunderstandings between otherwise well intending actors. Those rare cases can be dealt with through gentle, subtle intervention by those with authority, together with the disapproving stares of the other members of the community. Harsh, public sanctions are not needed (see e.g. Keizai-nin Ko-Entaku Kaigi 2016, 2017).

This narrative is often intertwined with the (seemingly mutually reinforcing) notion that Japanese society values harmony (wa) above all else. 'Foreigners' (i.e. Western people), so this narrative goes, are inherently adversarial, think only about themselves, and are too quick to demand their rights, even if this could disrupt the harmony of the collective. Japanese people, on the other hand, are more considerate of others, and elegantly give way wherever possible, ensuring that all members of society are happy (see e.g. Keizai-nin Ko-Entaku Kaigi 2016, 2017).

Obviously, the above narrative gives rise to significant questions, including who defines what constitutes 'harmony' within Japanese society at any given time, which social actors benefit from said 'harmony', and what (if any) mechanisms exist to ensure the interests of vulnerable actors. These are broader questions that are out of the scope of this paper (and out of the expertise of this author): suffice it to say there has been little pressure on the government to adopt binding standards in areas of business and human rights.

Of course, even without penal provisions, law and policy can potentially act as a catalyst for social change, insofar as government positions can play a role in setting the tone of popular discourse. This paper will examine three areas of business and human rights in Japan: regulation of excessive working hours, the import of illegal timber, and the rights of women in the workplace, as examples of the non binding approach the government has adopted. By and large, the 'carrots but no stick' approach has proven inadequate, at least in the immediate term: efforts in the areas of working hours and illegal timber over recent years have been ineffectual in bring about improvements, with certification schemes even arguably serving as a whitewashing effort. There has been some improvement in the area of women's rights, but that has been over the space of three decades, and Japan still remains at the bottom of the international league table in this area.

There has been surprisingly little written on these three issues based on the business and human rights framework, or even the framework of international human rights in general. The topics of excessive working hours and the treatment of women in the workplace are both subjects of intense public debate in Japan; however, when legal frameworks are made reference to, they are generally limited to domestic labour law—international law is rarely cited (see e.g. Arai et al. 2018). It is submitted that this is part of a broad trend within the Japanese legal community (including the judiciary), most of which tends to have little knowledge of international human rights standards (See e.g. Iwasawa 1998). Likewise, textbooks on international human rights law tend not to examine these issues in an indepth manner (see e.g. Shin 2013). Indeed, many corporate people have told this author that they believe the two issues to be 'labour issues, not human rights issues', and it would appear that this misconception is widespread. Of course, business and human rights is itself a relatively new field, with the UNGPs only having been adopted in 2011. Regarding the issue of illegal timber, it has received almost no attention outside of research published by international NGOs. This paper will examine government, corporate, and NGO documents, and engage in a qualitative evaluation of government measures in these three areas.

Japan had long been criticized by civil society for being one of only two G7 countries that had not adopted a National Action Plan on Business and Human Rights (NAP) in accordance with the UNGPs. In a surprise move, Japan announced at the UN Forum on Business and Human Rights in November 2016 that it would formulate a NAP, and the Foreign Ministry has reportedly commissioned baseline studies in relevant areas. Nevertheless, there remains a paucity of publicly available information regarding the direction of the NAP, and there is concern that it will continue with the current approach of providing only carrots, with no stick.

Karoshi: Death from Overwork

Japanese workers work extremely long hours, often described, quite literally, as 'murderous' (satsujin-teki). Data submitted by the government to OECD states that Japanese workers work an average of 1713 hours worked annually, putting Japan at 23rd out of 39 countries—however, this data seems to include all workers in any kind of form of work, e.g. students working part time (OECD 2018). Data collected by Keidanren, on the other hand, indicates that average working hours in member companies are in fact around 2000 hours, which would put Japan at fourth or fifth place in the OECD ranking (Keidanren 2018b). However, even the Keidanren figure does not appear to include the massive overtime (hours worked beyond the normal 40 hour work week) that Japanese workers are routinely expected to perform, often without claiming overtime pay—a practice widely derided by Japanese as 'service overtime'.

Labour Ministry data indicates that only about half of workers take all their annual leave days (a minimum of 10 days per annum) (Kosei Roudosho 2018a). More fundamentally, most companies do not have separate provisions for short term sick leave, meaning that workers who are sick and unable to come to work are forced to take annual leave. In addition, Japanese graduates starting in the corporate world are regularly warned against taking more than one or two leave days at a time, making, for example, a week long holiday impossible.

The above practices make accurate accounting of actual working hours difficult. Nevertheless, there is universal recognition that Japanese workers are forced to perform too many hours, and that this causes a multitude of physical and mental health problems. Indeed, Japan is well known for the internationally infamous phenomenon known as 'karoshi'—the Japanese term for 'death from overwork'. In 2017, the Labour Ministry, recognised

260 deaths as directly resulting from overwork.[3] In addition, 498 persons were also recognized as having mental health conditions resulting from overwork (including 84 suicides or attempted suicides resulting from overwork). The trend in recent years has been generally constant, meaning between 700 to 800 lives are either lost or seriously damaged every year from overwork.

These figures are widely understood to be a gross underestimate, as such recognition operates on the basis of very stringent criteria. Amongst others, the guidelines for 'karoshi' recognition require that the worker had performed 'around 100 hours of overtime' over the month immediately preceding death, or 'around 80 hours of overtime per month' over two to six months before death (Kosei Roudou-sho 2001: 7). This has resulted in both the 80 and 100 hour monthly overtime marks being commonly referred to as the 'karoshi line'.

There is of course a multitude of factors behind these working practices, not the least of which, it is submitted, the fact that pulling in long hours has evolved to a symbol of Japanese masculinity. The image of Japanese as being diligent, hard working, and ready to sacrifice themselves (sometimes quite literally) for the good of the collective is often juxtaposed with the 'foreigner' (the Westerner). who is lazy, selfish, and quick to use his 'so called rights' as an excuse to weasel out of hard work. There is no shortage of 'blame the victim' type narratives in popular discourse on karoshi, along the lines of how 'young people nowadays are too weak' and get sick or depressed at the drop of a hat. Other narratives aim at diffusing responsibility completely, arguing that society as a whole is to blame for having unreasonable expectations of ever faster services (therefore allowing companies to act as the victim and shirk any liability for the problem).

What is often overlooked is the fact that legislative and systemic protection for Japanese workers is utterly inadequate. Japanese labour law in principle provides for a 40 hour work week, but states also that workers may be required to perform overtime (or to work on weekends), subject to a limit agreed on by management and the relevant labour union in what is commonly referred to as an 'Article 36 Agreement' (after the Article in the Labour Law). Though this would appear to offer an element of protection against unreasonable demands on workers, the overwhelming majority of unions in Japan are company unions, i.e. they are made up

[3] Official recognition of a death or accident as having resulted from work carries with it payment from a government administered insurance scheme.

only of employees of one particular company, and are often reticent of taking strong stances against management. This results in a situation where workers are vulnerable to 'agreements' that are, to put it lightly, not in their interest.

In 2017, it was reported that a large number of leading manufacturers allowed workers to perform overtime far beyond the karoshi line. For example, the 'agreement at IHI reportedly allows for workers to perform up to 200 hours of overtime per month, Hitachi up to 150, and Sumitomo Heavy Industries up to 140. Toshiba allows 120, Mitsubishi Electrics 105, and Fujitsu, JFE Steel, and Mitsui Engineering and Shipbuilding all allow 100 hours of overtime per month. Toyota, Mazda, Nissan, Mitsubishi Motors, Kawasaki Heavy Industries, NEC, and Nippon Steel and Sumitomo Metal all allow for up to 80 hours of overtime' (Business & Human Rights Resource Centre 2017a). Indeed, 16 out of 17 companies on the Board of Keidanren in 2017 also had Article 36 Agreements that provided for overtime beyond the karoshi line, with NTT allowing up to 150 per month (Business & Human Rights Resource Centre 2017b).

Even the Article 36 Agreements are often flouted by companies (with the acquiescence of unions). The Labour Ministry does raise working hour issues with companies on the basis of complaints, but their recommendations are not legally binding, and further action (in particular referral for prosecution) is extremely rare.[4] In addition, there is no public record of which companies the authorities have raised concerns with, making it extremely difficult for prospective employees (or the general public) to gauge the practices of a particular company. In 2016, the Ministry announced that official unemployment offices would no longer carry job adverts of companies that were the subject of persistent complaints (Nikkei Shimbun 2016). This begs the question as to why this had not been the case before—and in any case the role of government unemployment offices in the Japanese employment system is not large, in particular with regard to new graduates.

Karoshi has been the source of much concern since at least the 1980s, but it was not until 2014 that the government finally adopted legislation aimed at combating the phenomenon. Nevertheless, the 'Promotion of Measures for Karoshi Act' is a prime example of diffusion of responsibility, stating in Article 3 that 'actual conditions concerning karoshi … are not

[4] In 2016, the Labour Ministry raised issues with 23,915 companies. (Kousei Roudosho 2017d).

necessarily sufficiently grasped, [and] this shall be done by encouraging public awareness of the importance of preventing karoshi … and deepening their interest in and understanding' of the phenomenon. Companies are required in the law only to 'endeavor to cooperate with the State and local public entities in promoting measures to prevent karoshi', and the general public appears to be equally responsible for the problem, with the law stipulating that 'citizens shall be aware of the importance of preventing karoshi … and endeavor to deepen their interest and understanding'. There is no mention of any binding measure on businesses, unions, or any entity: indeed, the only clear obligation in the law is for the government to prepare an annual report to parliament. The law has been a failure on its face, as, as stated above, the number of karoshi has remained constant in recent years.

The government also has a certification scheme under which companies that demonstrate measures aimed at shortening working hours and on other indicators related to worker safety and welfare can obtain official recognition from the Labour Ministry. This theme is heavily promoted by the government and the corporate world, and has an anime style logo to attract young, potential employees. However, the scheme has been the subject of widespread derision after a prominent 2015 case involving the suicide of a young worker, Matsuri Takahashi, at Dentsu, the leading advertising house in Japan. It came to light that despite the fact that karoshi cases at Dentsu had been recognized by the Labour Ministry as recently as 2013, Dentsu had still received certification under the scheme, in both 2013 and 2015. (Shimbun Akahata 2016, 2017) Takahashi, 24 years old at the time, had been forced to work 105 hours of overtime the month before her suicide. Takahashi's family sued Dentsu in court, and the company was ordered to pay a derisory sum of JPY 500,000—approximately USD 4400 (Business and Human Rights Resource Centre 2016a).

In late June 2018, over considerable public protest, the government rammed through parliament a bill that could weaken even further protections for workers. Though the bill would for the first time set a legal limit on working hours, the limit is extremely high—a total of 720 hours overtime per year, with a maximum of 100 hours overtime per month during 'peak times' (Kosei Roudou-sho 2018b). While the establishment of a ceiling on overtime is clearly a positive step, there has been considerable outcry at what is arguably the normalization of working up to the karoshi line.

Perhaps even more concerning is the creation of a new category of workers who would be exempt altogether from any regulation of working hours. Under the bill, employees with salary levels over a specified amount could be designated as 'highly skilled professionals', who would be paid according to specified targets (and not according to the hours they work). (Kosei Roudou-sho 2018b see proposed revisions to Labour Law Article 41) Though the amount of salary above which workers may be designated as such is currently stipulated at the relatively high level of three times the average salary, Keidanren is on record as demanding that employees receiving above 4 million yen—approximately the starting salary of most university graduates—should be exempt from any overtime pay (Hagiwara 2018).

In what is a seeming admission that an approach providing only for carrots has been insufficient, the bill provides for penalties for non compliance, including the potential of up to six months imprisonment (Kosei Roudou-sho 2018b, see proposed revisions to Labour Law Article 119). Only time will tell how strictly these provisions are enforced, and whether it will have an impact on the karoshi issue.

Import of Timber

Regulation of the import of timber is another area where the government approach of carrots at the expense of sticks has, up till this point at least, proven ineffectual. As noted by Global Witness in a report published in April 2016, Japan is the only country in the G7 not to explicitly outlaw the import of illegal timber, and up to 12 percent of imported timber is estimated as potentially having been illegally felled, giving rise to serious environmental and indigenous rights concerns in areas of Malaysia (Global Witness 2016: 5, 6).

In lieu of binding legislation to be enforced on companies, the government adopted in 2006 a voluntary scheme, under which companies that abided by government guidelines can receive the 'Goho Wood' ('goho' meaning 'legal') certification. The certification is widespread, covering most major importers, but as noted by Global Witness, 'the majority of companies only check documents that in practice don't ensure legality. … a wide range of documents are accepted … These documents are taken at face value' (Global Witness 2016: 6). For its part, the national government is required by legislation to purchase only legal timber, setting a good example: however, a survey conducted in 2014 found that over 26 percent of national government agencies and over 40 percent of local governments didn't even bother to verify the legality of imported timber (Chikyuu Ningen Kankyou Forum and FOE Japan 2014: 5).

In May 2016, shortly after the Global Witness report, parliament adopted a new law on timber import, widely promoted by the government as the 'Clean Wood Act'. The law does state that all businesses 'must endeavor' to use only legal timber (Article 5): nevertheless, none of its provisions are formulated in binding terms, and there are no penalties for companies or individuals that violate the law.

The law provides for voluntary registration of companies that use imported timber. Companies that register will be bound by the law's provisions and guidelines on confirming the legality of timber they use—however, there are no measures envisioned to encourage companies to register, save a public information campaign to 'promote understanding' amongst businesses and the general public (Article 4.3). Unlike working hours, there is no large scale certification scheme with anime like characters, making the incentive to register in terms of companies advertising themselves as 'good citizens' arguably even weaker.[5] In any case, the guidelines issued by the government upon the law coming into force in May 2017 are extremely vague—they make no mention of human rights, and would seem to allow nearly any document as proof that particular timber is legal, essentially allowing registered companies to continue as they had done before (Rinya-cho 2017). A group of 18 NGOs issued a statement upon adoption of the law, criticizing it as '[falling] far short of what is necessary' and noting that it 'fails to meet the standards already adopted by its G7 peers' (Global Witness et al. 2016: 1).

Only a few days before adoption of the May 2016 law, TOCOG published for public comment a draft sourcing code for timber to be used in the 2020 Olympics. The draft code was immediately criticized by several NGOs, who not only argued it was 'inadequate' and 'unsustainable', but also that the draft did not even fulfill the standards of the 2016 bill (Business and Human Rights Resource Centre 2016c). Though some changes were subsequently made to the draft before eventual adoption, in October, the quango organizing the construction of the new stadium for the Olympics announced it would not implement the new sourcing code, stating tender had already been issued (Business and Human Rights Resource Centre 2016d).

[5] Of course, some companies have used their registration under the scheme for promotion purposes; see Sumitomo Forestry 2017.

As the new law has only come into force in May 2017, it is too early to tell what, if any, impact it will have on the import of illegal timber to Japan—though skepticism is certainly warranted. As of 31 May 2018, most, though seemingly not all, of the seven of the major importers examined by Global Witness in 2016 had registered under the law (Nihon Gas Kiki Kenya Kyoukai 2018).

Women's Rights

The advancement of women's rights in the workplace (and in society as a whole) has ostensibly been one of the main platforms of the second Abe government (in power since 2012), and PM Abe has been active in stating that women must be given more positions of responsibility in the corporate world. It is notable that the impetus (stated clearly) behind these efforts is the low birth rate and the perceived economic need to ensure that women are able to continue working after having had children, as opposed to any rights based principle. Nevertheless, there has also been widespread embarrassment at the fact that the country remains at the bottom of the heap amongst advanced economies in nearly every single indicator of women's empowerment.

Cited most often is the fact that only 13.0 percent of managerial positions in Japan are held by women. By ways of comparison, the same figure was 43.4 percent in the United States, 36.0 percent in the United Kingdom, and 34.2 percent in Singapore (Naikaku-fu Danjo Kyodo Sankaku-kyoku 2018). Japan ranked a dismal 96th out of120 countries in 2015, and there has been little improvement since then (International Labour Office 2015: 19, 21). The only OECD country that performs worse than Japan on this indicator is Korea (a fact consistently highlighted by Japanese government and media reports on these issues). The civil service is even worse, with only 3 percent of managerial positions held by women (Naikaku-fu Danjo Kyodo Sankaku-kyoku 2014).

Only 3.4 percent of corporate board seats in Japan are held by women (Naikaku-fu Danjo Kyodo Sankaku-kyoku 2018), as compared to between 10 and 20 percent in most other OECD countries (ILO 2015: 11). According to data compiled by OECD, the wage gap between men and women in Japan in 2015 was 25.7 percent, nearly double the OECD average that year of 14.3 percent and once again putting Japan at the bottom save Korea (OECD 2018). The issue of course goes beyond the workplace: for example, the poverty rate of families headed by working single parents (predominantly women) is an astounding 50.9 percent, almost 2.5 times the OECD average of 20.9 percent. The average annual income of these households is a paltry JPY 1,790,000—not even USD 17,000 (Tokyo Shimbun 2014).

Japan ratified CEDAW in 1985, and adopted the Equal Employment Opportunity Act in the same year. Before this law, it was almost unheard of for women to have a non-support position in corporate Japan. Women were commonly referred to as the 'flower of the workplace', and it was widely understood that women who had graduated from two year junior universities had better job prospects than those who had degrees, as women who were younger than their male counterparts would be easier to supervise (and would be viewed more desirable as a marital partner). In that regard, the situation has of course improved significantly.

The 1985 law is limited in scope, and while it does contain language clearly prohibiting particular practices in the workplace, those practices are narrowly construed. In particular, thanks largely to advocacy by the corporate sector, there is no punishment for failing to abide by the law. While the law can be the legal basis for a civil lawsuit for a finding of unlawfulness and damages, this is of course incumbent upon the victim mounting the financial and emotional resources to take a case to court. Otherwise, the only real recourse a victim would have is to request the intervention of the Labour Ministry, which, as is the case with karoshi and other labour rights violations, usually makes only nonbinding 'recommendations for improvement' to the company concerned.

Japan does not have comprehensive legislation banning discrimination (on the basis of sex or other reasons)—an issue pointed out consistently by human rights treaty bodies—and Japan remains non state party to ILO Convention 111 (C111) prohibiting discrimination. Many observers point to the demands made upon Japan by the ILO upon ratifying ILO Convention 100 on equal pay for equal value work to reduce the wage gap between men and women, stating that this in turn led to lobbying by businesses to refrain from ratifying C111 (Tokyo Shimbun 2015). Japan is one of only 12 member states that have not ratified C111, and one of only two non state parties that are members of the OECD (the other being the United States). Japan has steadfastly refused to become party to the Optional Protocol to CEDAW (or to any of the individual complaints procedures in international human rights law), so that avenue for recourse is also closed for victims in Japan.

The above notwithstanding, progress has been made since 1985. Government data shows that, for example, women in middle managerial positions in companies over 1000 employees was a mere 1.6 percent in 1985; in 2014, it stood at 9.2. percent (Kosei roudou-sho 2015). Nevertheless, this figure is still extremely low by international standards, and it is fair to question whether it is at an acceptable level after more than thirty years after having adopted the 1985 law. An approach containing mandatory targets might have been (will be) more effective.

Though the public discourse on this issue has largely centred on the proportion of women in managerial positions, the current situation remains problematic in many areas. Sexual harassment and maternity harassment remain commonplace in corporate Japan; citing one government survey released in 2016, the Business and Human Rights Resource Centre noted that 'nearly a third of Japanese women have been subjected to sexual harassment at the workplace, including inappropriate touching and unwarranted advances. Nearly two thirds did not make any complaint about the harassment, either formal or informal, and approximately one in ten who did complain were penalized for having done so, including suffering demotion. In addition, over twenty percent of Japanese women reported suffering from pregnancy discrimination' (Business and Human Rights Resource Centre 2016b).

The 1985 law prohibits 'unfavourable treatment' for women who married or gave birth during their employment (Article 9). Despite this provision, for years women who took maternity leave were routinely subject to demotions upon their return, in effect penalized for having had children. The government did nothing to address this issue, and it was not until a landmark Supreme Court judgment in 2014 that this was defined as being prohibited by the law (Business and Human Rights Resource Centre 2015a). Subsequent to the ruling, the Labour Ministry issued updated guidelines stipulating that demotion was prohibited (Business and Human Rights Resource Centre 2015b). In late 2015, an NGO demanded improvement for women with irregular contracts, stating that only 4 percent of women in that situation were able to take maternity leave (Business and Human Rights Resource Centre 2015c).

As with the karoshi issue, there are of course copious amounts of narratives aimed at justifying current practices. Many of these are variants of the 'culture' argument, i.e. the notion that Japanese women have 'always' stayed at home while the men perform their duties as the breadwinners of the household. These arguments are nonsensical since, outside of the aristocracy, Japanese women were historically far more economically independent until 'modern' European norms were imposed by the Meiji government during the period of industrialization in the late nineteenth century. This is not to suggest that Japan was not a patriarchal society before then, but to point to the fact that the current model of a nuclear family, with the man working and the women staying at home performing a subservient role, is a relatively new phenomenon, and has hardly been a mainstay of Japanese history and culture throughout the centuries. Nevertheless, the government has made no attempt to point to those facts, choosing rather to justify its policies solely on the current economic realities. This is arguably unsurprising, since the right wing groups that are proactive in advancing the above unfounded narrative also form an integral part of Abe's support base.

In June 2014, the government announced it would set a target of 30 percent of all 'leadership' positions to be held by women by 2020. After a barrage of criticism, in particular by businesses, that the target was too ambitious, the government was forced to scale back its plans considerably. In late 2015, a five year plan was adopted aiming at women holding 15 percent of middle managerial positions in the corporate sector, and a somewhat meagre 7 percent in central government by 2020 (Business and Human Rights Resource Centre 2015d). One observer writes that 'while the Cabinet Office insists the 30 percent figure remains its general aim, the drastic lowering of expectations acknowledges poor progress to date' (Aoki 2015).

Also in 2015, parliament adopted the 'Act on Promotion of Women's Participation and Advancement in the Workplace'. The law obligates companies with more than 300 employees to prepare and submit to the government action plans on improving the position of women at the workplace (Article 8). The action plans are compiled by the government and published on a web based database. An incentive scheme is built into the law itself, with provisions specifying that companies that show particularly effective measures can, if they wish to apply, receive certification by the government and receive preferential treatment in the awarding of public contracts (Article 9). Once again, however, there are no penalties stipulated in the law for non compliance with any of its provisions.

The government stated in 2016 that 85 percent of required companies, a total of 13,087, had submitted action plans. Of those over 13,000 companies, only 46 received certification. It is unclear whether this is because the criteria for certification are strict (which may be desirable) or because most companies have not bothered with applying in the first place. A cursory examination of the database shows that the action plans of even the certified companies are general, even vague, and rarely go over one side of a page in bulleted text format (Kosei Roudo-sho 2018b). As with the other two areas examined in this paper, it is too early to gauge the efficacy of the 2015 law, but skepticism is warranted.

Conclusion

In terms of business practices impacting on human rights, the Japanese government has generally shunned binding legislation and strict enforcement for an approach based largely on voluntary standards and incentives. This approach has overall been ineffective, at least in the three areas examined in this paper—excessive working hours leading to karoshi, the status of women in the workplace, and the importing of illegal timber.

This is not necessarily to argue that certification or other methods are by definition ineffectual. The reasons for why the Japanese schemes have fallen short are no doubt complex, and warrant further research. However, it is the contention of the author that regimes based solely, or even predominantly, on positive incentives are bound to fail. Whether or not companies have inherent good will towards human rights is an open question, but regardless of intentions, serious efforts towards human rights on their part cannot simply be assumed. Carrots have a place, but without a stick to accompany them, they will always be insufficient in the arena of business and human rights.

References

Aoki, Mizuho: 2015, 'Japan drastically lowers its goal for female managers in government and private sector', 25 December 2015, Japan Times.

Arai, Ta-ichi et al.: 2018, Kajuu roudou, harassumento soshou [Legal cases pertaining to overwork and harassment], Chuou Keizai-sha, Tokyo.

Business and Human Rights Resource Centre: 2015a, 'Japan: Supreme Court rules against demotion of hospital worker on account of pregnancy', at https://www.business-humanrights.org/en/japan-supreme-court-rules-against-demotion-of-hospital-worker-on-account-of-pregnancy (last viewed on 28 May 2018).

———: 2015b, 'Japan: New guidelines finally outlaw "maternity discrimination"', at https://www.business-humanrights.org/en/japan-new-guidelines-finally-outlaw-maternity-discrimination (last viewed on 28 May 2018).
———: 2015c, 'Japan: Only 4% of women on irregular contracts take maternity leave', at https://www.business-humanrights.org/en/japan-only-4-of-women-on-irregular-contracts-take-maternity-leave (last viewed on 28 May 2018).
———: 2015d, 'Japan: Gov't abandons ambitious target for women managers', at https://www.business-humanrights.org/en/japan-govt-abandons-ambitious-target-for-women-managers (last viewed on 31 May 2018).
———: 2016a, 'Japan: Advertising giant causes karoshi of 24 year old employee and is fined USD 4400', at https://www.business-humanrights.org/en/japan-advertising-giant-causes-karoshi-of-24-year-old-employee-and-is-fined-usd-4400 last viewed on 28 May 2018).
———: 2016b, 'Japan: Government survey: one third of women suffer sexual harassment', at https://www.business-humanrights.org/en/japan-government-survey-one-third-of-women-suffer-sexual-harassment (last viewed on 28 May 2018).
———: 2016c, 'Japan: Olympics timber sourcing code 'inadequate and unsustainable", at https://www.business-humanrights.org/en/japan-olympics-timber-souring-code-inadequate-and-unsustainable (last viewed on 31 May 2018).
———: 2016d, 'Japan: High risk of illegal logging in Olympic stadium construction', at https://www.business-humanrights.org/en/japan-high-risk-of-illegal-logging-in-olympic-stadium-construction (last viewed on 31 May 2018).
———: 2017a, 'Japan: Workers work up to or beyond "karoshi line" in most Japanese manufacturers', at https://www.business-humanrights.org/en/japan-workers-work-up-to-or-beyond-karoshi-line-in-most-japanese-manufacturers (last viewed on 28 May 2018).
———: 2017b, 'Japan: Overtime beyond karoshi line allowed in nearly all Keidanren board companies', at https://www.business-humanrights.org/en/japan-overtime-beyond-karoshi-line-allowed-in-nearly-all-keidanren-board-companies (last viewed on 28 May 2018).
Chikyu Ningen Kankyou Forum [Global Environmental Forum] and FOE Japan: 2014, 'Mokuzai, mokuzai seisin no choutatsu in atatte no gouhousei no kakunin ni kansuru anke-to kekka mamotme' ['Summary of survey on verification of legality of procured timber products'], May 2014 at https://www.fairwood.jp/news/pr_ev/2014/gohosei_question_result201405.pdf (last viewed on 31 May 2018).
Edelman Japan, 'Shinrai chosa '2017 edelman trust barometer' ninon no chosa kekka happyou' [Trust barometer 2017, findings on Japan], 7 February 2017, at https://edelman.jp/news/20170207 (last viewed on 31 May 2018).

Global Witness: 2016, Willful Ignorance: how Japan's voluntary approach is failing to stop the trade in illegal timber, 2016, London.

Global Witness et al.: 2016, 'Japan's new law fails to meet G7 Äb0commitment to halt trade in illegal timber: Government must ensure robust regulations and broad industry participation', 25 May 2016.

Hagiwara, Hiroko: 2018, 'Zangyou-dai nashi choujikan roudou gouhouka no kodo puruofesshionaru seido, zenshokushu taishou ni naru kanousei mo' [Highly skilled professional system: no overtime pay, legalization of long working hours, may be expanded to all professions], 17 May 2018, Business Journal Japan, Tokyo.

International Labour Office: 2015, Women in Business and Management: Gaining Momentum, International Labour Office, Geneva.

Iwasawa, Yuji: 1998, *International Law, Human Rights, and Japanese Law: the Impact of International Law on Japanese Law*, Clarendon Press, Oxford.

Kaye, David: 2017, 'Report of the Special Rapporteur on the Promotion and Protection of the Right to Freedom of Opinion and Expression on his Mission to Japan', United Nations Human Rights Council A/HRC/35/22/Add.1, 29 May 2017.

Keidanren: 2017, 'Charter of Corporate Behavior', at https://www.keidanren.or.jp/en/policy/csr/charter2017.pdf (last viewed on 26 May 2018).

———: 2017b, 2017nen roudou jikantou jittai chousa shuukei kekka [2017 working hours survey, summary of findings], Keidanren, Tokyo.

Keizainin Ko-Entaku Kaigi: 2016, Tai de no sute-kuhoruda- enge-jimento puroguramu wo kaisai shimasu [Invitation to participate in stakeholder engagement programme in Thailand], http://crt-japan.jp/blog/2016/04/24/thai-stakeholder-engagement-program/ [last viewed on 29 November 2018].

———: 2017, Seizen-setsu to seiaku-setsu wo chouetsu shita jinken deyu- dirijensu puroguramu wo kaisai shimasu [Invitation to participate in human rights due diligence programme that goes beyond seizen-setsu and seiaku-setsu], http://crt-japan.jp/blog/2017/12/14/crt-due-diligence-seminar/ [last viewed on 29 November 2018].

Kosei Roudou-sho: 2001, Noukekkan shikkan oyobi kyoketsusei shinnshikkanntou (fushou ni ki-in surumono wo nozomu) no nintei kijun ni tsuite [Standards for recognition of brain or heart related disorders (excepting this resulting from accidents)], at http://www.mhlw.go.jp/new-info/kobetu/roudou/gyousei/rousai/dl/040325-11a.pdf (last viewed on 28 May 2018).

———: 2015, 'De-ta de miru hataraku josei no henka [Working women: data on changing trends]', at http://www.mhlw.go.jp/file/04-Houdouhappyou-11902000-Koyoukintoujidoukateikyoku-Koyoukintouseisakuka/0000087682.pdf (last viewed on 3 June 2018).

———: 2017a, 'Heisei 29nen roudou kumiai ishiki chousa no gaikyou [2017 survey regarding labour unions, summaru]'

———: 2017b, 'Roudou toukei youran D-18, nenji yuukyuu kyuuka no shutoku joukyou [Work related statistics D-18, percentage of taken annual leave]' at http://www.mhlw.go.jp/toukei/youran/indexyr_d.html (last viewed on 28 May 2018).

———: 2017c, 'Karoshitou no rousai hoshou joukyou [Payments of compensation regarding karashi etc.], at http://www.mhlw.go.jp/stf/houdou/0000168672.html (last viewed on 28 May 2018).

———: 2017d: Choujikan roudou ga utagawareru jigyouba ni taisuru kankoku shidou kekka [Results of recommendations to workplaces suspected of excessive working hours], at http://www.mhlw.go.jp/stf/houdou/0000172536.html (last viewed on 28 May 2018).

———: 2018a, Josei no katsuyaku suishin kigyou de-ta-be-su [Database of companies on empowerment of women], http://positive-ryouritsu.mhlw.go.jp/positivedb/ (last viewed on 31 May 2018).

———: 2018b, 'Hatarakikata kaikaku no jistugen ni mukete [Towards changes in how we work], http://www.mhlw.go.jp/stf/seisakunitsuite/bunya/0000148322.html [last viewed on 4 June 2018].

Naikaku-fu Danjo Kyodo Sankaku-kyoku [Cabinet Office, Gender Equality Bureau]: 2014. 'Kokka koumuin kanrishoku ni shimeru josei wariai no sui-i [Proportion of women managers in national civil service, trends], at http://www.gender.go.jp/about_danjo/whitepaper/h26/zentai/html/zuhyo/zuhyo01-01-06.html (last viewed on 28 May 2018).

———: 2018, Danjo kyokudo sankaku hakusho heisei 29nendo [White paper on gender equality, 2017], at http://www.gender.go.jp/about_danjo/whitepaper/h29/zentai/index.html#pdf (last viewed on 28 May 2018).

Nihon Gas Kiki Kensa Kyoukai [Japan Gas Appliances Inspection Association]: 2018, 'Kuri-n uddo-hou mokuzai kaaren jigyou-sha touroku [Clean wood act timber companies registration]', http://www.jia-page.or.jp/environment/cleanwood/directory/index.html (last viewed on 31 May 2018).

Nikkei Shimbun: 'Burakku kigyou no kyuujin kyohi kyouka [Strengthening of regulation of job adverts at 'black' companies]', 7 December 2016.

OECD Data, Hours worked, at https://data.oecd.org/emp/hours-worked.htm (last viewed on 28 May 2018).

Office of the United Nations High Commissioner on Human Rights: 2011, Guiding Principles on Business and Human Rights: Implementing the United Nations "Protect, Respect and Remedy" Framework, Geneva.

Rinya-cho [Forestry Agency]: 2017, 'Mokuzai kanren jigyou-sha no gouhou bassai mokuzaitou no rayon no kakuho ni kansuru handan no kijun to narubeki jikou wo sadameru shourei [Ministry order for timber companies regarding standards for decision making on legal timber etc.], 23 May 2017.

Shimbun Akahata, '15nen seizou kigyou, roudou jikan nen 2000jikan, tsuki 200jikan no zangyou kyoutei mo kinzoku-roukyou shirabe [Article 36 agree-

ments in manufacturers in 2015, 2000 working hours per year, 200 hours overtime per month 2000: metal workers union]', 16 February 2017.
———: 'Denstu wo "jitan kigyou" nintei, 07, 13, 15 kourou-shou ihou shiritsutsu [Ministry of health and welfare recognized Dentsu as "low overtime" in 07, 13 and 15, knowing illegal practices], 26 October 2016.
Shin, Hebon: 2013, Kokusai Jinken-hou: kokusai kijun no dainamizimu to kokunai-hou tono kyouchou [International Human Rights Law: Dynamism of International Standards and Coordination with Domestic Law], Sinzansha, Tokyo.
Sumitomo Foresty: 2017, 'First registered operator under the Clean Wood Act', 30 November 2017.
Tokyo Shimbun: 2014, 'Boshi setai hataraitemo hinkon sekai ni rei naku [Single mother households: working yet in poverty, seen nowhere else globally]', 15 October 2014.
———: 2015, 'ILO jouyaku to ninon fuutatu ga mihijun, towareru shisei [ILO conventions and Japan: two not ratified, country's position quetsioned], 14 January 2015.

CHAPTER 6

States' Rights to Development of Natural Resources Versus Indigenous People's Rights: Resource Corporations and Free, Prior and Informed Consent

Matthew Storey

Introduction

The aim of this contribution is to examine three principles of international law, and the municipal law manifestations of those principles that international resources companies (IRCs) are today required to navigate in order to operate legitimately. The principles that will be considered are: Permanent Sovereignty over Natural Resources (PSNR), commonly seen as being articulated in United Nations (UN) General Assembly Resolution 1803 on *Permanent Sovereignty over Natural Resources* (G.A Res 1803 (XVII) UN Doc A/5217 (Dec 14 1962). (the RPSNR); Indigenous Peoples' rights of Free Prior and Informed Consent (FPIC) to the developments affecting their lands as enunciated in the UN Declaration of the Rights of Indigenous Peoples (A/res/61/295 Ann. 1, Sept 13, 2007)

M. Storey (✉)
Melbourne, VIC, Australia
e-mail: matthew.storey@cdu.edu.au

J. Gomez, R. Ramcharan (eds.), *Business and Human Rights in Asia*,
https://doi.org/10.1007/978-981-15-7273-9_6

(UNDRIP); and, a corporation's responsibilities under the *UN Guiding Principles on Business and Human Rights* (A/HRC/8/5.) (the GP) and the contextualisation of these responsibilities in the International Council on Mining and Metals (ICMM) May 2013 Position Statement on *Indigenous Peoples and Mining* (the Position Statement).

The purpose of this examination is to explore the proposition that when faced with the potentially competing obligations to respect a nation's right to permanent sovereignty over its natural resources imposed under municipal legislation and to respect Indigenous Peoples' right to FPIC with respect to natural resource development on their lands imposed under the GP and the Position Statement, IRCs are caught in a potential dilemma. The paper concludes by suggesting that this conflict can best be resolved through incorporation of a more contemporary interpretation of PSNR being included in municipal resource legislation and the practice regarding its implementation. However, the paper also notes that, absent such legislative reform, the existing legislation in the two jurisdictions considered do allow for IRCs to give effect to the FPIC principle.

In reaching this conclusion the paper proceeds in three sections subsequent to this introduction. The first of these sections is in turn divided it four parts. The first part considers the origins and development of the principle of PSNR. The second part looks at the development of UNDRIP and places it in the context of developments in international law regarding PSNR. The third part considers the development of the notion corporate responsibility with regard to human rights that led to the endorsement of the GP and the subsequent development of industry codes of practice such as the Position Statement. The following section examines the application of these international law principles in municipal legislation. The *Philippine Mining Act of 1995* and the Western Australian *Mining Act 1978* and the associated (Australian) Commonwealth *Native Title Act 1993* are utilized for this purpose. The concluding section considers how the competing obligations under the instruments considered can be reconciled in the practical operating environment of an IRC. As noted earlier, the conclusion reached is that this reconciliation can best be achieved through modification of municipal legislation, but that it is open to IRCs to address this situation within the existing legislative structure.

International Legal Principles and Expectations

Permanent Sovereignty Over Natural Resources

Effective control over territory, and therefore the natural resources within that territory, is an integral aspect of sovereignty and therefore international legal personality. This is generally known as "Westphalian Sovereignty" from the Peace of Westphalia of 1648. (See also for example Art 1 Montevideo Convention on Rights and Duties of States 1933 165 LNTS 19; USTS 881). At first blush then the 1952 UN General Assembly Resolution 626 *The Right to Exploit Freely Natural Wealth and Resources (UN* General Assembly Res 523 (VI) UN Doc A/2119 (Jan 12, 1952) (The 1952 Resolution) and the subsequent 1962 RPSNR would seem otiose.

The rationale for the development of the concept of PSNR lies in the post-colonial context within which it occurred. PSNR evolved at the time that of the International Covenant on Civil and Political Rights (UN General Assembly, *International Covenant on Civil and Political Rights*, 16 December 1966, UNTS, vol. 999, p. 171) (ICCPR) and the International Covenant on Economic, Social and Cultural Rights (UN General Assembly, *International Covenant on Economic, Social and Cultural Rights*, 16 December 1966, UNTS, vol. 993, p. 3.) (ICESCR) was underway and that at that time there was debate around the inclusion of the appropriateness of the inclusion of reference to a right to self-determination "in covenants dealing with the rights of individuals" (Hyde 1956, 855). There was further debate about the inclusion in the definition of the right of self-determination of the principle of PSNR—economic self-determination.

Of course, common Art 1.2 of both the ICCPR and ICESCR ultimately provided:

> 1.2. All peoples may, for their own ends, freely dispose of their natural wealth and resources without prejudice to any obligations arising out of international economic co-operation, based upon the principle of mutual benefit, and international law. In no case may a people be deprived of its own means of subsistence.

As Hyde (1956, 855) goes on to note:

> Once the principle [of PSNR] became part of a draft article on self-determination, it was directly involved in the issue of colonialism and took secondary position in heated discussions of what the principle of self determination is and how it should affect the relations of colonial and non-colonial peoples.

It is against this background that the PSNR Declaration was adopted. The PSNR Declaration provides in part:

> 1. The right of peoples and nations to permanent sovereignty over their natural wealth and resources must be exercised in the interest of their national development and of the well-being of the people of the State concerned.
>
> 2. The exploration, development and disposition of such resources, as well as the import of the foreign capital required for these purposes, should be in conformity with the rules and conditions which the peoples and nations freely consider to be necessary or desirable with regard to the authorization, restriction or prohibition of such activities.
>
> …
>
> 4. Nationalization, expropriation or requisitioning shall be based on grounds or reasons of public utility, security or the national interest which are recognized as overriding purely individual or private interests, both domestic and foreign. In such cases the owner shall be paid appropriate compensation, in accordance with the rules in force in the State taking such measures in the exercise of its sovereignty and in accordance with international law ….

From this brief review of the history of the PSNR Declaration three matters become apparent. First, there has, virtually from its outset, been some tension over the inclusion of PSNR in (individual) human rights instruments. Second, the origins of the debate around PSNR lie in issues associated with the obligations a post-colonial state towards (generally) IRCs who secured rights in relation to resources located in the (former) colonial territory during the period of colonial rule. Thus, the issue of PSNR, from its outset has involved the relationship between a state and (international) private corporations. Third, the use of the term "peoples" in each of the Covenants and the PSNR Declaration, is informed in part by an understanding of the fact that the instruments were developed in the context of the management of the de-colonization process. Prior to independence, the occupants of a colonial territory are a "people". It is only subsequent to the act of self-determination leading to independence that a state is formed. However, as discussed below, the potential distinction between peoples and a state has influenced much of the subsequent development of international jurisprudence around PSNR.

The issue of whether PSNR vests in peoples or a state is considered by Duruigbo (2006) who suggests: "[t]he right to PSNR has been viewed alternatively as a right vested exclusively in peoples, solely in states (nations), or jointly in peoples and states."

The subsequent development of the concept of PSNR has reflected this diversity of views. The conceptual uncertainty has been exacerbated by divergence of opinion regarding the meaning of peoples. Duruigbo (2006, 52) again identifies the different interpretations:

> "Peoples" can refer to: (1) those under colonial occupation, (2) a portion of the population, especially indigenous peoples, (3) the whole of the population, or (4) a synonym for the state.

Contemporary jurisprudence has some shed some light upon the interpretation of these issues. As a starting point that in the subsequent *Armed Activities in the Congo* case (*Armed Activities on the Territory of the Congo (Congo v Uganda) (Judgment)* [2005] ICJ Rep 168) the ICJ expressly recognized the RPSNR as accurately stating contemporary international law (*Armed Activities in the Congo* at 251-2 [244]). A series of cases considered by the African Commission established under the African Charter on Human and Peoples Rights (The African Charter on Human and Peoples' Rights adopted Nairobi on 27 June 1981, entered into force 21 October 1986, 1520 UNTS 217) are important in this regard. Specifically those cases are: *Democratic Republic of the Congo v Burundi, Rwanda and Uganda*, Communication 227/99 29 May 2003; *Case Centre for Minority Rights Development (Kenya) and Minority Rights Group International obo the Endorois Welfare Council v the Republic of Kenya*, Communication No 276/2003 (*Endorois*) and *Social and Economic Rights Action Center and Center for Economic and Social Rights v Nigeria*, Communication 155/96.

So too are several matters considered by Inter-American Commission on Human Rights and the Inter-American Court of Human Rights established under the Organisation of American States. Specifically these cases are: *Yanomani (v Brazil)* case Inter-American Commission on Human Rights, Res 12/85, Case 7615, March 5 1985; Inter-American Commission on Human Rights, Report 40/04, Case 12.053 *Maya*

Indigenous Communities of the Toledo District v Belize, Oct 12, 2004; OAS Report No 75/02, Case 11.140 *Mary & Carrie Dann v United States, Dec 27, 2002 (The Western Shoshone Case);* Inter-American Court *Mayagna (Sumo) Awas Tingni Community v Nicaragua August 31,* 2001). 54 and, Corte Inter-Americana de Derechos Humanos, *Caso Comunid Indigena Yakye Axa v Paraguay.* Sentencia de 17 junio de 2005)

These cases support the proposition that while certainly PSNR still supports the right of states as representatives of their peoples to control (and if need be expropriate) the natural resources within their territory. However, the further development of international legal instruments relevant to PSNR and the development of (particularly regional) human rights jurisprudence around the exercise of state's "sovereign" rights in the allocation of natural resources has served to qualify this sovereignty. There is a clear trend in the jurisprudence to suggest that PSNR is vested in the state as a trustee or fiduciary (Duruigbo, 2006, 67–68; Schrivjer 2013, 95) and the state can be held to account as such. However, the jurisprudence also suggests that "the people" who are the beneficiaries of the PSNR are not necessarily the undifferentiated residents of the post-colonial state. Rather, the rights of communities within the broader population can be asserted as a foil to the state's exercise of PSNR. What should be noticed from the survey of the regional jurisprudence above, however, is that it is not suggested that the plaintiff communities have a competing sovereignty in natural resources but rather that the state's exercise of the sovereign rights vested in it is constrained by the necessity to have regard to the interest of the affected communities.

With this conclusion in mind it is apposite to consider the second key instrument upon which this discussion is centred; the *United Nations Declaration of the Rights of Indigenous Peoples.*

UN Declaration of the Rights of Indigenous Peoples (UNDRIP)

The UNDRIP was passed by the UN General Assembly on September 13, 2007. One hundred and forty-four member States voted in favour of the resolution adopting UNDRIP, eleven abstained, and four (Australia, Canada, New Zealand, and the United States) voted against it. Since 2007, all four of the countries who voted against the resolution, have reversed their positions and now officially endorse it.

The 46 articles of the UNDRIP cover a range of matters ad serve to recognise and protect indigenous peoples' rights to cultural integrity, education, health, and political participation. Of particular relevance to this discussion are UNDRIP's provisions that deal with self-determination and rights in respect of natural resources. To deal with the self-determination matter first. Article 3 of the UNDRIP, in familiar terms, provides:

> Indigenous peoples have the right to self-determination. By virtue of that right they freely determine their political status and freely pursue their economic, social and cultural development.

Article 3 is however qualified by the terms of Article 46.1 which relevantly provides:

> Nothing in this Declaration may interpreted ... as authorizing or encouraging any action which would dismember or impair, totally or in part, the territorial integrity or political unity of sovereign and independent States.

Article 4 provides some elaboration of this limited right of self-determination:

> Indigenous peoples, in exercising their right to self-determination, have a right to autonomy or self-government in matters relating to their internal and local affairs as well as ways and means for financing their autonomous functions.

The issue of natural resources is dealt with extensively in Articles 26–28. Article 26 provides:

> 1. Indigenous peoples have the right to the lands, territories and resources which they have traditionally owned, occupied or otherwise used or acquired.
>
> 2. Indigenous peoples have the right to own, use, develop and control the lands, territories and resources that they possess by reason of traditional ownership or other traditional occupation or use, as well as those which they have otherwise acquired.
>
> 3. States shall give legal recognition and protection to these lands, territories and resources. Such recognition shall be conducted with due respect to the customs, traditions and land tenure systems of the indigenous peoples concerned.

Article 27 provides for a requirement to establish a process to "adjudicate the rights of indigenous peoples pertaining to their lands territories and resources. Such a process is expressed to require the involvement of Indigenous peoples and the recognition of indigenous law and land tenure systems in the process of adjudication. Article 28 establishes a requirement for redress for land, territories and resources previously taken without indigenous peoples free, prior and informed consent.

Finally, Article 32 deals with the management of lands and natural resources:

1. Indigenous peoples have the right to determine and develop priorities and strategies for the development or use of their lands or territories and other resources.
2. States shall consult and cooperate in good faith with the indigenous peoples concerned through their own representative institutions in order to obtain their free and informed consent prior to the approval of any project affecting their lands or territories and other resources, particularly in connection with the development, utilization or exploitation of mineral, water or other resources.
3. States shall provide effective mechanisms for just and fair redress for any such activities and appropriate measures shall be taken to mitigate adverse environmental, economic, social, cultural or spiritual impact.

With this overview of the UNDRIP in mind, it is appropriate to focus attention on that aspect of the Declaration that gives effect to an Indigenous people's right to control natural resources within their lands. It will be recalled that this is contained in Article 32.2:

> States shall consult and cooperate in good faith with the indigenous peoples concerned through their own representative institutions *in order to obtain their free and informed consent* prior to the approval of any project affecting their lands or territories and other resources, particularly in connection with the development, utilization or exploitation of mineral, water or other resources. (Emphasis added)

Article 32.2 is one of a number in the declaration that use the "free, prior and informed consent" formulation (see also for example Arts 10, 11 19, 28, 29). The principle of Free, Prior and Informed Consent (FPIC) is explained in general terms by the following text developed by the United Nations Permanent Forum on Indigenous Issues and contained in the 2005 *Report of the International Workshop on Methodologies regarding Free, Prior and Informed Consent and Indigenous Peoples* (UN 2005a, [46]).

- ***Free*** should imply no coercion, intimidation or manipulation.
- ***Prior*** should imply that consent has been sought sufficiently in advance of any authorization or commencement of activities and that respect is shown for time requirements of indigenous consultation/consensus processes.
- ***Informed*** should imply that information is provided that covers (at least) the following aspects:

  - the nature, size, pace, reversibility and scope of any proposed project or activity
  - the reason(s) for or purpose(s) of the project and / or activity
  - the duration of the above
  - the locality of areas that will be affected
  - a preliminary assessment of the likely economic, social, cultural and environmental impact, including potential risks and fair and equitable benefit-sharing in a context that respects the precautionary principle
  - personnel likely to be involved in the execution of the proposed project (including indigenous peoples, private sector staff, research institutions, government employees and others)
  - procedures that the project may entail.

- ***Consent*** Consultation and participation are crucial components of a consent process. Consultation should be undertaken in good faith. The parties should establish a dialogue allowing them to find appropriate solutions in an atmosphere of mutual respect in good faith, and full and equitable participation. Consultation requires time and an effective system for communicating among interest-holders. Indigenous peoples should be able to participate through their own freely chosen representatives and customary or other institutions. The inclusion of a gender perspective and the participation of indigenous women are essential, as well as participation of children and youth, as appropriate. This process may include the option of withholding consent.

Consent to any agreement should be interpreted as indigenous peoples have reasonably understood it.

The Report (UN 2005a, [48]) goes on to suggest:

> Indigenous peoples should specify which representative institutions are entitled to express consent on behalf of the affected peoples or communities. In free, prior and informed consent processes, indigenous peoples, United Nations organizations and Governments should ensure a gender balance and take into account the views of children and youth, as relevant.

Anaya and Puig (2017) explore the notion in greater detail. They suggest there are four approaches to interpreting FPIC: the human rights pluralist approach; the consent or veto approach; the instrumentalist approach; and, the minimalist approach. The latter of these approaches:

> … regards consultation processes as a sizeable bureaucratic obstacle that hinders productive activity. Accordingly, consultations are reduced to obtaining input to validate the measure with ultimate state decision making power remaining substantially unaltered.
>
> According to this approach, instead of adding burdensome processes like consultation, states should minimize the risks and red tape to encourage long-term commitment of financial resources in indigenous communities. (Anaya and Puig 2017, 450–451)

Of the instrumentalist approach these authors suggest:

> This discursive methodology essentially treats the duty to consult as a body of rules with a fixed determinate meaning … the state acts as an imperfect optimizer of competing demands to be assessed, evaluated and examined. Formal institutions within the state make the decisions over policy and its consequences as well as over the long-term and aggregate needs of different communities. (Anaya and Puig 2017, 448)

Anaya and Puig (2017, 449–450) comment on the consent or veto approach that it asserts:

> A freestanding 'right to consent' as part of the consultative norm. Accordingly, protecting a choice of giving or withholding consent—not specifically safeguarding human rights.

> This position affirms a slice of sovereignty for indigenous peoples at the expense of the state and implies an absolute right to block a proposed measure that may otherwise be backed by ordinary majoritarian democratic decision making.
>
> ...
>
> Notwithstanding its deep concern for the advancement of the rights of indigenous people, the consent or veto approach tends to reduce the key outcomes of the process to obtaining or withholding consent, instead of safeguarding human rights.
>
> ...
>
> ... it eliminates the governments' policy space to make important decisions without indigenous peoples' consent—something that is difficult to reconcile with the basic idea of state sovereign decision making and prevailing understandings of pluralistic democracy.

However, the consent or veto approach is central to publicists such as Erueti (2017, 571) who view the rights contained in Articles 26 and 32 to control the natural resources located in their lands and for these not to be developed without the Free, Prior and Informed Consent of the relevant Indigenous peoples as lying in a decolonization model resonating with the discourse around the development of the concept of PSNR (discussed above) and informed not by the human rights model but rather "... is primarily directed at the negotiation between two nations of their terms of co-existence." To Erueti (2017, 571) this approach allows for a "stronger reading" of rights such as those contained in Articles 26 and 32.

The human rights pluralist approach favoured by Anaya and Puig (2017, 461) is described in the following passage:

> In keeping with the safeguard role of the duty to consult, consent by indigenous peoples is required whenever their substantive rights of land and resources ... or other internationally recognised rights will be materially and substantially affected by a measure promoted by the state. It follows that if the measure is ultimately designed or revised to avoid any substantial effect on indigenous peoples' rights, consent or agreement is not required. By the same token, consent or agreement can only be required for those aspects of a project that materially affect indigenous peoples' rights and not necessarily for the entire project.
>
> ...
>
> In all cases in which the state determines that consent is not required, the state has the burden of demonstrating either that no rights are being limited

or affected or if they are that the limitation is permissible under international law.

Anaya and Puig's rejection of FPIC as constituting an absolute right to veto proposals that affect their lands and resources on the basis of substantive satisfaction of human rights and recognition of the pre-eminent sovereign rights of the state is illustrative of Erueti's contention that a human rights-based approach to the interpretation of FPIC inevitably leads to a weakening of the right. It is also difficult to contemplate circumstances in which a proposal that affected the lands and resources of an Indigenous people that was not supported by those people would not constitute a *material* contravention of Articles 26 and 32 of the UNDRIP. If this is the case the utility of the approach suggested by Anaya and Puig is difficult to comprehend. Thus, it can be considered that on either approach the right to FPIC in the UNDRIP comprehends a right to consent, or not, to a mineral development on their traditional lands.

Notably, UNDRIP as a UN General Assembly resolution is considered 'soft law' and not binding on States parties except to the extent that its provisions are considered to articulate contemporary customary international law.

The jurisprudence around the PSNR discussed earlier suggest its terms have now been accepted as constituting contemporary customary international law. In this regard the regional jurisprudence also noted above suggest that developments that occur on the lands of Indigenous peoples without their consent constitute a violation of their property rights (For example the cases of: *Endorois*,; *Yanomani*, as well as *Maya*, and *Dann* all noted earlier). These conclusions are significant in determining the extent to which the UNDRIP provisions are a manifestation of contemporary customary international law.

Having thus considered the nature, scope and inter-connectedness between a State's PSNR and an Indigenous peoples' right to FPIC under UNDRIP it remains to consider the origins and nature of an IRC (as opposed to the host state) to respect these potentially competing obligations.

International Resources Companies' Obligations

Basis of International Legal Regulation of Corporations

That corporations can be considered to have rights at international law should be apparent from the earlier discussion regarding the debate on PSNR. The RPSNR was seen as a potential threat to the property rights of international corporations. That there was (is) an increasing *need* to involve corporations in the human rights framework is broadly acknowledged. This increasing need is commonly seen as being based on the increasing influence of global corporations and financial institutions and the corresponding (relative) decrease in the influence of States (Ruggie 2014; Wettstein 2012; Kwakyewah and Idemudia 2017).

The struggle for international legal jurists has been to formulate a basis for implanting and imposing *responsibilities*, particularly with respect to international human rights norms, on such rights-bearing corporations (Wettstein 2012, 744). Overwhelmingly, this struggle has been seen to be founded in the state-centric nature of international law itself (Miyawa 2006, 52; Wettstein 2012, 743). From this struggle, two approaches to imposing responsibilities on corporations have arisen.

The first, more traditional approach is to impose responsibilities by way of treaty like instruments. Arnold (2010, 373–4) suggests the International Labour Organisation's *Tripartite Declaration of Principles Concerning Multinational Enterprises* as one example of this approach. The better-known example is though the *Draft Norms on the Responsibilities of Transnational Corporations and Other Business Enterprises with regard to Human Rights* (UN Doc. E/CN.4/Sub.2/2003/12/Rev.2 (2003). (UN 2003, "the *Norms*"). The *Norms* "attributed to companies to companies … essentially the same range of duties that states have accepted for themselves under international treaties that they have ratified." (Ruggie 2014, 7). The *Norms* were however rejected by the Commission on Human Rights (Ruggie 2014, 7).

Subsequent to this, the Commission on Human Rights successfully sought the establishment of the position of Special Representative of the Secretary General on the issue of Human Rights and Transnational Corporations and Other Business Enterprises. (SRSG). The function of the SRSG was to clarify aspects of the UN Global Compact (UN 2005a, b). The Global Compact was a policy initiative of the UN Secretary-General launched in 2000. It sought "companies to embrace support and enact, within their sphere of influence, a set of core values in the areas of human rights, labour standards, the environment and anti-corruption." (Arnold 2010, 372).

In this respect the Global Compact represents the second approach to having corporations accept human rights responsibilities. This approach focusses upon the "voluntary" acceptance of these responsibilities by corporations.

The result of the work of the SGSR was the 2011 United Nations Guiding Principles on Business and Human Rights. (*Report of the Special Representative of the Secretary General on the issue of human rights and transnational corporations and other business enterprises, John Ruggie*, HRC, UNGOAR, 17th Sess, UN Doc A/HRC/17/31 (2011)—(UN 2011a, b—"the GP").

Before moving to consider the content of the GP it is worth noting, as Kwakyewah and Idemudia (2017, 154) do that proponents of the more treaty approach see the GP as "a parallel development and … not a substitute for moving towards a treaty". As these authors also note: "it is clear that 'soft norms' [such as the GP] are presently being privileged."

Content of the Guiding Principles

The GP are expressed to be "grounded in the recognition of" (GP, 1) three foundations: the State's duty to protect human rights; a corporation's responsibility to respect human rights; and, the necessity for the availability of a remedy for victims of any transgression of their rights. The corporation's responsibility to respect human rights is expressed to extend to all corporations irrespective of their size or scope of operations (GP, 15,—Principle 14). Some commentators note that the notion of a corporation's duty to respect human rights is vague in content so as to have questionable effect (Miyawa 2006, 34). However, it appears the duty to respect is, in essence, simply the obligation expected of all members of a society not to transgress, or collude in the transgression of the laws of the state. The novelty in the GP is that the laws in question are internationally recognised human rights. Principle 12 (GP, 13) states that the rights in question are "as a minimum", those contained in the International Bill of Human Rights and the ILOs *Declaration on Fundamental Principles and Rights at Work* (June, 1988). However, the commentary to this principle also notes that in particular contexts "business enterprises may need to consider additional standards"(GP, 14). United Nations' instruments concerning Indigenous Peoples are identified in this regard.

It is unnecessary for current purposes to review the entirety of the GP. However, several aspects are of particular relevance.

Principle 11 program provides:

> Business enterprises should respect human rights. This means that they should avoid infringing on the human rights of others and should address the adverse impacts with which they are involved.

Principle 22 in turn provides

> Where business enterprises identify that they have caused or contributed to adverse impacts they should provide for or cooperate in their remediation through legitimate processes.

Finally, Principle 23 provides in part:

> In all contexts business enterprises should:
>
> ...
>
> b) seek ways to honour the principles of internationally recognized human rights when faced with competing requirements

The commentary to Principle 23 (GP, 25) notes:

> Where the domestic context renders it impossible [to fully respect human rights] business enterprises are expected to respect the principles of internationally recognized human rights to the greatest extent possible in the circumstances ...

In summary and in the context of IRCs and Indigenous Peoples then it would appear that the GP creates an expectation on IRCs to respect the provisions of UNDRIP particularly with regard to FPIC but recognises that this may not be possible in certain "domestic contexts". However, if FPIC cannot be respected than an IRC is to participate in remediation of this human rights violation.

Although in some regards predating the GP, the publication of the GP prompted corporations in a number of sectors to develop Industry Standards (Ruiz-Lozano & Tirado-Valencia 2016). This process is contemplated within the GP itself. The responsibilities contained in the GP are explicitly referred to in the International Council on Mining and Metals (ICMM) May 2013 Position Statement on *Indigenous Peoples and*

Mining. As such the Position Statement can be seen as a manifestation of this process in the particular context of IRCs and Indigenous Peoples.

The ICMM Position Statement—Background

The ICMM is an international industry association comprising 27 mining and metals companies and 33 national and regional mining associations and global commodity associations. The ICMM was established to address core sustainable development challenges. It is headquartered in London. ICMM corporate members include: Anglo-American, BHP-Billiton, Freeport, Mitsubishi Materials, Newmont, and Rio Tinto. The Minerals Council of Australia (MCA) is one of the "member national associations". To be eligible for membership corporations must implement a Sustainable Development Framework that incorporates ten key principles and six positions statements. The ICMM conducts annual third party verified assessment of member corporations' progress against the commitments contained in the Framework. The results of the annual assessment are published (and publicly available).

The ten principles contained in the Framework can be summarised as follows:

1. Implement and maintain ethical business practices and sound systems of corporate governance.
2. Integrate sustainable development considerations within the corporate decision-making process.
3. Uphold fundamental human rights and respect cultures, customs and values in dealings with employees and others who are affected by our activities.
4. Implement risk management strategies based on valid data and sound science.
5. Seek continual improvement of our health and safety performance.
6. Seek continual improvement of our environmental performance.
7. Contribute to conservation of biodiversity and integrated approaches to land use planning.
8. Facilitate and encourage responsible product design, use, re-use, recycling and disposal of our products.
9. Contribute to the social, economic and institutional development of the communities in which we operate.

10. Implement effective and transparent engagement, communication and independently verified reporting arrangements with our stakeholders.

The Position Statements are intended to provide greater clarity to matters contained in the Principles. They go to matters such as: Climate Change, Water, Mercury Risk Management, Protected Areas and Indigenous Peoples. The Indigenous Peoples and Mining Position statement is said to clarify Principles 3, 6 and 9.

The ICMM Position Statement—Content and Analysis
The Position Statement is described setting out ICMM members' "approach to engaging with Indigenous Peoples and to free, prior and informed consent". (ICMM 2013, 1) The Position Statement describes FPIC as "a process and an outcome". The *process* is summarised as ensuring decisions are: made freely without coercion or manipulation; involve sufficient time; and, are on the basis of full information. "The *outcome* is that Indigenous Peoples can give or withhold their consent to a project ..." The requirements of the Position Statement should have been implemented by May 2015 but do not apply to projects that have started the approvals process at the time of adoption of the Position Statement (May 2013). Aside from these preliminary comments the Position Statement contains six "Recognition Statements" and six "Commitments". This discussion will focus only on those aspects dealing with the consent requirement. Essentially these are found in Recognitions Statements 4 and 5 and also Commitments 4 and 5. Reproducing (at least portions of) the text of these provisions is necessary in order to analyse them.

Recognition Statements 4 and 5

> 4. Successful mining and metals projects require the support of a range of interested and affected parties. This includes both the formal legal and regulatory approvals granted by governments and the broad support of a company's host communities. ... *States have the right to make decisions on the development of resources according to applicable national laws*, including those laws implementing host country obligations under international law. Some countries have made an explicit consent provision under national or sub-national laws. In most countries however, "neither Indigenous Peoples nor any other population group have the right to veto development projects that affect them", *so FPIC should be regarded as a "principle to be respected to*

> *the greatest degree possible in development planning and implementation*". (Emphasis added)
>
> 5. States also have an important role to play in the process of engaging with Indigenous Peoples. *They may be involved in determining which communities should be considered indigenous, in shaping the process for achieving FPIC and in determining how this relates to regulated processes for ensuring community participation in decision making.* Given their role in balancing the rights and interests of Indigenous Peoples with the wider population, states may also play an important role in supporting the resolution of disagreements that may arise between Indigenous Peoples and companies in the pursuit of FPIC. (Emphasis added)

Commitments 4 and 5

> 4. *Work to obtain the consent of indigenous communities* for new projects (and changes to existing projects) that are located on lands traditionally owned by or under customary use of Indigenous Peoples...These processes should neither confer veto rights to individuals or sub-groups nor require unanimous support from potentially impacted Indigenous Peoples (unless legally mandated). Consent processes should not require companies to agree to aspects not under their control.
>
> 5. Collaborate with the responsible authorities to achieve outcomes consistent with the commitments in this position statement, in situations where government is responsible for managing Indigenous Peoples' interests in a way that limits company involvement. *Where a host government requires members to follow processes that have been designed to achieve the outcomes sought through this position statement, ICMM members will not be expected to establish parallel processes.*

There are two (inter-related) issues arising from these provisions. The first is that, in the preambular text it is accepted that the "outcome" of FPIC consent is absolute: that is; it can be given or withheld. However, in Recognition Statement 4 and Commitment 4 while the giving of consent may be absolute, the consequence of the withholding of consent is not. This is because FPIC has become a principle to be respected "to the greatest degree possible" the Commitment is "to work towards it" as opposed to "not proceeding without it".

The authority cited in the Position Statement in this regard is the United Nations Department of Economic and Social Affairs (UNDESA), *Resource Kit on Indigenous Peoples Issues* (2008) (UNDESA 2008, "the

Resource Kit"). The Resource Kit is "designed to provide United Nations Country Teams with guidance as to how to engage with indigenous peoples and include their perspectives in development processes" (UNDESA 2008, 1).

The full paragraph in the *Resource Kit* to which the Position Statement refers should be appreciated. That paragraph reads:

> It should be noted that the FPIC process may include the option of withholding consent. It should also be noted that, in most countries, neither indigenous nor any other population group actually have the right to veto development projects that affect them. The concept of free prior and informed consent is therefore a goal to be pursued and a principle to be respected to the greatest degree possible in development planning and implementation. (UNDESA 2008, 18)

With the greatest of respect, taken in context, this paragraph out of a guide for UN Country Teams on how to involve indigenous peoples in development processes does ***not*** provide the ICMM with a legitimate basis to reduce FPIC to an "aspiration". This conclusion is emphasised by the earlier discussion around the increasing acceptance of FPIC as a feature of international law and a limitation on State sovereignty with respect to natural resources.

The second issue is the role of the State. The first point to note here is that the Position Statement accepts that the State has the right to develop resources in accordance with its (FPIC embracing or not) national laws. Further, even in the observance of FPIC (to the extent it is not trumped by the State right to develop resources), the State may have a role in identifying relevant parties and in shaping and regulating processes. If these processes are "designed to achieve" FPIC, the ICMM member is absolved of independent accountability in the event the design fails

In many respects one may be inclined to feel some sympathy for the position of the ICMM in this regard. It could be seen as merely acknowledging the state of the law in the jurisdictions within which its members operate, and those laws are based on the concept of PSNR.

The question of state sovereignty in the inter-relation between domestic law and international law is well travelled. The fundamental principle is that domestic law (including sub-national law) cannot be invoked as a justification for failure to perform a treaty (or other international legal)

obligation (*Pacta sunt servada*: Vienna Convention on the law of Treaties 1969 1155 NTSS 331, art 26 and 27).

As the earlier discussion on the GP suggested, a high-profile transnational corporation is unlikely to justify (for example) employment (directly) of child labour, causing massive environmental degradation, or the manufacture of internationally prohibited weaponry on the basis that the laws of the place of operation permit these activities. These are the very basis of the "respect" foundation of the GP. It will be recalled that the commentary on Principle 11 in Part II ("The Corporate Responsibility to Protect Human Rights") put the matter quite succinctly:

> The responsibility to respect human rights is a global standard of expected conduct for all business enterprises wherever they operate. It exists independently of States' abilities and/or willingness to fulfil their own human rights obligations and does not diminish those obligations. And it exists over and above compliance with national laws and regulations protecting human rights. (GP, 13)

Thus, it can be appreciated that, at least as an ethical proposition, there should be no distinction drawn in application of FPIC *even absent national laws giving effect to the principle*. Indeed, if reliance on the text of national laws provided sufficient guidance for ICMM members on ethical behaviour there would be no need for the Position Statement or even ICMM.

From this perspective the reliance in the Position Statement on the idea of "just following the local law" would appear unsupportable and contradictory.

A final, but significant, point to note in relation to the Position Statement is that it makes no reference to the notions contained in Principles 22 and 23 of the GP. It will be recalled that these principles created an expectation in corporations "when faced with competing requirements" to "honour the principles of internationally recognized human rights." Principle 22 created the expectation to "provide for or cooperate in [the] remediation through legitimate processes" of any "adverse impacts" the corporation had "caused or contributed to". Thus, the GP create an expectation that even when IRCs are obliged by national laws to not fully respect FPIC they will take steps to remediate this adverse impact. This concept is absent from the commitments contained in the Position Statement.

Conclusions as to International Legal Principles and Expectations

The following conclusions can be drawn from the foregoing discussion:

- A State's indisputable sovereignty over the natural resources within its territory is qualified by international legal expectation that the assertion of its sovereignty will bear used for the benefits of the peoples that constitute that State. In the same manner a State's general legislative sovereignty is qualified by international legal expectations that it will uphold a range of internationally recognised human rights norms.
- The rights of Indigenous Peoples to control development of the natural resources within their traditional lands and territories is increasingly accepted under international law, particularly in those states that have endorsed the principle of FPIC contained in the UNDRIP.
- Corporations, particularly IRCs are subject to an *expectation* that they will also respect these internationally recognised human rights norms, including FPIC.
- The ICMM Position Statement contemplates as acceptable an IRC not fully respecting the FPIC principle where this absence of respect is a feature of the relevant municipal natural resources regime.
- The authority of the ICMM Position Statement in this respect is questionable and does not address the expectation in the GP that, even when faced with the dilemma of a conflict between municipal legislation and internationally recognised human rights standards a corporation should take steps to remediate any adverse impacts of the IRCs operations.

With these conclusions in mind, the third part of this paper examines the mining regimes actually in place in both the Philippines and the Australian state of Western Australia.

The Municipal Regimes

The Republic of the Philippines

Background and Legislative Framework

The Republic of the Philippines is a nation of a high mineral prospectivity. Recent estimates suggest there are $US 840 billion in mineral reserves (Raymundo 2014). These reserves are primarily in non-ferrous metals such as copper, gold, lead nickel, silver and zinc (Holden 2005, 418). Indigenous Peoples constitute between 15%–20% of the total population (Holden and Ingelson 2007, 376). The main centres of Indigenous population are on Mindanao where the Lumad people, who constitute approximately two thirds of the total Indigenous population live and in the Cordillera of the island of Luzon where the Igorot people live (Holden and Ingelson 2007, 377). As Holden (2005, 422) notes: "[i]t is estimated that half of all areas identified in mining applications in the Philippines are in areas subject to Indigenous land claims".

There are three main pieces of legislation relevant to the current discussion: the *1987 Constitution of The Republic of the Philippines* (the Constitution); the *Mining Act* of 1995 (Republic Act No 7942) (the PMA); and, the *Indigenous Peoples Rights Act* of 1987 (Republic Act No 8371) (the IPRA).

The relevant provisions of the Constitution are:

Section 2 of Article XII which provides in part:

> … The exploration, development and utilization of natural resources shall be under the full control and supervision of the State. The state may directly undertake such activities, or it may enter into coproduction, joint venture, or production sharing agreements with Filipino citizens or corporations or associations at least sixty percent U.N. of whose capital is owned by such citizens.
>
> …
>
> The President may enter into agreements with foreign-owned corporations involving either technical or financial assistance for large-scale exploration, development and utilization of minerals petroleum and other mineral oils according to the general terms and conditions provided by law, based on real contributions to the economic growth and general welfare of the country.

Section 5 of Article XII, however, provides as follows:

> The State, subject to the provisions of this Constitution and national development policies and programs, shall protect the rights of the indigenous cultural communities and their ancestral lands to ensure their economic, social and cultural well-being.

Pursuant to the power under section 2 of Article XII the Philippine legislature enacted the PMA. This Act and the regulations (Administrative Orders—DENR AO97-24) promulgated under it by the Department of Environment and Natural Resources (DENR) created two relevant forms of "tenure": the Mineral Production and Sharing Agreement (MPSA) and the Financial Technical Assistance Agreement (FTAA). Both of these forms of title allow for a 25-year tenure for exploration and production purposes. The MPSA is limited to a maximum area of 16,200 hectares for exploration purposes whereas the FTAA provides for 81,000 hectares for exploration and 5000 hectares for production purposes. The MPSA is limited to 40% foreign ownership but the FTAA allows for 100% foreign ownership but requires a minimum investment commitment of US$50 million. It can only bear approved by the President of the Philippines (O'Callaghan 2009, 98–99). O'Callaghan also notes that both forms of title have four core elements. Two of these go to taxation arrangements and environmental matters. Relevantly the other two go to the operational arrangements and social issues. He describes these latter two elements as follows (O'Callaghan 2009, 97):

> An "operating contract" which stipulates the terms under which a company can explore and develop a mine, and which sets out the terms for the exploration, utilization and development of a resource, the sizer of the concession, the number of years a concession may be held and, most importantly their level of foreign ownership.

The second relevant element is:

> A "social and cultural contract" which includes appropriate treatment of indigenous peoples and communities, workforce skill development and labor laws.

The issue of treatment of Indigenous Peoples is also impacted upon by the second piece of relevant legislation; the IPRA.

Holland and Ingelson (2007, 379) summarise the IRPA as follows:

> IPRA is a powerful statute that provides for a wide range of indigenous Peoples trig hits such as the right to ancestral domain, the right to self governance and the right to cultural integrity .... IPRA created the National Commission on Indigenous People (NCIP), which is the 'primary government agency responsible for the formulation and implementation of policies, plans and programs to recognize, protect and promote the rights of. [Indigenous Cultural Communities—(ICC) and Indigenous Peoples]

Pursuant to the IPRA the NCIP promulgated NCIP Administrative Order 98-1 Part III section 7 of which:

> ... require[s] that the free prior and informed consent of an indigenous cultural community be obtained as a precondition for the exploration, for the exploration development, exploitation and utilization of natural resources that are the ancestral domain of an indigenous community. (Holden and Ingelson 2007, 380)

The following from O'Callaghan (2009, 102) describing the processes required under the IPRA to achieve FPIC is perhaps lengthy but comprehensive.

> The difficulty for investors is that the process is extremely bureaucratic. It includes endorsement by the Minerals and Geosciences Bureau (a separate bureaucratic process itself), negotiations with landowners, field based investigation conferences and reports, a range of mandatory activities for achieving consent (including development of a community consultative community), and the negotiation and signing of a memorandum of understanding (MOU). The MOU includes such commitments as the payment of royalty fees, employment, education, medical and health services, free light and water supply, security, social projects, infrastructure development, communications facilities and a conflict resolution mechanism. Finally, the [NCIP] may decide to either approve a project or reject it. If it rejects it the applicant must begin the entire process again or abandon it.

While clearly to O'Callaghan the process is "overly bureaucratic", read in the context of the earlier discussion of the FPIC provision of UNDRIP it would appear as an exemplar of an appropriate regime. The one possible qualification to this may be the role of the NCIP. The NCIP is comprised of seven Commissioners appointed by the President on the nominations from the Indigenous communities of seven defined regions (IPRA,

Chapter VII, s 40). A question may possibly arise as to whether a national body of this constitution would satisfy the Indigenous governance provisions of UNDRIP Art 18. Leaving this matter aside, clearly the relevant structures under the IPRA and Administrative Orders are based on recognition and application of FPIC.

The following section of the discussion however, reviews literature regarding the application of these legislative provisions.

Application of the IPRA and PMA

In contrast to the legislative provisions of the IPRA and its implementing Administrative Orders a preliminary review of the literature regarding the application of this regime suggests a darker picture. Holden and Ingelson (2007, 385) describe dislocated Indigenous communities "living under a bridge." The UN Special Rapporteur on the Situation of Human Rights and Fundamental Freedoms of Indigenous People reported in 2003 that there were reports of:

> Arbitrary detentions persecutions and even killings of community representatives, of mass evacuations, hostage taking, destruction of property, summary executions, forced disappearances, coercion and also rape by armed forces and so-called paramilitaries. (Stavenhagen 2003)

Writing in 2016, Simbulan (2016, 29) reiterates the allegations of the killings of Indigenous leaders as a consequence of mining developments and asks: "[w]hy are mining companies and their operations in the Philippines often accompanied by militarization and violence in the ancestral lands of indigenous peoples."

However, the relationship between IRCs and Indigenous Peoples in the Philippines is not reported as universally bleak. In 2005 Holden noted that in 1997:

> At its Tampkan property on the island of Mindanao, the Australian mining company Western Mining Corporation engaged in substantial efforts to gain the consent of the *Bla'an* communities. First, the mining project proponent made efforts to engage the communities as early as possible when it began the process of mine development; then, the mining company hired ethnographers and archaeologists to document the traditions of the indigenous community and the extent of its territory; finally Western Mining Corporation also engaged in efforts to improve the conditions of the *Bla'an*

> Peoples by providing them with education and medical facilities. (Holden 2005, 431–432)

Despite this positive note the question remains: how does the positive legislative regime in the Philippines translate into such (largely) reported negative outcomes?

Holden and Ingelson (2007, 389) comment:

> IPRA is based on the same principles as [UNDRIP]. IPRA as *legislation*, does describe indigenous peoples' rights; however, the problem lies not in the law, but with the government's reluctance to *enforce* the law.

Despite these apparent administrative shortcomings in the enforcement of the relevant Philippine legislation, the point must also be made that it is not apparent (at least from the available literature) that a potential concession holder is *obliged* to participate in the flawed application of a structurally sound regime. The fact that negotiations under IPRA occur *after* an application for a concession under the PMA is made imply a concession applicant will have a certain negotiation period to satisfy the requirements of IPRA before a final decision to proceed or not with the grant of a concession is made.

The following section of the discussion, which describes the regime in place in the Australian state of Western Australia, suggests that the "problem" there is by contrast not in the *enforcement* of the law but in the law itself.

Western Australia

The Native Title Act 1993 *(Cth.) ("NTA")*

Although the High Court of Australia decision in *Mabo & Ors v Queensland & Ors (Mabo No 2)* (1992) 175 CLR 1 established the possibility of the existence of native title rights in any given tract of land confirmation of this existence in any particular land requires a determination by (generally) the Federal Court of Australia (NTA s 13). The process of determining the existence of native title rights is a complex litigious process that requires extensive evidence regarding the continued existence and content of traditional laws and customs to support the asserted native title right. It also requires evidence of details of all tenure granted in the relevant land since the assertion of sovereignty in order to determine which, if any native title rights have been extinguished by inconsistent Crown grants (NTA ss 61 and 223). The process will usually take in excess of five years to conclude once initiated. Given these timeframes the NTA provides for a process of the administration assessment and registration of native title determination applications ("claims") pending ultimate finalisation of the matter by the Federal Court (NTA ss 184–191).

Once a native title claim is registered and upon ultimate determination of the claim by the Federal Court and native title holding community is afforded procedural rights in respect of any proposed (relevantly) grant of a mineral interest in their lands. These rights are afforded whether the native title rights (claimed or determined) amount to exclusive possession or non-exclusive possession rights. (Non-exclusive possession rights are those generally determined to co-exist with a pastoral lease). As the Australian Commonwealth government notes currently: "some 94 per cent of the landmass of north Western Australia is subject to a native title claim or determination, as is 62 per cent of north Queensland and 30 per cent of the Northern Territory" (C of A 2015, 19).

Once a native title claim is registered or determined the grant of a mining title can only proceed if either an Indigenous Land Use Agreement (ILUA) in respect of the proposal is negotiated or the Right to Negotiate (RTN) procedure is satisfactorily concluded.

Although technically complex, conceptually the ILUA is straightforward. It is a contract between the native title holding community and the state government and(or) putative miner authorising the grant and (usually) operating conditions a mining proposal will be subject to. It is possible for an ILUA to authorise both exploration and any subsequent production activities. The impact of the mining activity on any native title rights and interests is given statutory authorisation under the NTA (NTA ss 24BB—24EBA, particularly s 24 EB). Subject to the discussion below then, the ILUA process is a voluntary, largely unconstrained, mechanism for a proponent to negotiate the FPIC of an affected Indigenous community with respect to their lands.

The RTN procedure (contained in NTA ss 24 MB- 4MD and ss 25–44) is less straightforward. Under the RTN in order to make the grant of a mining title the state government must give public notice of its intention (NTA s 29). There is then a three-month period in which any native title claiming community can seek to have a claim registered. If the claim is registered the native title claiming community is entitled to commence negotiations with the state and the putative miner. Once a claim is registered (or if there is already a determination of the native title in the relevant area) there is a mandated period of three months negotiations, which must be undertaken "in good faith" (NTA s 35). The object of the negotiations is to reach an agreement as to the granting of the title. Under the NTA (s 33) negotiations at this stage can contemplate the ultimate agreement including the payment of "royalties" to the native title holding/claiming community. If an agreement is reached the title can be granted (NTA s 31). At the conclusion of the period, if no agreement is reached the state or the putative miner can seek arbitration of the matter (NTA s 35).

The arbitration is undertaken by the National Native Title Tribunal (NNTT), a statutory administrative body whose members are appointed by the Commonwealth Government for five-year terms (NTA, s 111). The NNTT can determine to approve, approve on conditions or not approve the proposed grant. However, the determination cannot include provisions relating to royalty payments (NTA s 38(2)). The criteria the NNTT is required to take into account in making its decision include the affect on the native title holding communities and their wishes as well as the "economic or other significance" of the grant and the "national interest" (NTA s 39).

Between 2012 and 2017 the NNTT dealt with over 100 applications to arbitrate the grant of a mining title because agreement could not be reached between the parties. On only two occasions has there been a determination by that the grant of a mining title cannot proceed. Those two matters were: Weld Range Metals Limited/Western Australia/Ike Simpson and Others on behalf of Wajarri Yamatji, [2011] NNTTA 172 (21 September 2011); and Western Desert Lands Aboriginal Corporation (Jamukurnu—Yapalikunu)/Western Australia/Holocene Pty Ltd., [2009] NNTTA 49 (27 May 2009).

A decision of the NNTT can be overruled by the relevant Commonwealth minister (NTA s 42) but such action has never been taken.

The Western Australian Mining Regime

Native Title aside, responsibility for land management (including the grant and regulation of mineral tenures) in Australia resides with the (subnational) state governments. While each state government has its own mineral titling regime they are in broad terms similar. The State of Western Australia (WA) has a regime typical in this respect and is also the location of much mining activity in Australia with total resource and export sales in

2016–17 of over A$105 billion (G of WA 2017). Total Australian resource and energy exports in 2016–16 were valued at $157 billion, accounting for 51% of Australia's goods and services exports (C of A Undated).

The WA mining regime is regulated under the *Mining Act 1978* (WA) (WAMA) and associated regulations. Section 9 of the WAMA declares property in (essentially) all minerals in the state vests in the Crown and s 155 makes unlawful exploration for or production of mineral unless authorised under the WAMA. Interestingly in these provision sis a clear assertion of PSNR that (in WA) dates back to before 1899.

The following passage from the WA Government's Mineral Statistics Digest provides a more practical representation of situation 'on the ground':

> In 2016–17, 42.5 million hectares of Western Australian land was covered by mining tenements—an increase of 13 per cent from 37.6 million hectares in 2015–16. Exploration licences accounted for about 80 per cent of the area covered by mining tenements. The number of exploration licences increased 11 per cent over the year from 4529 tenements in 2015–16 to 5020 tenements in 2016–17. Mining leases accounted for just 6 per cent (2.4 million hectares) of the total area. The number of mining leases fell 1 per cent from 5873 in 2015–16 to 5827 in 2016–17, although the area covered under these mining leases rose 1 per cent over the same period. (G of WA 2017, 9)

The WAMA itself does not contain any requirement to satisfy obligations arising from the existence of native title rights as a precondition to the grant or operation of a mineral tenement. Rather these obligations are set out in in ss 24AA and 24OA of the NTA. Under s 109 of *The Constitution of the Commonwealth of Australia*, any state Act that is inconsistent with Commonwealth legislation will be invalid to the extent of the inconsistency which operate to make invalid any grant of a mining title that has not been undertaken in compliance with the NTA.

Consideration of the WA Regime and the NTA

The mining titles regime and the NTA thus described has significant shortcomings. First, the fact that under the NTA an Indigenous people must be able to establish both the ongoing nature of their traditional laws and customs from the original assertion of British Imperial sovereignty in (generally) the late eighteenth century until the current and that there has been no inconsistent Crown grant on those lands during that period means that many Indigenous peoples (particularly in southern Australia) are largely denied access to the procedures under the NTA altogether. Second, is the RTN.

As described above, the RTN does not satisfy the requirements of FPIC as commonly understood. Although it must be accepted it does come closer to satisfying these requirements as described by Anaya and Puig (2017) as discussed above. Moreover, the fact that a putative miner can ultimately resort to arbitration which, in over 98 percent of cases will determine that the grant of the title can proceed without any conditions as to royalties for an affected Indigenous community impacts upon the entire process. An Indigenous people and the putative miner will enter into negotiations with the knowledge that unless an agreement is reached within the mandated negotiation period the alternative is an arbitrated outcome as sought by the miner.

This fact also affects the context of the negotiation of an ILUA. Just as with negotiations under the RTN, an Indigenous people and the putative miner will enter upon negotiations aimed at achieving an ILUA in the knowledge that should those negotiations not be successful the path leading to a determination by the NNTC is always available to the putative miner. This significantly undermines the Indigenous peoples' negotiation position and calls into question whether any resulting consent can in fact be described as "free".

These factors noted, it must also be noted that, at least the ILUA process, leaves it open to a putative miner to work to achieve a genuine consent That is while their tenement application remains on foot and are provided administrative protection from the ambitions of their competitors while they do so under the priority provisions of the WAMA (ss 67 and 105A).

Analysis and Comparison of the Municipal Regimes

The examination in this section of the discussion has revealed significant similarities, and a number of differences, between the two municipal regimes under consideration. Both regimes assert state (Crown) ownership of mineral resources. Interestingly in the Philippines the granting of a concession under the PMA operates as a contract between the government, who retains joint ownership of the mineral and the operator. By contrast in Western Australia the granting of a productive title (Mineral

Lease) bestows on the grantee the right to work and win the Crowns minerals in situ and having extracted them also bestows title to them (accompanied by a legal obligation to pay taxes and royalties). The distinction may be founded in the earlier origins of the WA regime which is indicative of a less active role for government.

However, both regimes contain provisions that recognise that the state's right to grant interests in "its" minerals is necessarily qualified (to some extent) through consideration of the wishes and interests of affected Indigenous communities. The extent of recognition of Indigenous peoples' rights in this regard is, on the face of the relevant legislation, notably different. Significantly, in both regimes there are available avenues through which an IRC can reach an agreement with an affected community that satisfies the FPIC requirements. Further, both regimes have in place some "priority" protection for an IRC while it is engaged in these processes. There are, however, also avenues through which it appears (anecdotally in the case of the Philippines) an IRC can avoid the satisfaction of the FPIC obligations if it so chose. These alternative avenues and the aspirational character of the ICMM Position Statement's commitment constitute the "soft place" suggested in the title to this paper.

The final section of this discussion considers the implications of the conclusions reached in each of the preceding sections of the examination as well as proposing suggestions for further research in this field.

Conclusion

The conclusions of this discussion may be fairly simply stated. First, as noted earlier, a State's indisputable sovereignty over the natural resources within its territory is qualified by international legal opinion that the assertion of its sovereignty will bear used for the benefits of the peoples that constitute that State. This qualification is particularly manifest in the context of Indigenous peoples affected by natural resource development proposals who have a right to grant, or withhold the free, prior and consent to any such proposal.

Further IRCs (and other corporations) are under an *expectation* to uphold these principles even when relevant municipal legislation and practice does not specifically provide for them. In cases where there is conflict between the expectation placed on IRCs and State practice, IRCs are expected to put in place remediation measures to ameliorate this conflict. The ICMM's Position Statement acknowledges FPIC but portrays it as largely aspirational. It does not address the issue of remediation in circumstances where the aspirational FPIC cannot be satisfied.

The two municipal regimes considered both incorporate consideration of the wishes and interests of affected Indigenous communities in decisions regarding the approval of grants of mining interests' However, in both cases these regimes also provide mechanisms (legislative or—apparently—practical) by which FPIC obligations can be avoided. There is some suggestion that the existence of these mechanisms can undermine more broadly the practical implementation of the FPIC principle.

From these conclusions two additional matters arise. The first is that this discussion has been limited to an examination of the architecture of the relevant international and municipal regimes. There has been no opportunity to consider the application of the principles contained in the regimes in practice, at least apart from secondary reports in academic literature. This deficiency has significant implications. It is impossible in this discussion to consider whether those IRCs that have assumed the obligations under the ICMM's Position Statement are in fact utilising the mechanisms provided for in municipal regimes that allow for the full application of FPIC or whether the other avenues are utilised. There is some suggestion that in fact the mechanisms that allow for FPIC are utilised by ICMM members. The reference to the practice of WMC by Holden (2005) is an example of this.

The second additional matter that arises is that this discussion has not been able to examine the scenario where an IRC fully respects FPIC and the relevant Indigenous community freely determines to *withhold* consent. Presumably in this scenario in due course the state would negatively determine the IRCs development application and seek another applicant, possibly one who may not be as conscientious regarding the FPIC requirements. This scenario suggests that the fundamental issue to be examined is state practice and IRC practice, while relevant is only one factor to be investigated.

This second matter underscores one final conclusion that can be drawn from this discussion That is simply that the necessity to examine IRC practice stems at its core from a failure of state regulation. This failure may arise from the alleged reluctance to enforce the relevant aspects of the municipal regime suggested in relation to the Philippines or it may arise from the deficiencies in the architecture of the regime suggested in relation to Western Australia. In either case, a code of practice such as the ICMM Position Statement suggests a willingness on the part of IRCs to accept the responsibility to *respect* human rights imposed by the *UN Guiding Principles*. Once this is accepted, it becomes clear that the real core of the problem of ensuring the enjoyment of contemporary human rights lies in the failure of states to accept their duty to uphold human rights through the passage and enforcement of effective legislative regimes.

References

Articles

Anaya, S James and Puig, Sergio. 2017. 'Mitigating State Sovereignty: The Duty to Consult with Indigenous Peoples', *University of Toronto Law Journal* 67 (4): 435–464.

Arnold, Denis. 2010. 'Transnational Corporations and the Duty to Respect Basic Human Rights' *Business Ethics Quarterly* 20(3): 371–399.

Duruigbo, Emeka. 2006. 'Permanent Sovereignty and Peoples' Ownership of Natural Resources in International Law', *George Washington International Law Review*, 38: 33–100.

Erueti, Andrew. 2017. 'The Politics of International Indigenous Rights', *University of Toronto Law Journal* 67 (4): 569–595.

Holden, William. 2005. 'Indigenous Peoples and non-ferrous metals mining in the Philippines', *The Pacific Review*, 18 (3), 417–438.

Holden, William and Ingelson, Allan. 2007. 'Disconnect between the Philippine Mining Investment Policy and Indigenous Peoples Rights', *Journal of Energy and Natural Resources Law* 25 (4): 375–391.

Hyde, James N. 1956. 'Permanent Sovereignty over Natural Resources", *American Journal of International Law* 50: 854–867.

Kwakyewah, Cynthia and Idemudia, Uwaafiokun. 2017. 'Canada-Ghana Engagements in the Mining Sector: Protecting Human Rights or Business as Usual', *Transnational Human Rights Review* 4: 146–170.

Miyawa, Maxwell. 2006. 'The International Dimension of the Right o Development: Where is the Gapping Crack of Accountability for Non-State Actors', *The Transnational Human Rights Review* 3: 39–75.

O'Callaghan, Terry. 2009. 'Regulation and Governance in the Philippines Mining Sector', *Asia Pacific Journal of Public Administration*, 31 (1): 91–134.

Raymundo, Roberto. 2014. *The Philippine Mining Act of 1995: Is the law sufficient in achieving the goals of output growth, attracting foreign investment, environmental protection and preserving sovereignty?* De la Salle University Research Presentation, March 2014. http://www.dlsu.edu.ph/conferences/dlsu_research_congress/2014/_pdf/proceedings/SEE-III-026-FT.pdf.

Ruggie, John G. 2014. 'Global Governance and "New Governance Theory": Lessons from Business and Human Rights', *Global Governance* 20: 5–17.
Ruiz-Lozano, Mercedes and Tirado-Valencia, Pilar. 2016. 'Do industrial companies respond to the guiding principles of the Integrated Reporting framework? A preliminary study on the first companies joined to the initiative', *Spanish Accounting Review*, 19(2): 252–260.
Schrijver, Nico. 2013. 'Self-Determination of Peoples and Sovereignty over Natural Resources and Wealth' chapter in *Realizing the Right to Development: Essays in Commemoration of 25 Years of the United Nations Declaration on the Right to Development*, United Nations: 95–102.
Simbulan, Roland. 2016. 'Indigenous Communities' Resistance to Corporate Mining in the Philippines' *Peace Review*. 28 (1): 29–37.
Stavenhagen, Rodolfo. 2003. *Report of the Special Rapporteur on the Situation of Human Rights and Fundamental Freedoms of Indigenous People*, prepared by the UN Commission on Human Rights, 59th Session, 2003 (4/2003/90/Add.3).
Wettstein, Florian. 2012. 'CSR and the Debate on Human Rights: Bridging the Great Divide', *Business Ethics Quarterly*, 22(4): 739–770.

Organisational Publications

Commonwealth of Australia (C of A). 2015. *Our North, Our Future, White Paper on Developing Northern Australia*, Government Publication. https://www.industry.gov.au/data-and-publications/our-north-our-future-white-paper-on-developing-northern-australia.
Commonwealth of Australia, (C of A). Undated. *Department of Industry, Innovation and Science. Australian Mineral Commodities.* Government. https://www.industry.gov.au/resource/Mining/AustralianMineralCommodities/Pages/default.aspx.
Government of Western Australia (G of WA). 2017. *Mineral and Petroleum Statistics Digest 2016–2017*, Government Publication. http://www.dmp.wa.gov.au/Documents/About-Us-Careers/AboutUs-StatisticsDigest_2016-17.pdf.
International Council on Mining and Metals (ICMM). 2013. Position Statement on *Indigenous Peoples and Mining*. https://www.icmm.com/website/publications/pdfs/commitments/2013_icmm-ps_indigenous-people.pdf.

Legal Materials

Australia

The Constitution of the Commonwealth of Australia, 1901.
Mining Act 1978 (WA).

Native Title Act 1993 (Cth.).
Mabo & Ors v Queensland & Ors (Mabo No 2) (1992) 175 CLR 1.

REPUBLIC OF THE PHILIPPINES

1987 Constitution of The Republic of the Philippines.
Indigenous Peoples Rights Act of 1987 (Republic Act No 8371).
Philippine Mining Act of 1995 (Republic Act No 7942).

INTERNATIONAL MATERIALS

TREATIES

The *African Charter on Human and Peoples' Rights* adopted Nairobi on 27 June 1981, entered into force 21 October 1986, 1520 UNTS 217.
International Labour Organization (ILO), *ILO Declaration on Fundamental Principles and Rights at Work*, June 1988.
Montevideo Convention on Rights and Duties of States 1933 165 LNTS 19; USTS 881.
UN General Assembly, *International Covenant on Civil and Political Rights*, 16 December 1966, UNTS, vol. 999, p. 171.
UN General Assembly Resolution 1803 on *Permanent Sovereignty over Natural Resources* (G.A Res 1803 (XVII) UN Doc A/5217 (Dec 14 1962).
UN Declaration of the Rights of Indigenous Peoples (A/res/61/295 Ann. 1, Sept 13, 2007).
UN General Assembly Resolution 626 *The Right to Exploit Freely Natural Wealth and Resources* GA Res 523 (VI) UN Doc A/2119 (Jan 12, 1952).
Vienna Convention on the Law of Treaties 1969 1155 NTSS 331.

UNITED NATIONS MATERIALS

United Nations. 2003. *Draft Norms on the Responsibilities of Transnational Corporations and Other Business Enterprises with regard to Human Rights* (UN Doc. E/CN.4/Sub.2/2003/12/Rev.2 (2003).
United Nations. 2005a. *Extract from United Nations Permanent Forum on Indigenous Issues, Report of the International Workshop on Methodologies regarding Free, Prior and Informed Consent and Indigenous Peoples.* (New York, 17–19 January 2005), UN Doc E/C.19/2005/3 (2005), [46]. https://undocs.org/E/C.19/2005/3.
United Nations. 2005b, UN Commission on Human Rights, *Human Rights Resolution 2005/69.*

United Nations. 2011a. *UN Guiding Principles on Business and Human Right* (A/HRC/8/5.).

United Nations. 2011b. *Report of the Special Representative of the Secretary General on the issue of human rights and transnational corporations and other business enterprises, John Ruggie*, HRC, UNGOAR, 17th Sess, UN Doc A/HRC/17/31 (2011).

United Nations Department of Economic and Social Affairs (UNDESA) 2008. *Resource Kit on Indigenous Peoples Issues*. https://www.un.org/esa/socdev/unpfii/documents/resource_kit_indigenous_2008.pdf.

International Cases

Armed Activities on the Territory of the Congo (Congo v Uganda) (Judgment) [2005] ICJ Rep 168.

Case Centre for Minority Rights Development (Kenya) and Minority Rights Group International obo the Endorois Welfare Council v the Republic of Kenya, Communication No 276/2003 (*Endorois*).

OAS Report No 75/02, Case 11.140 ***Mary & Carrie Dann v United States***, *Dec 27, 2002 (The Western Shoshone Case)*.

Democratic Republic of the Congo v Burundi, Rwanda and Uganda, Communication 227/99 29 May 2003.

Inter-American Commission on Human Rights, Report 40/04, Case 12.053 ***Maya Indigenous Communities of the Toledo District v Belize***, Oct 12, 2004.

Inter-American Court ***Mayagna (Sumo) Awas Tingni Community v Nicaragua*** August 31, 2001.

Social and Economic Rights Action Center and Center for Economic and Social Rights v Nigeria, Communication 155/96.

Corte Inter-Americana de Derechos Humanos, *Caso Comunid Indigena **Yakye Axa v Paraguay***. Sentencia de 17 junio de 2005).

Inter-American Commission on Human Rights, Res 12/85, Case 7615 ***Yanomani (v Brazil)***, March 5 1985.

CHAPTER 7

Effect of the Minimum Wage on Employment Security: The Case of Precarious Workers in Myanmar

Hanh Nguyen, Min Zar Ni Lin,
and Samukelisiwe Ngwenya

Introduction

Ensuring remuneration for a decent living and favourable conditions of work for all labourers is an important component of labour rights. The International Covenant on Economic, Social and Cultural Rights in 1966 provides that workers must have the right to 'fair' and sufficient wages that

H. Nguyen (✉)
Yangon, Myanmar

Hanoi, Vietnam
e-mail: james@asiacentre.co.th

M. Z. N. Lin
Yangon, Myanmar

S. Ngwenya
Beijing, China

J. Gomez, R. Ramcharan (eds.), *Business and Human Rights in Asia*,
https://doi.org/10.1007/978-981-15-7273-9_7

allow themselves and their families to have a decent living. This provision is increasingly crucial in the era of dramatic transformation in the employment structure as the proportion of people with precarious work, or 'unsecure' employment, is on the rise. It is generally recognised that besides employers, it is the duty of states to have overall responsibility for upholding the rights of workers, especially the precarious ones who are exposed to the highest risk of wage insecurity and irregular working hours. Given certain market conditions, including the low bargaining power of workers, a minimum wage policy is welfare enhancing for low-income workers (Robinson 1933; Stigler 1946; Hungerbühler and Lehmann 2009).

In Myanmar, the implementation of the Minimum Wage Law since late 2015 is indicative of the government's commitment to transform the labour market by improving workers' welfare and facilitating productivity growth. Given the dynamic changes within the market and the increasing pressure from both workers and foreign entities, including a strong tide of labour activism since late 1980s, setting a minimum wage was an essential step. Following a series of tripartite consultations with worker representatives, employer representatives and government officials, the first daily minimum wage was set at MMK 3600 (approximately USD 2.70) at the rate of MMK 450 (approximately USD 0.30)[1] per hour which applied to workers across all sectors, industries and territories of Myanmar. A year after the minimum wage initiation, the Centre for Economic and Social Development (CESD)[2] conducted an assessment to evaluate the effects of the legislation on worker welfare and firm productivity.

Although employment security has remained a concern in Myanmar, there is a lack of adequate research on this matter. In order to fill that gap, this research paper aims to provide an understanding of precarious workers in food processing and garment factories in Myanmar, including their demographic characteristics and welfare response to the minimum wage. A precarious worker is defined by the lack of an employment contract and a less than minimum wage salary. By framing the concept in this way, the paper provides policy implications for designing employment and income redistribution schemes in Myanmar, since the country's social protection systems and the protection of workers' rights are still at an early stage.

[1] Currency exchange used is from December 2015; USD 1: MMK 1311.1.

[2] Centre for Economic and Social Development (CESD) is an independent think tank that supports evidence-based policy making in Myanmar. CESD's work is focused on five themes: Food security policy and rural development, governance, labour market reform, macroeconomic reform and natural resource management.

This paper is structured into five main sections that are all geared towards gaining more insights on the income effect of the 2015 Minimum Wage on precarious workers in Myanmar. First, it provides a review of existing literature on employment security, international legal frameworks that stipulate rights and benefits of labourers as well as studies on effects of minimum wages. The paper then gives a background on how the labour dynamics within key economic sectors in Myanmar were faring before the implementation of the Minimum Wage Law. The next section continues the analysis on labour rights-related legislation in Myanmar and the country's path to a minimum wage setting in 2013. This paper then presents key findings on the effect of a minimum wage on precarious workers by looking at the collected data and research methodology, profiles of precarious workers in the study and the effects of a minimum wage on precarious workers. The last section gives some insights into the development of employment policies that advance human rights in business in Myanmar. These findings aim to inform further direction of research on labour market reforms in Myanmar and Asia region.

Employment Security, State Responsibility and Wage Setting

The International Covenant on Economic, Social and Cultural Rights (ICESCR) in 1966 provides that workers must have the right to 'fair' and sufficient wages that allow themselves and their families to have a decent living. This provision requires that the wage that will be paid to the worker is in line with any applicable collective bargaining agreements and with local 'living wage' norms. However, changes in employment relations system since 1990s in most countries have led to a change in the structure of jobs, thus negatively affecting employment security (Katz 1993; Kuruvilla and Erickson 2000). A research by Lee and Kuruvilla (2001) found that the proportion of people who have full-time permanent employment has been decreasing while part-time, temporary and contingent employment is becoming more common. This decline in 'secure' employment—a component of the more global notion of job security—is explained by social critics and particularly critics of globalisation (Virtanen et al. 2002). Precarious work, or 'unsecure' employment, includes the threat to continued employment due to organisational changes, such as closure, redundancy or outsourcing, and limited access to social welfare due to the lack of secure employment contract.[3] This trend has called for both legislative and institutional intervention to prevent further erosion in employment security.

As emphasised in the United Nations Human Rights Council's Guiding Principles on Business and Human Rights (BHR/UNGPs), states have overall responsibility for upholding the rights of all labourers within their territory and/or jurisdiction through effective policies, legislation, regulations and adjudication. BHR/UNGPs also refer to the Declaration on Fundamental Principles and Rights at Work by the International Labour Organization (ILO) as one of the foundational principles for corporate responsibility. This includes freedom of association and the effective recognition of the right to collective bargaining, the elimination of forced or compulsory labour, the abolition of child labour and the elimination of discrimination with respect to employment and occupation. Well before that, the ILO defines minimum wage as 'the minimum amount of remuneration that an employer is required to pay wage earners for the work performed during a given period, which cannot be reduced by collective agreement or an individual contract' (ILO 1970). This provision emphasises protection for the low-paid workers, often the most vulnerable in the sectors, by shifting the earning distributions in their favour.

There are two main schools of thoughts in the literature on the effects of minimum wages. The first strand concludes that a minimum wage is welfare enhancing given certain market imperfections. A popular assumption, initially made by Robinson (1933) and Stigler (1946), is that employers have monopoly power over wages. Rutkowski (2003) explained how wage inequality decreases with the implementation of the minimum wage as the wage effects were concentrated in the bottom income quartile. Then in 2009, by studying the minimum wage in the presence of search frictions in labour market and an optimised tax schedule, Hungerbüehler and Lehmann conclude that a minimum wage mechanism was efficient when the bargaining power of employees is sufficiently low. Indeed, according to the OECD (1998), most cases of minimum wage result in the compression of the earnings distribution.

[3] http://www.ilo.org/global/topics/employment-security/lang%2D%2Den/index.htm.

The second school of thought, however, argues that a minimum wage hike can lead to economic welfare loss and negative impacts on workers' employment. Neoclassical economists see the minimum wage setting as a distortion of labour markets, grounded in the view that the wage agreed upon by the worker and employer is welfare maximizing for both. Furthermore, it has been seen when a minimum wage can unintentionally cause the dis-employment effects, hurting the low-paid workers it is supposed to protect. Theoretical explanation for this effect has to do with setting the minimum wage above the market equilibrium rate, then, subsequently forcing the firms to fire unskilled workers whose value of the labour product is below the newly fixed minimum wage. Arango and Pachón (2004) and Freeman (1996) found that minimum wage substantially lowered employment in Puerto Rico. Likewise, Maloney and Nunez (2000) found similar results in other Latin America countries. In response to the minimum wage policies, firms often reduce working time and increase work intensity (Couch and Wittenburg 2001; Linneman 1982). In China, minimum wage adjustments have significantly reduced working hours especially for women as the employers often suppressed wage increase upon the weakest group of workers (Sun et al. 2015).

Despite the variety of potential impacts, within the scope of this study, the authors will only focus on the income effect of minimum wages. Dis-employment effect can only be observed through a time series data which is not available due to the data scarcity in Myanmar. In this regard, differences in income of workers before and after the minimum wage as a proxy for income effects of a minimum wage in Myanmar will be examined through a self-reported cross-section of 525 observations. In addition, this study expands the concept of employment security to other monetary and non-monetary incentives that workers receive, including bonuses, charges and trainings. Further research and data collection are needed to explore the full effects of a minimum wage in Myanmar.

Labour Market Dynamics in Myanmar

Myanmar has a young and relatively cheap labour force (See Oxford Business Group 2016). According to the 2014 Myanmar Population and Housing Census, the youth population in Myanmar was estimated at more than 17 million people. Myanmar's labour market is dynamic in that there has been considerable growth in the past seven years since economic and political liberalisation. Development of entry-point and labour-intensive industries like garment and food processing has the potential to transform the Myanmar economy by creating a conducive environment for a more efficient use of the country's abundant human capital. In 2017, the garment sector employed over 320,000 workers, which constituted 1.4 per cent of the country's total labour force, compared to nearly 260,000 workers in 2015 (MGMA 2017). Most of these workers are unskilled youth, predominantly women, migrating from rural locations to Yangon where 95 per cent of the garment factories are located. Besides the apparel industry, food processing is one of the most important sectors for job creation in Myanmar. According to the CESD's Enterprise Survey in 2015, most workers in the food processing industry were male and 60 per cent of the workforce in the industry was unskilled.

Although there has been an increase in the labour force in the industry and service sectors, it is important to consider some of the areas in which the labour market is lagging. For instance, the labour force participation rate was at 64.7 per cent in 2015; however, in 2017 the rate decreased to 61.5 per cent. This shift affected unemployment rate, raising it from 0.8 to 2.1 per cent. These figures indicate the challenge to create jobs in Myanmar. Securing jobs is a major problem, especially in rural areas where employment is dominated by the agricultural sector and typically does not involve a formal contract.

Despite being more formalised than rural jobs, the industrial sector in urban areas cannot guarantee employment security for workers. Garment and food processing industries in Myanmar have high annual labour turnover rates, estimated at 57 per cent and 39 per cent respectively (CESD 2015). Like informal workers, employees in those industries are likely to move from one manufacturer to another without any notice for a small salary increase (ILO 2015). Industrial relations are another major issue as there is very little consideration for social aspects of those factories. In the apparel sector, relatively high incidence of crime and theft, often preying upon rural female migrant workers, combined with high transportation and housing costs, exacerbate the stress level of workers. Meanwhile, in the food processing sector, the basic pay is less than the minimum wage while the working conditions, including non-discrimination treatment by supervisors, access to facilities (i.e. toilets, drinking water) and workplace safety, are not adequate. This highlights another aspect of worker rights that needs to be addressed by the government.

A Myanmar's Path to Minimum Wage Setting

The setting of the minimum wage in 2013 was indicative of the government's commitment to improve workers' welfare and labour productivity. In fact, Myanmar was one of the earliest countries in Southeast Asia to promulgate the Minimum Wage Act in 1949 following its independence in 1948. The act recognised the importance of labour movement during the independence struggle that began in late 1930s. However, the government failed to enforce the legislation despite the formation of the Minimum Wage Council in 1953 and attempts to set wage rates in the agricultural sector and cigarette-making businesses in 1950s (Than 2007).

Labour activism and its impacts on government accountability are the main driver of the recent minimum wage establishment. Under the military government in 1988, labour activists came to the forefront of the prodemocracy movement. This led to the formation of the Federation of Trade Unions of Burma (FTUB) in 1991, which actively lobbied for human rights and sought for international support. In 2013, FTUB established the Confederation of Trade Unions of Myanmar. Soon after that, many other worker associations were established across the country, registering some 400 basic-level unions (ITUC 2013). During the period of political liberalisation that began in 2011, networks of local trade union activists took advantage of new opportunities to organise workers into trade unions as a force for further political and economic changes (Henry 2015).

In 2012, a new law on the Settlement of Labour Dispute Law was adopted, which provided dispute resolution mechanisms through conciliation and arbitration. However, confrontations between workers and employers continue to rise as the agreements reached through the conciliation process are neither respected nor enforced as binding agreements (ITUC 2013). According to the Action Labour Right's survey report in 2016, there were 447 garment worker strikes nationwide between 2012 and 2014. As the government came to realise that the majority of strikes were not due to political aspirations but more motivated by low wages, they started to look more favourably upon fixing the minimum wage, in accordance with the law passed in March 2013. At the same time, the government was also conscious of restoring its international legitimacy by respecting and promoting labour standards—a statutory condition required by the United States Government to lift the sanctions on Myanmar.

As a result, a new law on minimum wage was introduced in 2013 as a key component of economic and social reforms, setting the rate at MMK 3600 (approximately USD 2.70) per day in June 2015.[4,5] A major challenge in determining the optimal minimum wage rate was the lack of labour statistics that countries usually rely upon when they estimate living wage and other conditions of labour market. Myanmar had to use formal mechanisms under tripartite National Minimum Wage Committee comprising of five worker representatives, five employer representatives, 12 government representatives and five independent experts to determine the wage rate acceptable for both workers and employers.[6] In essence, the minimum wage determination was undertaken in accordance with two objectives: to meet the basic needs of working families engaging in the production, trade and service sectors; and to strengthen productivity and competitiveness of the workforce in these sectors.'[7] The minimum wage legislation affects all formally registered firms with a minimum of 15 workers in any industrial sector across Myanmar. As a result, workers in labour-intensive industries like garment and food processing became the main beneficiaries of the minimum wage policy.

In addition to the Minimum Wage Law, the Social Security Law was enacted in 2012 replacing the previous legislation in 1954. The social scheme covers employees working for firms with more than five employees, of which employers and employees are required to contribute respectively 3 per cent and 2 per cent of their total wages. As such, it amended

[4] National Minimum Wage Fixing Committee proposed the rate at K. 3600 in end of June 2015, when the prevailing exchange rate for USD 1 was equal to MMK 1110. The Committee announced it nationwide and waited 60 days for public feedback and questions. Then, the government made official notification on 28 August 2015.

[5] Recently the committee began the review process of the minimum wage in 2017 and a new minimum wage of MMK 4800 came into effect on the 14th of May 2018.

[6] As a follow-up, the government requested CESD to take a rapid assessment on living wage conditions in three urban centres, namely Yangon, Mandalay and Bago, to know the prevailing market prices. After that, the Department of Labour conducted household surveys in all 15 states and regions to understand household expenditures and their living conditions. All these findings were presented to the Committee in parallel to regular sessions of social dialogue that the Ministry was hosting for the representatives of workers and employers to put their positions on the table. When the negotiations for the minimum wage started, the workers demanded MMK 8000 per day while the employers suggested MMK 1500. After a series of consultations and an analysis of the findings, in August 2015 the committee finalised the minimum wage at MMK 3600 (USD 2.70) per eight-hour working day which then came into effect on the 1st of September 2015.

[7] Union of Myanmar. *Pyidaungsu Hluttaw Law No. 7: Minimum Wage Law*. 22 March 2013. Preamble.

contribution rates and benefits for medical care, maternity leave and workplace injuries and introduced new family benefits (Lynn 2017). The Social Security Board (SSB) has implemented the Social Security Law after two years in 2014. Up to 2017, three hospitals and 101 clinics have been opened throughout 13 states/regions to provide medical treatment and other benefits for workers and their families. However, there are some concerns about the way SSB operates, especially in terms of their financial sustainability (Lynn 2017).

More recently, the Pyidaungsu Hluttaw (Assembly of the Union) enacted the Myanmar Investment Law[8] in 2016, which emphasised the obligation of investors to support the rights of their workers and staff. Accordingly, an investor shall ensure 'the entitlements and rights in the labour laws and rules, including minimum wages and salaries, leave, holidays, overtime fees, damages, compensation of the workman, social welfare, and other insurance related to workers in stipulating the rights and duties of employers and employees and occupational terms and conditions in the employment contract.' The new Investment Law plays an important role in shaping business behaviour in Myanmar, providing directions for what companies are permitted and required to do regarding labour rights. However, further guidance and enforcement are needed to enable enterprises to respect human rights in Myanmar.

The Effect of Minimum Wage on Precarious Workers in Myanmar—Findings from the Worker Survey

This section describes the results of the analysis of the effect of the minimum wage enforcement on precarious workers in Myanmar conducted using the data from the CESD's 2016 Worker Survey. There are two major concepts that need to be redefined in this section. First, the 2013 Myanmar Minimum Wage Law defines wage as 'the fee, wage or salary entitled to be obtained by an employee for carrying out hourly work, daily work, weekly work, monthly work or any other part-time work with an employer.' Wage shall include overtime fee or bonus paid by the employer, or other remunerations and benefits which may be determined as income.[9] A minimum

[8] Before 2016, the Foreign Investment Law and Myanmar Citisen Investment Law were separately enacted in 2012 and 2013 respectively.

[9] According to the 2013 Myanmar Minimum Wage Law, wage shall not include: (i) travel allowances; (ii) pension payments and gratuities for service; (iii) social security cash benefits; (iv) allowances for accommodation and meals, electricity charges, water service charges and

wage is therefore understood as the wage that excludes overtime payments. Following up to the Minimum Wage Law, the Notification no. 2/2015 by the National Committee for Minimum Wage provides guidlines on how to calculate the minimum wage. Accordingly, the proposed minimum wage is set at MMK 3600 (USD 2.70) at the rate of MMK 450 (USD 0.30) per hour for an eight-hour work day for all workers, irrespective location and type of work. This paper refers to the minimum wage as the monthly compensation of MMK 108,000 (USD 81) for eight-hour work for duration of 30 working days.

Second, since there is no legal definition of precarious workers, this paper defines precarious workers as employees who had no employment contract and received less than a minimum wage. This definition is in line with the ILO's understanding of precarious work as the work uncertainty as to 'the duration of employment, multiple possible employers or a disguised or ambiguous employment relationship, a lack of access to social protection and benefits usually associated with employment, low pay, and substantial legal and practical obstacles to joining a trade union and bargaining collectively'[10] (ILO 2011).

The Data

The empirical analysis explores the data from the 2016 Worker Survey conducted by CESD and the Yangon University of Economics (YUE)[11] in Hlaing Thayar industrial zone.[12] The Survey collected data on employees' wages and benefits before and after the minimum wage enforcement. As such, worker's income is divided into two components: basic salary and other allowances, including overtime benefit, attendance bonus, productivity and skill bonus, housing, transportation and lunch charges.

duties and taxes; (v) medical treatment allowances and creation allowances; (vi) compensation for dismissal from work and compassionate allowance; (vii) Other fees not considered wage in accordance with the Law.

[10] ILO provides characteristics of precarious conditions: (i) Low wage, (ii) Poor protection from termination of employment, (iii) Lack of access to social protection and benefits usually associated with full-time standard employment, (iv) Lack of or limited access of workers to exercise their rights at work.

[11] The survey was conducted by 400 final year economics students from the Yangon University of Economics guided by 20 economics lecturers from the same university and 12 survey researchers from the CESD. The survey period was from July to August 2016 and funded by the International Development Research Centre (IDRC).

[12] Hlaing Thayar is the largest zone in Myanmar with about 1.4 million acres of land, hosting over 500 firms with over 50,000 workers operating in the zone (See Appendix 1).

The Survey also gathered information about other non-monetary incentives, such as working days and overtime hours, trainings, savings and loans.

As a result, a cross-section dataset of 525 observations from workers in food processing and garment factories was collected 11 months after the implementation of the Minimum Wage Law in 2015. (See Annex I, Tables 7.3 and 7.4) The gender distribution of sample in the survey was predominantly female, representing 69.7 per cent of the respondents. The average age of respondents was 28.2 in garment factories and 25.5 in food-processing factories. Although the legal age of labour in Myanmar is above 14,[13] 0.3 per cent of the observations fell under the age of 15. Both the garment and food processing factories have large shares of workers with middle school education (70 per cent of the respondents). This result clearly indicates the urgent need for worker training within the industrial zones and firms. Detailed demographic information of the selected respondents is presented in the Appendix 2.

The CESD's 2016 Minimum Wage Survey was the first survey in Myanmar to empirically demonstrate changes in workers' welfare under the minimum wage policy. The survey focuses on the case of Hlaing Thayar Industrial Zone to represent the industrial sector in Myanmar. This selection ensures external validity of the findings despite the time and resource constraints. However, the Survey is built on limited the existing studies and data on wage and precarious work in Myanmar. Though the self-reported data is useful in providing workers' perspectives on a minimum wage, it is not sufficient to validate the reported information. In addition, the cross-section data could not reveal the dis-employment effect of the minimum wage. As a result, it is necessary to combine this dataset with existing literature and practices regarding labour issues in Myanmar to have a more comprehensive overview of industrial workers' welfare.

Precarious Workers before the Minimum Wage Setting

This sub-section provides descriptive information on the precarious workers in the survey in order to answer two questions: (i) what is their demographic profile?; and (ii) which factors attributed to their employment insecurity?. Though precarious workers in this paper are defined as

[13] In Myanmar, the Shops and Establishments Act of 1951 prohibited children under 13 years old from working in industrial settings. However, as of January 2016, the Factories Act and Shops and Establishments Act were amended and the minimum age for employment was raised to 14. Children 14–16 years old are not allowed to work in hazardous work and not allowed overtime; however, garment and food processing work are not regarded as hazardous.

employees who earned less than the minimum wage (MMK 108,000) and had no employment contract, these criteria could not provide a comprehensive understanding about their background and socio-economic status. Exploring profiles of those workers helps identify the most marginalised labour groups, serving the purpose of this paper to design social policies that target precarious workers in Myanmar.

Table 7.1 provides demographic information and employment status of 176 precarious workers in the survey before the minimum wage. The precarious group, dominated by female workers, was characterised by young workforce with low education level, low union participation rate and limited savings. Specifically, before the minimum wage, nearly 65 per cent of the precarious workers were female; some 75 per cent of those workers were under 30 years old. While 19 per cent obtained higher education (reported to have registered at a university), the majority had educational qualifications of high school or below. 13.07 per cent of such workers

Table 7.1 Profile of precarious workers before the minimum wage

	Number of respondents	*Percentage*		*Number of respondents*	*Percentage*
Gender			*Position*		
Female	114	64.77	Cleaner/	10	5.68
Male	62	35.23	Security	6	3.41
			Driver	5	2.84
Age			General	23	13.07
Under 20	40	22.73	worker	106	60.23
20–24	51	28.98	Helper	19	10.80
25–29	34	19.32	Operator	7	4.54
30–34	23	13.07	Amin/HR	24	13.64
35–39	14	7.95	Other	152	86.36
40+	14	7.95		48	27.27
			Union member	128	72.73
Education					
	13	7.39	Yes		
	65	36.93	No		
	65	36.93			
	33	18.75	*Saving*		
Primary and below			Yes		
Secondary			No		
High school					
Higher education					
Observations	176	100	*Observations*	176	100

were helpers, 60.23 per cent were operators while some 10 per cent held HR and Admin positions. Other positions, including cleaner, security staff, driver and general worker, altogether made up for 12 per cent of the precarious workers in the survey. Most of the workers in this group reported to neither have savings (73 per cent) nor participate in any labour union (86 per cent).

Information on the profile of precarious workers provides useful explanation for their unsecure employment status. The first component of precarious work—earning less than a minimum wage—was attributed to low educational levels and lack of work experience. In fact, 22 per cent of the precarious workers before the minimum wage had only one year of experience or less. Moreover, their gender status can be another factor that accounted for their low payment since on average, women earn less than men in Myanmar.[14] The second component—lack of employment contract—can be explained by the working positions and union membership participation. While most of the precarious workers held unskilled and easy-to-replace positions, their lack of participation in labour union minimised their bargaining power over the course of employment contract. Moreover, low saving rate could potentially lead to their continued unsecure status due to debt bondage.

Effects of the Minimum Wages on Precarious Workers in Myanmar

This sub-section provides an analysis of changes in welfare of precarious workers to determine whether the minimum wage in Myanmar is target efficient. A total sample of 525 observations is divided into two groups: precarious and non-precarious, based on their basic salary and employment contract status before the minimum wage. In theory, a minimum wage should not only enhance the income of the lowest earners, but also protect their rights by securing contracts and other employment benefits. Therefore, this section will also examine other aspects of workers' welfare enhancement, including employment bonus, training and employment promotion.

Before the minimum wage, the income gaps between non-precarious workers and precarious ones were 1.6 with regard to basic income and 1.5

[14] According to the 2015 Myanmar Labour Force Survey, on average, a female worker earned MMK 96,700 (USD 69) per month or 33% less than their male counterparts.

with regard to total income. After the minimum wage implementation, the gaps shrunk to 1.3 and 1.2 respectively. Income improvement in the precarious group reduced the percentage of those workers in the survey from 33.5 per cent to 7.4 per cent after the legislation. In fact, their basic salary was clustered at the minimum wage as 47 per cent of the precarious workers reported to receive the exact amount of the minimum wage after the minimum wage enforcement. However, 16.5 per cent of those workers, majority of whom were operators, helpers, cleaners and security staff, reported that they received less than the minimum wage even after the law was implemented. This finding indicates that most of the surveyed firms complied with the minimum wage law, with the exception of a few factories.

Together with the increase in basic salary, more workers secured their employment contract after the minimum wage. Of those precarious workers who did not have an employment contract before the minimum wage, 35 respondents or 20 per cent received one after the legislation. The self-reported cross-section from the survey also shows some occupational enhancement of precarious workers. For instance, 23 out of 176 precarious workers (13 per cent) reported that they got a promotion after the minimum wage law, including the 7 helpers and 4 general workers who were promoted to production operators and the 3 operators who received admin and HR jobs. This trend shows positive employment effects of the government's policy on reducing the skill gap between different segments of employees.

The Competitive Wage Determination theory by Stigler (1946) suggests that if the employers pay labour of given skills and application, a minimum wage must have one of the two effects: workers whose services are worth less than the minimum wage are discharged; or the productivity of low-efficiency workers is increased. Table 7.2 shows that after the minimum wage, workers who belonged to the precarious group experienced a substantial efficiency boost reflected in 135.1 per cent increase in the attainment of the skill and productivity bonus. This bonus increase is significantly higher than one received by the non-precarious group and the changes in other monetary incentives, such as overtime benefit, attendance fees, housing, transportation and lunch charges. These findings imply that firms can effectively boost workers' productivity by offering a skill-based bonus.

In-depth interviews with garment employers and workers show that firms increased their production target up to the average of 30 per cent. For instance, at a garment factory in Hlaing Thayar, the production target used to be 80–100 pieces for 40 people per line before, but increased to 150–200 pieces for 30 people per line after the minimum wage. Some supervisors fear that the minimum wage will have a greater impact on

Table 7.2 Changes in income and incentives after the minimum wage

	Per cent increase after MW (precarious) (%)	*Per cent increase after MW (non-precarious) (%)*
Basic salary	56.33	25.11
Overtime benefit	65.81	55.89
Attendance fee	5.69	-8.67
Skill and productivity bonus	135.10	88.89
Housing, transportation and lunch charges	27.34	16.73
On-the-job training (number of workers)	-13.33	-35.09
Outside training (number of workers)	-63.64	-5.88

operators who are less skilled, so they put more pressure on them to reach the targets. Contrary to the productivity bonus, there was a drastic decrease in the number of workers from the precarious group that received in-house and out-of-work trainings. In fact, although the provision of training to the workers is minimal at all factories in the Hlaing Thayar Industrial Zone, the number of precarious workers who received in-house training dropped by 13 per cent after the minimum wage enforcement while ones who attended out-of-job training declined by 64 per cent.[15]

Giving Effect to UNGPs Through Better Employment Policies

The above findings have important implications for promoting the BHR/UNGPS, advocating for the protection of human rights and creating more conducive work environments. Despite aiming at business enterprises, the Guiding Principles include operational provisions that a state may take in order to fulfil their duty to protect against human rights violations by third parties. This includes enacting and enforcing laws and creating a regulatory environment that facilitates business respect for human rights.

[15] In garment and food processing factories in Myanmar, in-house training or on-the-job training is mostly for new workers. Therefore, the decrease in in-house training can be due to the fact that surveyed workers themselves do not need further training as they are already familiar with their positions.

The launch of the BHR/UNGPS in 2011 coincided with the opening up of Myanmar which was characterised by significant economic and political changes. In fact, Myanmar has demonstrated its commitment to upholding the principles of protecting its workers and ensuring that both local and transnational businesses put human rights at the forefront of their operations. As the research findings have indicated, the labour reforms include the Minimum Wage Law (2013) and the Social Security Law (2012) which were both aimed at improving the working conditions and the well-being of workers in Myanmar.

As the country continues to generate more investment in labour-intensive sectors and as the flow of foreign direct investment continues, it is important that Myanmar ensures its integration into the responsible global value chains. In order for the business environment to thrive and generate economic growth, the needs and rights of workers have to be prioritised. More specifically, precarious workers should be at the central focus of employment policies as those are the segment that has limited protection from social security policies.

One of the main challenges is how all provisions are implemented and enforced. In this regard, the government of Myanmar needs to monitor compliance with the Minimum Wage Law and take corrective measures to deal with noncompliance. This process should go hand in hand with the formalisation of the economy. Additionally, the government should provide policy coherence and consistent communication of the actions taken between their ministries and departments. Moreover, the implementation of sound employment policies should take into consideration other employment regulations of industrial relations, land, tax and corporate laws.

Conclusion

The chapter documents the positive effects of a minimum wage in increasing basic salary and skill-based bonus, thereby securing the employment benefits of precarious workers in Myanmar. The Minimum Wage Law in 2013 resulted from a strong wave of labour activism and increasing international pressure to ensure worker rights. Tellingly, the minimum wage is supposed to protect the rights of the most vulnerable workers in Myanmar. The survey data suggests that the minimum wage enforcement led to a decrease in the percentage of precarious workers, who were predominantly female and low-educated workers, from 33.5 per cent before to 7.4 per cent after the minimum wage. The income gaps between non-precarious workers and precarious workers were consequently reduced. Together with increases in basic salary, more workers secured their employment contract and experienced a substantial increase in skill and productivity bonus. However, 16.5 per cent of those workers reported that they still received less than the minimum wage after the law has been implemented. Additionally, there was a drastic decrease in the number of those workers receiving both in-house and out of work training.

This study provides new insights into the human rights and business nexus. Specifically, it indicates the interconnected problems of ensuring economic rights for workers together with other aspects of employment security, such as contract, training and working hours. This is an area that needs to be further explored and expanded based on the framework of BHR/UNGPs. Future research will help inform and enhance legislation and policy-making process regarding employment and worker rights.

Crucially, this study has an important implication for advancing state accountability in Asia where the application of BHR/UNGPs remains limited. In this context, Myanmar can be a critical case study since the social protection scheme is being developed at the very early stage. More evidences with adequate and accurate data are necessary to track the accountability and effectiveness of state governance over the implementation of social security policies.

Annex 1

Table 7.3 Number of workers and enterprises in 2015 and 2016 in Hlaing Tharyar Industrial Zone, Yangon

No.	*Type of Business*	*No of Workers in 2015*	*No of Workers in 2016*	*No of Enterprises in 2015*	*No of Enterprises in 2016*
1.	Food Stuff	10629	12322	171	157
2.	Textile and Garment	65011	71699	121	175
3.	Engineering works	3189	3521	34	59
4.	Chemical products	3137	3175	38	61
5.	Stationery and Printing	1122	1275	15	20
6.	Forestry products	1170	1486	39	42
7.	Metal and Oil products	1424	870	35	26
8.	Packaging	4613	–	19	–
11.	Miscellaneous	29803	35926	446	503

Source: Hlaing Thayar Labour Exchange Office and Industrial Management Committee (2016)

Table 7.4 Demographic information of respondents

	Number of respondents	*Percentage*	*Note*
Sector			
Food processing	240	45.71	Three respondents denied to answer their current sector
Garment	282	53.71	
N/A	3	0.57	
Age			
Under 20	90	17.14	Two respondents were under 15 years old at the survey time
20–24	166	31.62	
25–29	112	21.33	
30–34	77	14.67	
35–39	43	8.19	
40–44	15	2.86	
45+	22	4.19	
Gender			
Female	366	69.71	49.58 per cent of respondents from food processing were female
Male	159	30.29	
Education			
Read & Write	9	1.71	
Primary	41	7.81	
Secondary	174	33.14	
High school	191	36.38	
Higher education	110	20.95	
Change the job in the last 12 months			
Yes	66	12.57	
No	459	87.43	
Observations	525	100	

References

Carlos Arango & Angélica Pachón, 2004. "Minimum Wages in Colombia: Holding the Middle with a Bite," BORRADORES DE ECONOMIA 003224, BANCO DE LA REPÚBLICA.

Centre for Economic and Social Development (2015). Myanmar Labour Issues from the Perspective of Enterprises: Findings from a CESD survey among food processing and garment manufacturing businesses. Yangon: CESD.

Couch, K.A. and Wittenburg, D.C., 2001. The response of hours of work to increases in the minimum wage. *Southern Economic Journal*, pp. 171–177.

Freeman, R.B., 1996. The minimum wage as a redistributive tool. *The Economic Journal*, *106*(436), pp. 639–649.

Hungerbühler, M. and Lehmann, E., 2009. On the optimality of a minimum wage: New insights from optimal tax theory. *Journal of Public Economics*, *93*(3–4), pp. 464–481.

International Labour Organisation. 2011. Policies and Regulations to Combat Precarious Employment. Geneva: ILO

International Labour Office. 1970. Concerning the Minimum Wage Fixing Convention, 1970 (No. 131), and the Minimum Wage Fixing Recommendation, 1970 (No. 135). *General Survey.*

International Labour Office. 2015. Myanmar garment sub-sector value chain analysis.

International Trade Union Confederation (ITUC) 2013. Countries at risk: 2013 Report on Violations of Trade Union Rights. Brussels: ITUC.

Katz, H.C., 1993. The decentralization of collective bargaining: a literature review and comparative analysis. *ILR Review*, *47*(1), pp. 3–22.

Kuruvilla, S. and Erickson, C., 2000. The impact of globalization on industrial relations in Asia: A comparative review and analysis. In *12th IIRA World Congress, Tokyo, Japan.*

Lee, A. and Kuruvilla, S., 2001. Changes in employment security in Asia. *Global Business Review*, *2*(2), pp. 259–287.

Linneman, P., 1982. The economic impacts of minimum wage laws: a new look at an old question. *Journal of Political Economy*, *90*(3), pp. 443–469.

Lynn, K. Y. 2017. Workers Welcome changes to social security system. *Frontier Myanmar.* 10 November. 2017. Web. 10 May. 2018.

Maloney, W.F. and Nunez, J., 2000. *Measuring the impact of minimum wages: Evidence from Latin America.* The World Bank.

Myanmar Garment Manufacturer's Association (MGMA) 2017. "Background about MGMA". Available at: https://www.myanmargarments.org/background-of-mgma/

Nicholas, H., 2015. "Trade union internationalism and political change in Myanmar," Global Change, Peace & Security, Vol. 27, No.1, 69–84.

OECD. 1998. Information on minimum wage setting and trends, and a summary of research on the impact of minimum wage regulations in OECD countries. *Employment Outlook, Paris.*

Oxford Business Group. 2016. The Report: Myanmar 2016 Economy.

Robinson, J., 1947. The Economics of Imperfect Competition (London, 1933). *Robinson The Economics of Imperfect Competition 1933.*

Rutkowski, J., 2003. The minimum wage: curse or cure. *Photocopy, World Bank, Washington, DC.*

Stigler, G.J., 1946. The economics of minimum wage legislation. *The American Economic Review*, *36*(3), pp. 358–365.

Sun, W., Wang, X. and Zhang, X., 2015. Minimum wage effects on employment and working time of Chinese workers—evidence based on CHNS. *IZA Journal of Labor & Development*, *4*(1), p. 19.
Than, T.M.M., 2007. *State dominance in Myanmar: The political economy of industrialization*. Institute of Southeast Asian Studies.
Virtanen, P., Vahtera, J., Kivimäki, M., Pentti, J. and Ferrie, J., 2002. Employment security and health. *Journal of Epidemiology & Community Health*, *56*(8), pp. 569–574.

CHAPTER 8

Access to Remedy for Corporate Human Rights Abuses in Indonesia

Iman Prihandono and Fajri Hayu Religi

Introduction

As a member state of the UN Human Rights Council, which has encouraged the adoption of the UNGPs Resolution, Indonesia has a strong moral commitment to implement UNGPs. Moreover, Indonesia actively involved in proposing the Resolution on the Legally Binding Instrument which aims to establish binding instruments of law at the international level, so that corporations can no longer avoid their obligation to respect human rights. At the international level, following the resolution on the adoption of UNGPs in 2011, in its Universal Periodic Review (UPR) report in May 2017, Indonesia received a number of recommendations (UN HRC 2017), of which four related to Business and Human Rights, which includes preventing child labour (UN HRC 2017: 139.108), and the need to further strengthen Indonesia's commitment on human rights dimension in business activities and to lead regional efforts in this issue.

I. Prihandono (✉) • F. H. Religi
Surabaya, Indonesia
e-mail: iprihandono@fh.unair.ac.id

J. Gomez, R. Ramcharan (eds.), *Business and Human Rights in Asia*,
https://doi.org/10.1007/978-981-15-7273-9_8

Indonesia's position at international level is sufficient to show how important the issue of Business and Human Rights for Indonesia. In addition, several conditions at the national level also affect the urgency of UNGPs implementation in Indonesia. First, Indonesia is one of the favourite destinations for foreign investment in the world. The size of the population and the growing number of middle classes is an attractive market. In addition, the high number of population provides workers with competitive wages compared to other countries. More importantly, Indonesia has the abundant natural resources products.

The Indonesia Investment Coordinating Board (BKPM) data shows the value of investment (foreign and domestic) has increased from IDR612.6 Trillion (2016) to 692.8 Trillion (2017), where as much as 13.1 per cent is a new investment (BKPM 2018). The Indonesia Statistic Centre data also shows Indonesia's economic growth in 2017 increased to 5.7 per cent, which is the highest since 2014 (5.02 per cent) (Cabinet Secretariat Republic of Indonesia 2018). This condition indicates an increase in economic activity supported by business activities of business actors and corporations in Indonesia. The increasing value of foreign investment in Indonesia, at the same time provides information on increasing the presence of foreign business actors. From the business and human rights perspective, this situation requires the Indonesian government to have the same business and human rights instruments for all business actors. Indeed, some home countries of foreign companies operating in Indonesia already have business and human rights standards that must be observed.

Apart from the two urgencies for UNGPs implementation in Indonesia as described above, there is one strong reason why UNGPs should be a priority. Indonesia has a binding international obligation contained in various ratified human rights instruments. All of these instruments require states to ensure that the fulfilment of human rights is not violated by any person, or group of persons, including corporations and business actors. This has also been emphasized by the United Nations High Commissioner for Human Rights during his visit in Jakarta on 7 February 2018. H.E. Zeid Raa'ad Al Hussein emphasised: "I urge the Indonesian government and corporations involved in mining activities of large-scale natural resources, plantations and fisheries business, to refer to UNGPs by ensuring that business activities are not carried out in ways that violate the rights of the community" (UN HRC 2018: 139.38).

This article examines the latest development in Indonesian regulations that promotes respect to human rights by companies operating in Indonesia. In particular, this article analyse two regulations, namely the Supreme Court Regulation No. 13/2016 on Guideline in Handling Corporate Crime (SCR 13/2016) and the Presidential Regulation No. 13/2018 on the Disclosure of Corporate Beneficiary Owner (PR 13/2018). This article seeks to analyse to what extent these two regulations may help victims of corporate abuses to obtain remedies, and what are the potential obstacles. The first part discusses recent development in business and human rights regulation in Indonesia. It is followed by examination of both the SCR 13/2016 and the PR 13/2018 respectively. Conclusion and suggestion is presented in the last section.

Business and Human Rights Situation in Indonesia: An Overview

Referring to the three pillars in UNGPs, the general conditions of Business and Human Rights in Indonesia can be described as follows:

First, regarding the obligation of the State to protect. In general, the rule of law relating to business activities that can impact the fulfilment of human rights is spread into different laws and regulations. Legislation containing obligations for business actors can be found in environmental, labour, land, mining, industrial and forestry laws. Similarly, Indonesia has ratified almost all major international human rights treaties.

In term of legal instruments, it is actually sufficient to ensure that business activities do not cause negative impact on human rights. But the implementation of this law remains ineffective, so that corporate rights violations by corporations remain. The drawbacks of the implementation of this law is due to several factors, these are:

1. The regional autonomy is considered as one of the factors driving conflict induced by business activities. The transfer of authority to grant business permits from the central government to the local government makes an assessment of the compliance of business activities with environmental, labour and social regulations becoming looser. This is because local governments tend to facilitate the granting of business licenses, by reason of increasing local revenue. In many cases, land concessions overlap, or granted on the land

rights of local communities (Konsorsium Pembaruan Agraria 2014, p. 10).

2. The lengthy bureaucratic chains between the central and regional governments make the monitoring system inefficient. Oversight tasks are often assigned to civil servants in local government, without adequate training and resources. So that labour inspectors, environment, plantation and industry officials tend to allow violations to occur. This tendency appears from very few cases where business actors are given warning sanction or revocation of business permit. Weak supervision of law enforcement also creates new problems, namely illegal business activities. Cases of illegal mining, illegal logging, and forest burning have an even greater impact than the consequences of licensed business activities. Often local governments have just taken legal steps after they have been victimized (Wiratraman 2007).
3. Some laws do not provide a sufficiently clear protection of human rights with respect to business activities. The Manpower Act, for example, has been filed several times with judicial review to the Constitutional Court. Similarly, the criminal article in the Plantation Law is declared invalid by the Constitutional Court. Even some legal regulations deliberately provide opportunities for human rights violations, such as granting mining concession licenses in protected forest areas. Unclear rules provide incentives for the emergence of environmental destruction, violations of the rights of workers and indigenous peoples (Riyadi et al. 2015).

In general, the remedies through courts still have some challenges for victims of human rights violations by corporations, among them are (Ahsinin et al. 2016):

1. Access to the courts is still a problem, because the victims of environmental pollution and land acquisition for example are often located in areas far from access to transportation and communication.
2. The formal process of handling cases in courts is still a barrier to recovery efforts. These formal barriers vary from the standing of the plaintiff, to the obstacles of proof that are not easy for the victim community.

3. The enforcement of court decisions is still not effective so as to delay the recovery for victims. This is evident in the case of the Supreme Court's decision in the case of formulated milk formula, the case of the clean water law of Jakarta citizens and the disclosure decision of Land Concession for Business Purposes (HGU) information.
4. The court case investigation has not yet considered the aspects of human rights involved. A case is solely inspected in accordance with its material offense, such as environmental law, mining, land. It is rare for judges to consider that environmental destruction is a violation of human rights.

Till date, initiatives to encourage the implementation of UNGPs in Indonesia are carried out by a number of Ministries and civil society organisations. The Ministry of Foreign Affairs of Indonesia is one of the pioneers in introducing and encouraging the implementation of UNGPs at national level. At international level the Ministry of Foreign Affairs is also actively participating in the Annual Business and Human Rights Forum organized by the United Nations. However, there has been no action for the implementation of Business and Human Rights in the form of national regulations. In mid-2017, the National Commission on Human Rights (Komnas HAM) and the Institute for Policy Research and Advocacy (ELSAM) initiated the launch of the Indonesian National Business and Human Rights Action Plan (NAP). This NAP is set forth in Komnas HAM Regulation No. 1 of 2017 on National Action Plan on Business and Human Rights (Komnas HAM 2017).

Supreme Court Regulation No. 13 of 2016 on Guideline in Handling Corporate Crimes

The Supreme Court Regulation No. 13 of 2016 (SCR 13/2016) is enacted to settle the main problem in the issue of corporate crimes in Indonesia. This problem is the lack of procedural law in dealing with corporate crimes. Based on a number of Indonesian laws and regulations, the court may found corporation responsible for criminal offences and may be imposed by various sentences, such as fines, compensation, and closure of business operation. However, although corporate crimes has been defined in almost seventy different laws and regulations, the practice among the law enforcement bodies (police, prosecutors, and the court) in handling the case are varies (Fathan 2017). One of the most contentious issues when handling corporate crime is in determining to what extent the company is liable for the offence committed by its executives; and more importantly, how to separate the criminal act of corporate executives and the company itself (Suhariyanto 2017).

In dealing with this issue, the SCR 13/2016 provides a guideline for the court in determining whether a company is at fault for crime. There are three situations in which the court may hold the company liable for committing crimes, these are (SCR 13/2016: Art. 4(2)):

1. the company obtain benefit or interest from the crime or the crime was committed for the interest of the company;
2. the company was silent to a crime;
3. the company failed to take necessary steps to prevent, to prevent larger impacts from occurring and to ensure compliance with the law to prevent a crime from occurring.

A company may be sentenced to pay certain amount of fines upon found guilty for committing crime. The court may order an imprisonment against the executives of the company, if the company fail to pay the fines. Apart from fines, the court may also impose additional sentences, these includes: (a) the seizure of assets which obtained from the criminal offence (SCR 13/2016: Art. 31); (b) compensation; and (c) restitution (SCR 13/2016: Art. 32). A company may also be sentence to restore the damages it caused arising out of the crime (SCR 13/2016: Art. 33). Victims of corporate crimes are entitled to obtain restitution in accordance with national regulation on restitution (SCR 13/2016: Art. 20). If company fails to pay restitution within a certain period of time, the prosecutor may seize the company's assets and to put into public auction for the payment of restitution (SCR 13/2016: Art. 32(4)).

In its face, the SCR 13/2016 is an important tool to provide an alternative remedy mechanism for the victims of corporate wrongdoings in Indonesia. As mentioned before, there are at least seventy laws and regulations that imposed criminal liabilities for companies operating in Indonesia. This includes the Law on Environment Management, the Law on Forestry, the Law on Mineral and Coal Mining, the Law on Plantation, the Law on Fisheries, the Law on Human Trafficking and the Law on Anti Corruption. Indeed, corporations have been involving in a number of criminal offences including those related to environment pollution and degradation, forestry, plantation, fisheries and human trafficking. Unfortunately, since the enactment of the SCR 13/2016, there have been a small number of criminal cases brought by the prosecutor against companies. Likewise, out of this small number of criminal case, it was only in one case that the victims of corporate human rights abuse succeeded to obtain restitution.

Before the SCR 13/2016 was enacted, there are two cases where corporations were found guilty for criminal offences. The first case was the corruption case involving PT Giri Jaladhi Wana, a company appointed to operate a public market facility in the city of Banjarmasin, South Kalimantan Province. The company was found at fault for violation the Law on Anti-Corruption, and to pay fines at IDR1.3 billion. Apart from fines, the company was also sentenced by 6 (six) months suspension of its business operation. The second case was an environment pollution case brought against PT Dongwoo Environmental Indonesia. The company operated waste management facility, and polluting the underground water resources in the area near to its facility. The court sentenced the company's Director Mr. Kim Young Woo with imprisonment and to pay certain amount of fines. Likewise, the court ordered permanent closure of the company's facility.

Since the enactment of the SCR 13/2016, there has been no criminal cases brought against corporation. In July 2017, the Indonesian Commission for Corruption Eradication (KPK) announced that it will resume criminal investigation against PT Duta Graha Indah—a construction company—and has made the company's director as the suspect for corruption. The company was charged under the Anti-Corruption Law for marking-up the value of the project, which caused loss to the state's budget (Firmanto 2017). This case would be the first case to use the SCR 13/2016. Unfortunately, the SCR 13/2016 has not been utilised in other public interest cases, such as criminal offence as stipulated under the environment, forestry, plantation, or labour laws.

On the other hand, the government has been succeeded in pursuing civil liability of companies for causing forest fires. There are five cases in which the court was in favour of the Ministry of Environment and Forestry. For instance, in the case against PT National Sago Prima, the court ordered the company to pay fines and compensation for environmental rehabilitation at IDR1.07 trillion. In the case of PT Kalista Alam, the Supreme Court uphold the decision of the lower courts and ordered fines and compensation to the company totalling at IDR366 billion (Case Register 651 2015). Likewise, in the case of PT Waringin Agro Jaya, the court found that the company is liable for the forest fire in the area of 1.802 hectares, and therefore must pay fines and compensation totalling at IDR758 billion (Jong 2017).

The aforementioned example shows that the government seems to prioritise civil liability mechanism in holding companies responsible for the harm they caused, rather than pursuing criminal liability. However, despite the advantages of pursuing liabilities of company in civil court, it has limitation. Based on the Law on Environment Protection and Management, government can bring a lawsuit against polluters or any parties that caused harm to the environment, but the government is not able to claim for financial compensation. It is only able to claim compensation for the purpose of environment restoration and rehabilitation (Law 32/2009: Art. 91). Thus, to obtain compensation, victims of environmental pollution and degradation must file an independent lawsuit or a class action (Law 32/2009: Art. 87). Unfortunately, not many victims of environment pollution or destruction case have the resources to file a lawsuit.

Therefore, the SCR 13/2016 may provide alternative for the victims of corporate abuse to obtain remedy, particularly through restitution mechanism. As mentioned above, the restitution procedures under the SCR 13/2016 is subject to the related law and regulation. Under Indonesian law, restitution is a compensation provided by the perpetrator or third party to the victims or their family member (Law 31/2014: Art. 1(11)). Furthermore, the victims of criminal offences have the rights to obtain 3 (three) types of restitution, these are: (a) compensation for the loss of assets or income; (b) compensation for suffering injury arising out of the crime; and/or (c) recovering the cost of medical and/or mental health treatment (GR 7/2018: Art. 19). Application to obtain restitution may be submitted by the victims, their family members or their legal representative. A victim may submit its application for restitution to the Protection of Witness and Victim Body (LPSK). The application may be filed before or after the perpetrator of criminal offence is found liable by the final judgment of the court (GR 7/2018: Art. 20(1)).

The LPSK will conduct substantive examination on the application, and will issue a recommendation to accept or refuse to continue the process of the application (GR 7/2018: Art. 26). In the case that the application is submitted after the final court verdict to the crime is obtained, the LPSK will submit its recommendation for the granting of restitution to the relevant court. The court will examine and decide the granting of restitution in accordance with the Supreme Court Regulation (GR 7/2018:

Art. 31). On the other hand, in the case that the application for restitution is submitted before the final court judgment, the LPSK will submit its recommendation for restitution to the prosecutor. The Prosecutor will then include the application of restitution together with the LPSK recommendation in its indictment (GR 7/2018: Art. 27). The court will then examine the criminal case in conjunction with the restitution application.

Nevertheless, despite the existence of legal instrument to obtain restitution for the victims of corporate crimes, obtaining restitution may not always be an easy task. The first challenge to the restitution procedure comes from the prosecutor itself. In the prosecutor's opinion, restitution has a similar character with fines imposed in criminal offences (Fathan 2017). The second possible obstacle is that the victim bears the burden of evidence. Victims must provide evidences of damage and injury they have suffered (GR 7/2018: Art. 21(3)). In relation to crimes, most likely the victims are lacking of resources to gather relevant evidence. Finally, perhaps not many victims are aware that they have rights to obtain restitution in a criminal case, particularly when involving corporations.

Based on 2016 data, the LPSK facilitated 152 applications for restitution, with the total amount at IDR3.2 billion. The restitution application was dominated by victims of human trafficking, and followed victims of torture and degrading treatment (Hukum Online 2016). In 2017, the LPSK succeeded in facilitating 55 restitution applications, amounting at approximately IDR1.08 billion. Out of these applications, 54 were human trafficking cases, and 1 domestic violence case (Antara 2018). These numbers indicates that, restitution mechanism has been utilised very dominantly in human trafficking cases, but very less in other criminal cases.

In 2013, workers of a cooking pan factory—mostly under age—that is located in Tangerang, Banten Province were found by the Police in bad conditions. They were locked in the factory without access to proper sanitation and food. The workers were forced to work 18 hours a day, yet they has not received wages. The factory owner, Mr. Yuki Irawan was charged for violating the Law on Child Protection for employing children and the Industrial Law for operating without licence. The court found the factory owner guilty for committing crime. Mr. Yuki Irawan was sentenced to 11 years in prison and a fine of IDR500 million (Fidrus 2014). Unfortunately, the court rejected the Prosecutor's application for restitution which amounted at IDR17.8 billion (Hukum Online 2014).

In 2015, an investigation by Associated Press journalists revealed modern slavery practices in Indonesia fishery industry in Benjina, an island located in Maluku Province. Fishermen from Myanmar, Cambodia, Laos and Thailand were forced in an excessive working hours in the fishing boats, suffered from mental abuse and torture, living in a bad condition and working without payment (IOM 2015). Following this investigation, the Indonesian Police arrested 5 (five) Thai nationals, identified as the captain of fishing boats. The Police also arrested 2 (two) Indonesian nationals, the acting CEO of PT Pusaka Benjina Resources—a company which run the fishing operation in Benjina (Jakarta Post 2015). The court found the alleged suspects guilty for committing crimes under the Law on Human Trafficking and the Law on Anti Slavery. The fishing boat captains were sentenced for 3 years of imprisonment and to pay fines at USD12.2500,- each. Likewise, they also have to pay restitution for the victims totalling at USD67.8000,-. The personnel of PT Pusaka Benjina Resources were sentenced 3 years in jail and ordered to pay restitution ranging from USD3.700,- to USD26.000,- for the abused fishermen (Leonard 2016).

The above two cases shows a different result in restitution claim. Restitution claim by victims in cooking pan factory was rejected, but restitution claim by victims of human trafficking in fishing industry was granted. The above cases also provide a good example which shows that victims in human trafficking cases tend to be more successful in obtaining restitution than in other criminal cases. To sum up, although SCR 13/2016 provide a clearer guide for law enforcers to hold companies liable for committing crimes, its implementation to help victims to obtain remedies remain challenging. First, SCR 13/2016 has not been utilised to hold companies liable for committing crimes which has significant impact on human rights, such as pollution and environment degradation, land grabbing, illegal logging, forest fires, children and woman rights, and labour protection. Second, it is true that SCR 13/2016 guarantees victim's rights to claim restitution, yet not all victims of criminal offences are able to obtain restitutions.

Presidential Regulation No. 13 of 2018 on the Implementation of the Principle of Knowing Beneficial Owners of Corporations

In March 2018, the government issued Presidential Regulation No. 13 of 2018 on the Implementation of the Principle of Knowing Beneficial Owners of Corporations in Relation to the Prevention and Eradication of Money Laundering and Terrorism Financing Crimes (PR 13/2018). This regulation is established on the basis that corporations can be used directly or indirectly as a vehicle to commit money laundering and terrorism financing crimes (Secretariat 2018). The PR 13/2018 is aiming at identifying the ultimate benefit holder or Beneficiary Owner (BO) of a company. Under the PR 13/2018, BO is defined as an individual who may appoint or dismiss board of directors, board of commissioners or other similar organ. It has the ability to control the corporation, directly or indirectly entitled to and/or receives benefits from the corporation and the actual owner of the company's funds or shares (PR 13/2018: Art. 1). A corporation may includes limited liability company, foundation, association, cooperative, limited partnership, partnership and other type of business entities (PR 13/2018: Art. 2(2)).

PR 13/2018 obliges the disclosure of information on BO to the competent authority. This obligation lies with the founder or the director (or similar organ of corporation); the notary or other party authorized by the founder or director (PR 13/2018: Art. 18(3)). The information of BO must be accompanied by a letter of statement on the correctness of the submitted information (PR 13/2018: Art. 18(2)). In addition, the corporation must disclose the information on BO when it has assigned the beneficial owner. In the event that the corporation has not assigned the BO at the time of the submission of (a) establishment; (b) registration; or (c) approval of business licences, it may submit a letter of statement on the corporation's willingness to convey the information on BO to the relevant authority (PR 13/2018: Art. 19(1)).

Furthermore, the submission of BO information is carried out through the Corporate Administration Service System, an online system operated by the Ministry of Justice and Human Rights (PR 13/2018: Art. 19(3)). For companies that have performed its business operation, the principle of recognizing the BO is performed by submitting any change of information to the Authority through the Corporate Administration Service System. This information must be submitted no later than three working days since the change take place (PR 13/2018: Art. 20(1–2)). Companies must up date information on BO regularly (PR 13/2018: Art. 21). The information on BO is to be supervised by the competent authority in cooperation with the Indonesian Financial Transaction Reporting and Analysis Centre (INTRAC) (PR 13/2018: Art. 23(4–5)). A Company that failed to comply with obligation to disclose its BO shall be subjected to sanctions in accordance with the provisions of relevant laws and regulations (PR 13/2018: Art. 24).

Prior to PR 13/2018, the Ministry of Energy and Mineral Resources has issued a Ministerial Regulation of Energy and Mineral Resources No. 48 of 2017 on the Oversight of Exploitation in the Energy and Mineral Resources sector (MR 48/2017). MR 48/2017 was enacted in accordance with the Law No. 4 of 2009 on Mineral and Coal Mining and the Government Regulation No.35 of 2004 on Oil and Gas Upstream Business Activities. MR 48/2017 is a regulatory tool by the government to obtain information on the change of ownership and direct control of the oil and gas companies operating in Indonesia. These changes include the transfer of participating interest and/or share transfer and the changes of directors and/or commissioners (MR 48/2017: Art. 2).

MR 48/2017 requires the disclosure of BO for all mining licences holder when submitting application for the extension of mining license. In relation to the ownership of shares, MR 48/2017 provides that all companies must disclose individuals/beneficiary holders, so as to counter tax evasion, money laundering and terrorism financing. Any transfer of participating interest in all mining companies must first obtain the Ministry approval, and assessed by the Special Taskforce for Upstream Oil and Gas Business Activities (*SKK Migas*) (MR 48/2017: Art. 3). The Minister's approval will only be given provided that the company disclose its BO (MR 48/2017: Art. 3(3)d). The transfer of shares in a mining company operating in processing and/or purification of mineral must also obtain the Ministry's approval (MR 48/2017: Art. 14(2)).

Both PR 13/2018 and MR 48/2017 are significant for business and human rights interrelation in Indonesia. These regulations provide mechanism for government and the public to track down the person(s) who take benefit from the corporate business operations. Indeed, without these regulations it would be difficult to identify corporate owners. These owners are hidden behind the complex webs of corporate structure. Under PR 13/2018, investigation on BO may be commenced in an allegation of money laundering. Based on the Law No. 8 of 2010 on Countermeasure and Eradication of Money Laundering, money laundering is a financial transaction that involved money or assets which is suspected to be coming from criminal offences (Law 8/2010: Art. 1.5.c). A criminal offence, which falls within the money laundering practice, is crimes committed in environment and forestry (Law 8/2010: Art. 21 (w–x)). This provision is in accordance with the criminal responsibility of corporations as stipulated by Law No. 32 of 2009 on Environment Protection and Management. Apparently, the PR 13/2018 is paving the path to identify the BO who is taking benefit from environmental crime committed by the company. Likewise, MR 48/2017 may also help to identify the real owners of mining companies who are taking benefit from environmental and forestry crimes.

However, tracking the BO may not be an easy tasks, this is due to several reasons. First, although the public in general may request the disclosure of BO (PR 13/2018: Art. 29), acquiring this information must be conducted in accordance with the Law No. 14 of 2008 on Public Information Disclosure. Based on this law, application to obtain public information must be submitted to the relevant public body (Law 14/2008: Art. 22(1)). Subsequently, the relevant public body shall record the name and address of the applicant, the subject and the format of the requested information. Likewise, the relevant public body will determine the method of providing the requested information (Law 14/2008: Art. 22(2)). If the requested party refuses to provide the information, the applicant may file a lawsuit to the civil court (Law 14/2008: Art. 4(3–4)). Likewise, the requesting party may file a lawsuit to the administrative court if the requested party is a government body (Law 14/2008: Art. 47). However, the enforcement of court judgement in the public information case may not be simple. There was a case where a government body refuse to disclose the requested information. This was the case in the disclosure of the HGU Map. Forest Watch Indonesia (FWI) submitted an application to the Commission for Public Information Disclosure. The FWI requested that the HGU Map must be disclosed to the public. This Map is important because there have been a number of land conflict between the local communities and palm oil plantation companies. The land concession given for the palm oil plantations are overlapping with land rights of local communities. In July 2016, the Commission for Public Information Disclosure decided that the National Land Agency must disclose the HGU Map to the public. However, the National Land Agency seemed reluctant to provide the requested Map. Subsequently, the FWI brought the case to the administrative court. In March 2017, the Supreme Court handed down its judgment and ordered the National Land Agency to disclose the HGU Map. Unfortunately, the government has not disclosed the document.

Secondly, if information on BO is located in foreign countries, this information may be obtained through states cooperation (PR 13/2018: Art. 27(2)(c)). This cooperation is conducted based on international treaty between states (PR 13/2018: Art. 26(3)). The exchange of information on BO between two different jurisdictions may be executed through the Automatic Exchange of Information (AEOI) and the Mutual Legal Assistance (MLA) mechanism. The AEOI is aiming at combating tax evasion. The AEOI mechanism provides an exchange of non-resident financial account information with tax authorities in the country of residence of the account holders, any countries which joining the AEOI will send and receive information without sending special request. The AEOI allows the tax office to detected tax evasion. Indonesia implements AEOI through Minister of Finance Regulation No. 39/PMK.03/2017 on Information Exchange Procedures under the International Agreement. To date, Indonesia entered into AEOI agreement with Hong Kong in 16 June 2017 (Baker McKenzie 2017).

As for the MLA, it is regulated under the Law No. 1 of 2006 on Mutual Assistance in Criminal Matters and the Law No. 15 of 2008 on Ratification of Treaty on Mutual Legal Assistance in Criminal Matters. Unfortunately, not all countries have cooperation on the exchange of information in criminal matter with Indonesia. Up to present, Indonesia entered into MLA with Australia, China, South Korea, Hong Kong and India. Within the ASEAN framework, a Regional Treaty on Mutual Legal Assistance in Criminal Matters is signed by Brunei Darussalam, Cambodia, Indonesia, Laos, Malaysia, Philippines, Singapore and Vietnam (Law 15/2008). Thus, other than these countries, it may be difficult to obtain information on corporate BO which located in foreign jurisdictions.

Conclusion

Based on the above analysis on both the SCR 13/2016 and the PR 13/2018 it is suffice to say that these legal instruments may help victims of corporate abuse to obtain remedy. The SCR 13/2016 for instance, it provides guidance for the law enforcement bodies (Police, Prosecutor and the Court) in handling criminal cases against corporation. As mentioned above, there are a number of Laws in Indonesia which contain criminal liabilities for corporation. Companies can be criminally liable for causing pollution and environmental destructions, failing to pay minimum wages to their employees, or involving in slavery and human trafficking. Unfortunately, three years since the SCR 13/2016 was issued, there have been no criminal cases brought against corporation. There is only one potential case brought by the Corruption Eradication Commission, which based on the Anti-Corruption Law. Considering the negative impacts that companies may cause to the environment, labour, and indigenous/local communities, there should be more criminal case brought against companies.

Similar situation may also occur with the PR 18/2018. This regulation provides the procedures to identify and track the benefit-holder of corporations. Although its main objective is to combat money laundering and terrorism financing, this regulation may be useful for the victims of corporate abuse in environment and forestry related crimes. In the context of business and human rights, information on the company ownerships is important in identifying who should be held liable for the company's abusive conduct. Indeed, companies have been taking the advantages of the complex corporate structure. It enables companies to hide financial transactions and the real owners who taking control of the company's operations (Nuruliza 2016). However, since this regulation has just been issued early this year, its effectiveness remains to be seen.

Despite opportunities offered by both the SCR 13/2016 and the PR 13/2018, these regulations contain a number of potential hurdles for the victims of corporate abuse. Both of these regulations contains long procedures and exhaustive for victims in obtaining remedies. This situation includes the long process in obtaining restitution, and information on corporate BO. The SCR 13/2016 offers an opportunity for the victims of corporate crimes to obtain restitution. However, obtaining restitution may involve a long administrative process and exhaustive court examination. Except in the human trafficking case, restitution has never been granted to victims of corporate crimes. Similarly, the PR 13/2018 contains a relatively complex procedure to obtain information on corporate BO. Although information on company's BO must be opened for public, there has been a case where the requested public information has not been provided. In the case where the requested party refused to disclose information, the requesting party must file a case to the court. Furthermore, the process to obtain information on corporate BO may become more complicated if the requesting party is located in foreign jurisdiction. Obtaining information on corporate BO may be complex and resources exhaustive, therefore, is not accessible for victims of corporate abuse.

Having the above concerns in mind, we propose that the process of obtaining restitution and information on corporate BO must be made simple. In relation with restitution process, we propose that the prosecutor office should be given authority to include the payment of restitution in its indictment. This has been implemented in the human trafficking cases. The Law No. 21 of 2007 on Human Trafficking provides authority for the prosecutor to submit restitution claim in its indictment. Providing the prosecutor with authority to include restitution claim will fast track the restitution process. Perhaps, there should be an amendment to the law and regulations which relate to restitution process. In criminal cases which involve corporate abuse, there should be special procedures for restitution. The special procedure may be applied in particular criminal offences which committed by corporation. This offence may include pollution, environmental degradation, labour rights, land grabbing, and forest fires.

Likewise, procedures to obtain information on corporate BO must also be made simple. One of the drawbacks in PR 13/2018 is that it does not contain sanction for companies who fail to disclose its BO. Indeed, under Indonesian legal system, sanctions may only be imposed by Law. Therefore, we propose that the obligation to disclose BO should be included in the Corporation Law. Under this law, sanction may be imposed for companies that fail to comply with obligation to disclose BO. With this sanction, legal suit to obtain information on BO will be unnecessary. Therefore, at the end it will shorten the process in obtaining the information on corporate BO.

References

Laws and Regulations

Law No. 14 of 2008 on Public Information Disclosure.
Law No. 15 of 2008 on Ratification of Treaty on Mutual Legal Assistance in Criminal Matters.
Law No. 32 of 2009 on Environment Protection and Management.
Law No. 8 of 2010 on Countermeasure and Eradication of Money Laundering.

Law No. 31 of 2014 on the Amendment of Law No. 13 of 2006 on Victim and Witness Protection.

Government Regulation No. 7 of 2018 on Granting of Compensation, Restitution and Assistance to Witness and Victim.

Presidential Regulation No. 13 of 2018 on the Implementation of the Principle of Knowing Beneficial Owners of Corporations in Relation to the Prevention and Eradication of Money Laundering and Terrorism Financing.

Ministerial Regulation of Energy and Mineral Resources No. 48 of 2017 on the Oversight of Exploitation in the Energy and Mineral Resources sector.

Supreme Court Regulation No. 13 of 2016 on Procedures in Handling of Corporate Crime.

Court Decision

Case Register No. 651 K/PDT/2015 (*PT Kalista Alam v. Ministry of Environment and Forestry*).

Internet Text

Antara News. 2018. *LPSK Catat 55 Penerima Restitusi Selama 2017*. https://www.antaranews.com/berita/676657/lpsk-catat-55-penerima-restitusi-selama-2017.

Baker McKenzie. 2017. *Indonesian Tax Authorities Finally Entered an Automatic Exchange of Information Agreement with Hong Kong*. https://www.bakermckenzie.com/en/insight/publications/2017/06/indonesian-tax-authorities-finally-entered/.

Cabinet Secretariat Republic of Indonesia. 2018. *Tertinggi Sejak 2014, BPS: Pertumbuhan Ekonomi 2017 Capai 5,07%*. http://setkab.go.id/tertinggi-sejak-2014-bps-pertumbuhan-ekonomi-2017-capai-507/.

Fathan Qorib. 2017. *Penolakan Permohonan Restitusi dan Tantangannya di Peradilan Pidana*. http://www.hukumonline.com/berita/baca/lt5965f975b0114/penolakan-permohonan-restitusi-dan-tantangannya-di-peradilan-pidana.

Fidrus, Multa. 2014. *Tangerang 'slave' factory owner gets 11 years*. http://www.thejakartapost.com/news/2014/03/26/tangerang-slave-factory-owner-gets-11-years.html.

Firmanto, Danang. 2017. *KPK Tetapkan PT DGI Tersangka Korporasi dalam Kasus Rumah Sakit*. https://nasional.tempo.co/read/894051/kpk-tetapkan-pt-dgi-tersangka-korporasi-dalam-kasus-rumah-sakit.

Hukum Online. 2014. *Tim Advokasi Buruh Kuali Kecewa dengan Putusan Hakim*. http://www.hukumonline.com/berita/baca/lt53340cd488069/tim-advokasi-buruh-kuali-kecewa-dengan-putusan-hakim.

Hukum Online. 2016. *Perdagangan Orang, Korupsi dan Kekerasan Seksual Dominasi Permohonan ke LPSK*. http://www.hukumonline.com/berita/baca/lt5863727261a79/perdagangan-orang%2D%2Dkorupsi-dan-kekerasan-seksual-dominasi-permohonan-ke-lpsk.

International Organization for Migration. 2015. *Human Trafficking in the Fishery Sector: The Benjina Case*. https://indonesia.iom.int/human-trafficking-fishery-sector-benjina-case.

Jong, Hans Nicholas. 2017. *Government wins in forest fire case*. http://www.thejakartapost.com/news/2017/02/09/government-wins-in-forest-fire-case.html.

Komisi Nasional Hak Asasi Manusia. 2017. *Rencana Aksi Nasional Bisnis dan Ham Asasi Manusia, Komnas HAM dan ELSAM*. https://www.komnasham.go.id/files/20180214-rencana-aksi-nasional-bisnis-dan-$DH79.pdf.

Leonard, Daniel. 2016. *8 Men Sentenced to 3 Years in Jail for Enslaving Fishermen*. http://www.thejakartapost.com/news/2016/03/11/8-men-sentenced-3-years-jail-enslaving-fishermen.html.

Nuruliza, Anissa Tri. 2016. *Disclosure of Ultimate Beneficiary Ownership in Indonesia*. Masters Thesis, Tilburg University, http://arno.uvt.nl/show.cgi?fid=142486.

Sekretariat Kabinet Republik Indonesia. 2018. *Cegah Pencucian Uang, Inilah Perpres Penerapan Prinsip Mengenali Pemilik Bermanfaat dari Korporasi*. http://setkab.go.id/cegah-pencucian-uang-inilah-perpres-penerapan-prinsip-mengenali-pemilik-manfaat-dari-korporasi/.

The Jakarta Post. 2015. *Seven Arrested in Benjina Case*. http://www.thejakartapost.com/news/2015/05/12/seven-arrested-benjina-case.html.

United Nations Human Rights Council. 2017. *Addendum*: Report of the Working Group on the Universal Periodic Review Indonesia A/HRC/36/7/Add.1, Recommendations by Panama, Tunisia, Kenya, and Myanmar. https://www.ohchr.org/EN/HRBodies/HRC/RegularSessions/Session36/Pages/ListReports.aspx.

United Nations Human Rights Office of The High Commissioner. 2018. *DisplayNews*: Opening remarks by UN High Commissioner for Human Rights Zeid Ra'ad Al Hussein at a press conference during his mission to Indonesia, Jakarta, 7 February 2018. http://www.ohchr.org/EN/NewsEvents/Pages/DisplayNews.aspx?NewsID=22637&LangID=E.

Journal and Publications

Ahsinin, Adzkar et al., *Perhutani Dan Hak Asasi Manusia: Studi Atas Empat Kasus Penanganan Konflik BUMN Perhutani Ditinjau Dari Perspektif Hak Asasi Manusia*, ELSAM, 2016: p. 51.

Indonesia Investment Coordinating Board, *Realisasi Penanaman Modal PMDN-PMA (Triwulan IV dan Januari-Desember Tahun 2017)*, 30 December 2018.

Konsorsium Pembaruan Agraria, *Membenahi Masalah Agraria: Prioritas Kerja Jokowi-JK Pada 2015*, Catatan Akhir Tahun, 2014: p. 10.

Riyadi, Eko, Anisah, Siti, and Ali, Mahrus, *Menjangkau Keterkaitan Hukum Bisnis Dan Hak Asasi Manusia: Kajian Awal*, in Ifdhal Kasim (Ed.), *Menjangkau Tanggung Jawab Korporasi Eksplorasi Hubungan Bisnis dan Hak Asasi Manusia*, ELSAM, 2015: p. 46.

Suhariyanto, Budi, *Corporate Criminal Liability Based on Corporate Culture Model and Implicatons for Welfare of Community*. Recht Vinding Journal. Vol. 6, No. 3. December 2017: pp. 443–44.

Wiratraman, R. Herlambang Perdana, *Neoliberalisme, Good Governance dan Hak Asasi Manusia*, Jentera Law Journal, 15th Ed., No. IV, May 2007: p. 28.

CHAPTER 9

Land Grabs in ASEAN: Access to Remedies in Agribusiness Industry

Socheata Sao

Introduction

Alleged business-related human rights violations, particularly land grabs, are rife in ASEAN (Mohan 2015; Pietropaoli and Maria 2015; Middleton and Pritchard 2013). Most complaints received by State-based complaints mechanisms in AMS concern land rights violations (Pietropaoli 2015; Kaufmann et al. 2013: 13). For instance, most of the complaints submitted to Myanmar's National Human Rights Commission since its establishment in 2011 involved arbitrary land confiscations by the government and military (APF 2015: para 1). Essentially, land grabs have been the most critical among major forms of business-related human rights violations in ASEAN (Pietropaoli and Maria 2015: 11–16; Kaufmann et al. 2013: 13, 25–26).

In recent decades, AMS governments have allocated sizeable lands for economic land concessions or long-term leases for large-scale agribusiness plantations run by foreign and local investors. Such land allocations, often

S. Sao (✉)
Melbourne, VIC, Australia
e-mail: socheata.sao@monash.edu

J. Gomez, R. Ramcharan (eds.), *Business and Human Rights in Asia*,
https://doi.org/10.1007/978-981-15-7273-9_9

carried out with minimal or no compensation or prior consultation with affected local communities, have resulted in widespread land conflicts. In this context, the growth of large agribusiness plantations that produce sugarcane, palm oil and rubber have coincided with alleged arbitrary land confiscations and forced evictions of hundreds of thousands in the region, most of whom are smallholder farmers and indigenous peoples (Neef 2016; Chao 2013). After being dispossessed and evicted from their lands, sometimes by force, affected people often lose their livelihoods and suffer far-reaching human rights violations, including State-sanctioned violence, criminalisation and even murders (Middleton and Pritchard 2013; see also FPP 2017; Equitable Cambodia and IDI 2013: 55–57; CCHR 2013: 35–36). Many affected people then struggle for years to seek justice and redress, often to no avail.

Under the UN 'Protect, Respect and Remedy' Framework and the UNGP, in addition to the State's duty to protect and businesses' responsibility to respect human rights, States and businesses involved in human rights violations must provide effective remedies for victims (Ruggie 2008; OHCHR 2011). In response to widespread business-related human rights abuses, there have been efforts by AMS governments through regulatory reforms and attempts by relevant stakeholders, including businesses, to foster corporate governance and corporate social responsibility in ASEAN (Thomas 2015; Kaufmann et al. 2013). These attempts, while providing some relief, are not yet sufficient to address the problems and remediate victims' grievances (Middleton and Pritchard 2013). While business-related human rights abuses continue to arise, especially in land-related sectors, there seems to be a region-wide lack of access to remedies for victims, especially in the CLMV (Ibid.: 42–43).

This chapter[1] thematically discusses the current state of affairs regarding access to remedies for victims of land-grabbing in the agribusiness industry in ASEAN, following the launch of the UNGP in 2011. In doing so, alleged land grabs in agribusiness investments in ASEAN are first discussed; some main causes of the abuses are highlighted. Then this chapter will examine some of the available avenues for victims to seek redress in AMS. Due to the space limit, this chapter will focus on Cambodia, Laos and Myanmar. Thereafter, it will highlight some major barriers facing victims seeking remedies. It will discuss what has been done by AMS and

[1] This chapter offers research and analysis conducted as part of the author's doctoral thesis at Monash University, Australia.

relevant stakeholders to address these barriers and outline some of the challenges. This chapter argues that, at present, there remains a lacuna in access to remedies for victims of land-grabbing in the agribusiness industry in ASEAN. There is thus an urgent need for AMS, ASEAN and businesses to explore additional forum(s) that is accessible and effective for victims to seek remedies.

Literature Review on Access to Remedies for Victims

The general lack of corporate accountability and remedies for victims of business-related human rights violations, including land grabs, have urged the UN human rights bodies, governments, academics, civil society organisations (CSOs) and other stakeholders, including businesses, to strengthen the implementation of the UN Framework's third pillar on access to remedy. At the UN level, there have been initiatives to improve access to remedies for victims. The "Accountability and Remedy Project" (ARP) was commenced in 2014 to enhance more fairness and effectiveness of domestic legal remedies for gross business-related human rights violations. It currently comprises of three phases dealing respectively with judicial mechanisms (ARP I), State-based non-judicial mechanisms (ARP II) and non-State-based grievance mechanisms (APR III) (OHCHR 2018b). In APR I, a final report with guidance to States on how to strengthen judicial mechanisms was issued in June 2016 (OHCHR 2016). For APR II, the Office of the United Nations High Commissioner for Human Rights (OHCHR) submitted in June 2018 its final report on State-based non-judicial mechanisms, containing its general observations on the role of these mechanisms in ensuring accountability and access to remedy and recommended "policies objective" for States, along with an explanatory addendum (OHCHR 2018c, d). The OHCHR is currently working on APR III (OHCHR 2018e). Since 2014, an open-ended intergovernmental working group has been tasked with the drafting of an international legal instrument on business and human rights to ensure enforceability of business human rights responsibility, accountability and remedies for victims (OHCHR 2018a; BHRRC 2013).

Academics and legal practitioners have also made various proposals for improving corporate accountability and access to remedies for victims (Calderón-Meza et al. 2016). There are calls for enforcing international criminal liability for gross corporate human rights abuses at the International Criminal Court (Kaeb 2016; Scheffer 2016) and enabling international civil liability for business-related human rights abuses through the establishment of international civil courts (Hackett and Moffett 2016; Wetzel 2016; Steinitz 2014). There are also proposals for resolving business and human rights cases through international arbitration either under the international investment law regime or private international arbitration between affected people and responsible investors (Amado et al. 2018; Cronstedt et al. 2017; Calderón-Meza 2016).

For continental Asia, Chung (2016) proposes an Asian-Pacific Court of Human Rights with jurisdiction over States and non-State actors, including businesses (Chung 2016). In ASEAN, the regional focus of this chapter, CSOs have called for the establishment of an ASEAN human rights court (Koshy 2016). In fact, the idea of creating a "Southeast Asian Court of Human Rights" was proposed earlier in 2009 (Phan 2009). This chapter will contribute to above efforts at improving access to remedies for victims, particularly access to effective remedies for victims of land grabs in ASEAN, an issue this chapter now turns.

Alleged Land-Grabbing in the Agribusiness Industry in ASEAN

Agribusiness is an important sector for the economic growth and poverty reduction in many AMS. However, this sector has been mired in far-reaching human rights abuses and impacts, particularly regarding land (FPP 2015, 2016a, 2017; Chao 2013). For instance, while rubber plays a significant role in the economies of Cambodia, Laos and Vietnam, the industry has been embroiled in alleged land grabs by business interests (Dao 2015; Kenney-Lazar 2012; Global Witness 2013). For instance, the Hoàng Anh Gia Lai (HAGL) and Vietnam Rubber Group (VRG), a Vietnamese corporation and State-owned company respectively, and their affiliated companies own vast rubber plantations in these countries. However, their rubber concessions and business activities have resulted in large-scale land confiscations, often without consultation or sufficient compensation to affected local communities, and infringement of indigenous peoples' rights. Said abuses were reportedly severe in Cambodia and Laos (Global Witness 2013: 2–3; see also Howe and Park 2015). Similarly, there are well-documented large-scale land confiscations, forced evictions and other human rights abuses in Myanmar's rubber industry (Global Witness 2015).

In Cambodia, land and human rights activists claimed that most of the land granted as economic land concessions (ELC) for sugarcane plantations were taken from small-scale farmers (Borras et al. 2016: 33–34; Equitable Cambodia and IDI 2013: 1). In a high-profile case, the grant of two adjacent ELCs in Koh Kong province in 2006 for a sugarcane plantation run by two Cambodian companies, both were majority owned by a Thai sugar corporation, led to land expropriation and forced evictions of hundreds of poor Cambodian families. Violence, loss of livelihoods and various human rights violations reportedly ensued (Equitable Cambodia and IDI 2013: 55–56; CCHR 2013: 30). This case was only resolved in March 2018 (Soth 2018c), after decade-long struggles for remedies both inside and outside of Cambodia (ERI and CLEC 2013: 9–14). Meanwhile, hundreds of other farmer families in the same province who were similarly affected by sugarcane plantation investments are still seeking acceptable remedies (Pech 2018a, b; Soth 2018a).

A similar reality is experienced by farmers and indigenous communities affected by land grabs and associated human rights abuses in agribusiness industry in other parts of Cambodia (Soth 2018b) and in other AMS (FPP 2015, 2016a, 2017; Chao 2013). For instance, Indonesia's palm oil industry, which is dominated by Malaysian and Singaporean investors, is also mired in alleged large-scale land grabs and indigenous peoples' rights violations, among other harms (Johnson 2015; Colchester and Chao 2013). Subsidiaries of Malaysian and Singaporean palm oil giants (namely, Sime Darby, Golden Agri-Resources (GAR) and Wilmar International) and their supplier companies have been reportedly involved in massive land confiscations which often occurred without a free, prior and informed consent (FPIC) of affected indigenous communities. This violates the FPIC requirement of the Roundtable on Sustainable Palm Oil (RSPO) to which these companies are members (FPP 2013; see further, Colchester and Chao 2013). Recently, Wilmar was reportedly implicated to a shooting of two farmers in one of its plantations in Central Kalimantan, where its subsidiary has been in a land dispute with the local communities since 2013 (FPP 2018). Alleged land grabs and rights abuses by palm oil companies also occur in the Philippines, for instance, in Palawan (FPP 2016a: 14–15; FPP 2015).

Main Causes of the Abuses

In ASEAN, one of the main causes of business-related human rights abuses, including land-grabbing, is arguably AMS' preferencing of economic growth over human rights protection (Gilson 2018: 54; Pietropaoli and Maria 2015: 5; Pietropaoli 2015; Carling et al. 2015: 5–7). The pursuit of economic growth has often resulted in human rights violations, adversely impacting many poor and marginalised people across the region. Laws are sometimes used to support AMS' respective economic agendas, often with an undue focus on attracting investment in land- and natural resources-related sectors (Pietropaoli 2015; Lim and Mukherjee 2015: 35). In the agribusiness sector, some AMS governments enforced land-related policies and legislation that permitted them to expropriate or requisition lands from landholders and allocate the lands to investors. Consequently, some otherwise legitimate land possessors or land users lost their rights to their land and became vulnerable to land confiscation and eviction for agribusiness plantations (Neef 2016: 8).

In the meantime, human rights remain a sensitive and less prioritised topic which AMS tend to overlook (Pietropaoli 2015; Thio 1999: 1). In turn, there is a lack of political commitment by some AMS to seriously tackle human rights issues (Jones 2014; Ginbar 2010). Other factors which contribute to, and sometimes intensify, the above problems include widespread corruption, weak governance, lack of respect for the rule of law and lack of regulatory capacity in AMS, especially in the CLMV (Kaufmann et al. 2013: 28–32; see also, Mohan 2015).

Available Avenues for Victims to Seek Redress

This section discusses available grievance mechanisms for victims affected by land grabs in the agribusiness industry in ASEAN. In line with the UNGP, this section examines what judicial, State-based non-judicial and non-State-based grievance mechanisms currently exist in AMS, particularly in Cambodia, Laos and Myanmar.

Judicial and State-Based Non-Judicial Mechanisms

Cambodia

According to the NGO Forum on Cambodia (NGOF 2016a), there are six formal complaint bodies for resolving land disputes in Cambodia. Most land disputes, including alleged arbitrary land takings, are first reported to the commune/sangkat councils which exist at commune level across Cambodia. These councils, however, lack formal dispute resolution procedures and decision-making authority (Ibid.: 8). Consequently, unresolved disputes are passed on to land dispute resolution bodies, depending on the legal status of the disputed land. Disputes over (yet) untitled lands that arose within areas undergone systematic land registration are handled by the administrative commissions. Lacking decision-making power, these administrative commissions are limited to conciliating the parties' differences. Disputes that cannot be settled are then forwarded to the National Cadastral Commission. Disputes over untitled lands that arise outside areas undergone systematic land registration are resolved by cadastral commissions which exist at both district/khan, provincial/municipal and national level. The district/khan-level cadastral commissions can only reconciliate the disputing parties. If no resettlement is reached after three attempts, the dispute is passed hierarchically to the next levels. At the top level, the National Cadastral Commission can issue a decision, which a dissatisfied party can appeal at the court (Ibid.: 9–10). Land disputes that are beyond the authority of the National Cadastral Commission, or that cannot be resolved by other land complaint bodies, are handled by the National Authority for Land Conflict Resolution (NALDR). Regardless of its rather vague jurisdiction, most high-profile (ELC-related) land disputes have been referred to the NALDR for settlement (NGOF 2016b: 4). In May 2016, a Special Unit for Dealing with Land Disputes was established under the Ministry of Land Management to settle pressing land disputes in rural Cambodia through conciliation (NGOF 2016a: 11). Finally, the courts have jurisdiction over disputes of registered land and appeal cases regarding the National Cadastral Commission's and NALDR's decisions (Ibid.: 11–12).

Following international pressure regarding rampant land grabs and human rights abuses in Cambodia's sugar industry, the EU (see Borras et al. 2016), the major market for Cambodia's sugar, and the Cambodian government created an inter-ministerial working group in 2014 to address highly complex and long-standing land disputes between affected local communities and sugarcane ELC-companies in three provinces (Hodal 2014; see also, Pech 2018b). As noted previously, the decade-long Koh Kong sugarcane plantation case was resolved by the inter-ministerial working group in March 2018.

To recap, Cambodia has various complaints mechanisms that may be used to resolve business-related land conflicts, depending on the legal status of the land. However, the ability of these mechanisms to resolve the disputes remains limited. Paradoxically, the existence of these many mechanisms has reportedly caused confusion and difficulties for affected people to access them, partly because they operate under unclear jurisdictional lines (CCHR 2014: 6; see also Grimsditch and Henderson 2009). Other key factors that undermine these mechanisms include a lack of independence and impartiality due to political interference or corruption, particularly in the judiciary; lack of capacity; unpredictability or inconsistency of their decisions; and difficulties in implementing and enforcing the decisions (ICJ 2017: 3–4; CCHR 2014: 6–7). Notably, the inter-ministerial working group seems to present some potential in filling the remedies gap of the current institutional grievance mechanisms.

Laos

There are customary or informal, semi-formal and formal complaint mechanisms in Laos (UNDP 2011b: 75). Village Mediation Units (VMUs), which are semi-formal mechanisms, exist at the village level to resolve minor disputes between villagers (UNDP 2011a: 83). However, due to their lack of expertise, decision-making authority, capacity and credibility, the VMUs are not a popular dispute resolution mechanism among Lao people. In most communities, the most common and preferred systems to resolve local-level disputes are informal mechanisms, using customary law systems and practices (UNDP 2011b: 75). Yet, customary mechanisms are generally “ill-equipped” for resolving disputes involving “outsider” parties (Ibid.: 97). Difficulties arise, for instance, where the other party is a powerful company. Disputes that cannot be resolved by customary mechanisms and the VMUs can be forwarded to higher level State bodies. For instance, unresolved disputes at the VMUs can be passed to the District Mediation Units (DMUs). Yet, even if disputes reach the DMUs, which is not often the case, they too may not be capable to handle the cases (LIWG 2014: 1). The last and most formal complaint mechanism is the courts (UNDP 2011b: 76). However, Laos courts are generally perceived as non-independent, corrupt and too costly for the poor (UNDP 2011a: 107, 112).

Affected people may also file a petition to a State administrative body or the National Assembly when State officials have made decisions that violate the law or adversely affect the interests of the community (UNDP 2011a: 83–84). While providing an additional option, especially for local communities affected by arbitrary land requisitions by the State, the petition option is also costly and potentially risky. This is because it does not address the dispute in an amicable manner as many communities would prefer (LIWG 2014: 1, 2; UNDP 2011a: 102). Moreover, it is likely that affected communities eventually submit a petition to the same administrative office that allocated their land to the investor in the first place. This raises issues regarding the conflicts of interest and independence of the office (LIWG 2014: 1). Consequently, Laos communities affected by arbitrary land requisitions have limited viable options to access remedies (Golay 2015: 240–241).

Myanmar

At the bottom level, land disputes, including alleged land grabs, are arbitrated through formal State-based non-judicial mechanisms at township offices operated by the General Administration Department (GAD). Given the GAD is also responsible for land acquisitions, this raises questions regarding conflicts of interest and its independence and impartiality in arbitrating land acquisition cases. This also potentially undermines the likelihood that affected people are awarded remedies or reparations. Consequently, the GAD is not seen as an effective redress mechanism (ICJ 2018: 29).

State-based complaint mechanisms have been established by the legislature and executive to investigate and resolve the massive land confiscation complaints in Myanmar. These bodies include the Farmland Investigation Commission (FIC), the Land Utilisation Management Central Committee (LUMCC) and the Central Reinvestigation Committee for Confiscated Farmlands and Other Lands (CRCCF), along with other related regional and state committees (Bernard 2017). Established in June 2016, the CRCCF replaces and undertakes the responsibilities and mandates of the FIC and its recommendation-implementing body, the LUMCC (Bernard 2017: 11). The CRCCF operates at all levels in Myanmar. Its composition includes GAD officials and civil society or community representatives at lower levels and Parliament Members at the

Union level. At present, the CRCCF committees' exact scope and authority remain unclear while their priorities seem to vary in each state and region in Myanmar (NAMATI 2017: 1, 8).

Initially, the CRCCF resolved to settle all land confiscation cases within the first six months of its mandate (Htet Naing Zaw 2016). However, the CRCCF has faced several shortcomings that hinder its work. As Bernard (2017) notes, one major issue is the lack of communication between its various level committees regarding case decisions and implementation of the decisions. Another problem involves its inadequate systematic dissemination of information and updates regarding cases received and/or handled. Without sufficient updates on their cases, complainants use various redress pathways causing extra workloads for other complaint bodies (Bernard 2017: 12). Moreover, the unclear line of authority and continually shifting case priorities of its committees in different regions and states cause confusion and create a barrier to remedies for affected people (NAMATI 2017: 8). Lastly, alleged conflicts of interest in the CRCCF committees (Bernard 2017: 13) inevitably affect its independence and impartiality as a complaint mechanism.

Affected people also submitted thousands of complaints to Myanmar's National Human Rights Commission (NHRC). The NHRC could assist the parties in conciliating their dispute, investigate alleged human rights violations and make recommendations on its findings to relevant State authorities. However, it has been criticised for its lack of power and, more notably, its limited role in securing remedies for victims (ICJ 2018: 26; Aguirre 2017; Min and Kuan 2016). Other institutions such as the Parliament's Rule of Law and Tranquillity Committee and ombudsman offices may provide additional avenues for remedies; however, they too have provided little relief (Bernard 2017: 13; Aguirre 2017).

The courts are rarely considered an option for redress due to their perceived lack of independence and impartiality. Most people avoid the courts, especially in cases where the State or the military is involved, which is common in land confiscations and related human rights violations. Fear of retribution among the people in Myanmar is prevalent as judicial harassments are reportedly perpetrated to those seeking justice and redress against the State or the military (ICJ 2018: 25–26; Aguirre 2017). Consequently, there is next to no public trust in the judicial system (ICJ 2018: 4, 19). Corruption is also rampant in the judiciary (Ibid.: 19), as Aguirre (2017) emphasised, "particularly at the township level where most people access it". While going to courts is costly and time-consuming, the prospect of affected people awarded remedies or reparations is negligible. Consequently, rather than resorting to courts, affected people often opt for other means for relief or simply give up their cases (ICJ 2018: 26).

As discussed above, although there are many complaint mechanisms in the countries discussed, their effectiveness as a grievance mechanism remains a problem. Although State-based mechanisms for legal redress are quite diverse and uneven among AMS (Kaufmann et al. 2013; Middleton and Pritchard 2013), the situation regarding access to remedy is quite similar across ASEAN. In most AMS, courts often either lack independence, impartiality, capacity or willingness to address human rights and politically sensitive cases, which are precisely the case for land-grabbing. Where cases are accepted, courts also often fail to provide timely and appropriate remedies to affected people. On the other hand, existing State-based non-judicial mechanisms are flawed in different ways and are not yet able to provide effective access to remedies for affected people seeking redress. Major weaknesses in existing judicial and other State-based mechanisms include corruption or conflicts of interest, lack of capacity, overlapping or unclear lines of responsibilities and jurisdiction among the different complaint bodies, complex procedures for lodging complaints, unpredictable or inconsistent decisions, and difficulties in enforcing the decisions or judgements. On the other hand, while being able to receive complaints and investigate cases, NHRCs in ASEAN are limited to issuing findings and recommendations which do not offer practical relief to affected people.

Given the lack of prospect of gaining remedies through State-based complaint mechanisms, victims must resort to other means to voice their grievances and seek appropriate redress. Those means include petitions to relevant ministries, the National Assembly, powerful ruling elites and related foreign embassies; public protests; international campaigns; and the media (Scurrah and Hirsch 2015: 2; Baird 2017). In Vietnam, apart from using the media and organising public demonstrations (Kerkvliet 2014), affected people use intermediaries such as retired State officials to help them negotiate with State authorities regarding arbitrary land requisitions. In the short-term, this strategy may be an alternative to Vietnam's State-based complaint mechanisms, especially the courts, that are currently unable to provide effective remedies to affected people (Gillespie 2014, 2017). These "self-help" mechanisms or "collective actions" have had mixed results though. While sometimes there are successful outcomes, these approaches often trigger various risks (for example, State-sanctioned violence or criminalisation) to affected people trying to seek relief. Moreover, some members of affected communities, especially women, who are unable to sustain in these protests or collective actions may be excluded from a settlement package later (Scurrah and Hirsch 2015: 2).

Non-State-Based Grievance Mechanisms

Following the introduction of the UNGP, businesses have been increasingly pressured to address human rights violations associated with their activities and remediate victims' grievances. In ASEAN, some businesses have set up company- or operational-level grievance mechanisms in recent years. For instance, VRG, the Vietnamese company involved in alleged large-scale land-grabbing in Cambodia and Laos, established a complaint mechanism in 2014 (Global Witness 2014). GAR, a Singapore-based palm oil giant, also established a complaint handling system in 2015 (GAR n.d.). In the Philippines, some agribusiness companies may be legally obliged by the Philippines's Revised Code of Corporate Governance to establish a company-level grievance mechanism to settle internal-corporate and third parties-related disputes (Lim and Mukherjee 2015: 47). Yet, at present, company-based or operational-level grievance mechanisms have done little in providing remedies to victims. Conversely, they are said to be biased toward the company and fail to protect human rights (ERI n.d.; Chau 2018).

Affected people may also seek remedies in industry-based complaint mechanisms. For example, local communities affected by palm oil plantations can seek redress under the RSPO complaint mechanism against RSPO's member companies, which are often more likely held accountable and more responsive to complaints (Persch-Orth and Mwangi 2016: 1). Nevertheless, many of the complaints submitted to the RSPO complaint mechanism remain unresolved (see e.g., Balaton-Chrimes and Macdonald 2016: 6–7). For instance, a complaint submitted to the RSPO mechanism against Wilmar's subsidiary in the land dispute mentioned earlier has not been resolved. Abuses reportedly continue to occur, even leading to abovementioned shooting incident (FPP 2016b, 2018).

In Cambodia, a novel process to resolve business-related land conflicts has been introduced by the Independent Mediation Group (IMG), a privately-funded NGO. IMG is using mediation to settle a long-standing land dispute between six indigenous communities affected by a foreign rubber company. At the time of writing, the pre-mediation stage has been concluded and the first negotiation stage has succeeded in part. The mediation process will continue until the end of 2018. Despite this early success, there are some key issues that need to be addressed, such as trust-building, communication with the parties, power balance between the parties, and capacity-building, particularly community representatives' negotiation skills (Poch 2018). Other challenges also include the project's sustainability and the government's endorsement and enforcement of the mediation outcome. Consequently, at this juncture, the mediation approach is seen as a "test case" (ICJ 2017: 30).

Mediation is also used to resolve lengthy land disputes between HAGL and thirteen indigenous communities in Ratanakiri province, Cambodia. The mediation, which is being run by the Compliance Advisor Ombudsman (CAO) of the International Finance Cooperation (IFC), has made some breakthroughs. Since 2015, a series of agreements have been reached between the parties, where HAGL promised, among others, to halt land clearance or development on disputed lands; establish an operational grievance mechanism; provide compensation or if so required return the communities' lands; and support the villagers in securing title to their lands. The case has not been concluded, however (CAO 2018). In the meantime, whether these promises can be actually delivered is unclear. For instance, while HAGL promised to return lands to affected indigenous communities, the Cambodian government claimed that contested lands actually belonged to the State. Thus, it is up to the government whether to return the lands to affected communities (Thuon 2018: 162).

Access to Remedies Within ASEAN

There is no ASEAN regional grievance mechanism that can receive complaints about business-related human rights violations in general, or instances of land grabs in particular. The ASEAN Intergovernmental Commission on Human Rights (AICHR) does not have investigative power or a complaint mechanism. It is unlikely that the AICHR could undertake human rights investigation in the foreseeable future (Aguirre 2017; Scurrah and Hirsch 2015: 6). Meanwhile, establishing a regional human rights court seems to be improbable. As Mohan (2015: 156) notes "[g]iven the CLMV States' historical resistance to binding human rights commitments, the prospect of an ASEAN human rights court seems far off".

In the absence of a regional human rights grievance mechanism, affected people, assisted by international and local NGOs, have sought other means to seek redress in ASEAN, especially in cases involving transnational business-related human rights violations. For instance, Cambodian farmers affected by sugarcane plantations owned by Thai sugar corporations made several complaints to the Thai NHRC. Although this body is limited to issuing findings and recommendations, its acknowledgement of the human rights violations perpetrated against affected Cambodian farmers has played an important role in their journey to seek redress. It essentially paves the way toward extraterritorial access to remedies for business-related human rights violations in ASEAN. Recently, a groundbreaking lawsuit was filed on behalf of hundreds of Cambodian farmers in the Thai court against the Thai sugar giant Mitr Phol for alleged land grabs and associated human rights abuses in its plantations in Cambodia (IDI 2018a, b).

Major Barriers to Access to Remedy in ASEAN

For most farmers and indigenous communities affected by arbitrary land confiscations or land grabs in ASEAN, the first major barrier to accessing remedies is the lack of formally recognised rights to their land. These people are unable to claim legally recognised rights to the land they possess, occupy or use. This is either because the property system of some AMS do not recognise informal or customary land tenures, or weaknesses and loopholes exist in their land-related legislation. Thus, when the State expropriates the land and subsequently evicts these people from places that they have occupied or possessed 'illegally', that is, without a formal ownership title, possessory rights or legally recognised land use rights, the State may deny that its measures constitute an arbitrary taking of property. This is because affected people do not have any land to be deprived of in the first place (Neef 2016: 8, 17–48, 58; Fitzpatrick 2015: 77–78). This, in turn, deprives affected people the right to redress in their home State. As mentioned in the HAGL case above, although the company agreed to return the lands, the State argued that the lands did not belong to affected communities from the beginning. It is thus at the State's sole discretion to decide whether to allocate to them the lands they perceived to be theirs. The lack of formally recognised land rights also potentially puts affected people at a disadvantage when negotiating with companies (FPP 2017: 4).

Similar difficulties are also experienced by people who lack evidential documents to attest their property and land rights (NAMATI 2017).

Furthermore, the implementation of land-related laws has been poor, uneven and/or selective across AMS, especially in the CLMV (see, e.g. Kaufmann et al. 2013). For instance, while Cambodian laws recognise and protect possessory rights, in practice, such rights are often ignored and violated (HRN 2012: 12). Consequently, although affected people may be able to prove their legitimate possessory right to the land, such right may not be necessarily enforced.

Compounding the above problems is the lack of an effective grievance mechanism for affected people to seek redress. As discussed earlier, existing State-based grievance mechanisms in AMS face various institutional and procedural weaknesses and challenges. The existence of multi-layer complaint bodies in some AMS, but with overlapping and blurred responsibilities and jurisdiction, creates another barrier for affected people seeking redress. Political interference in State-based grievance mechanisms in some AMS leads to a 'culture of impunity' for human rights violators, while affected people and their lawyers are sometimes subject to threats, reprisals and judicial harassments. This situation creates a barrier for victims to access domestic remedies and further diminishes the already minimal confidence and trust they have in existing State-based complaint mechanisms, especially the courts (Scurrah and Hirsch 2015: 4–5). Other barriers include corruption or conflicts of interest, weak rule of law and lack of regulatory and governance capacity. Non-State-based grievance mechanisms, on the other hand, have provided limited relief to affected people. Meanwhile, at the ASEAN level, there is no human rights complaint mechanism through which victims can seek redress.

Lastly, affected people often lack awareness or knowledge regarding their rights and redress routes, legal aid and resources to pursue their cases. Poverty is a major obstacle for affected people to seek redress, especially in poorer AMS. While NGOs may provide them with some limited supports, NGOs' activities have been increasingly restricted in various ways in AMS. In turn, this will further weaken affected people's capacity and confidence to seek remedies (Scurrah and Hirsch 2015: 2).

Efforts to Address Barriers to Access to Remedy

There have been efforts in some AMS to improve recognition of customary tenures and land rights. Supported by international donors, land reforms were carried out in some AMS, e.g. Laos and Cambodia, aiming to improve tenure security in these countries. The results, however, have been controversial (Hirsch and Scurrah 2015: 19; see also, Dwyer 2015). Recently, new land-related policies and legislation have been introduced in AMS to strengthen land rights. For instance, in 2016, Myanmar unveiled a new National Land Use Policy. Its 2012 Farmland Law and Vacant, Fallow and Virgin (VFV) Land Management Law have been under revisions. Introduced in September 2018, the Law Amending the VFV Land Management Law raises significant concerns. Among other impacts, it will put millions, particularly indigenous communities, at risk of eviction and landlessness (TNI 2018). Laos has also taken up its National Land Policy, compiled the National Master Plan on Land Allocation and undertaken land-related regulatory reform; for instance, Land Law revision (LIWG 2017a, b, 2018). Laos draft land law revision, in which civil society are involved, is expected to clarify how customary land rights and communal tenures can be secured and ensure a fair prior compensation for land requisitions by the State (LIWG 2017b: 2–3). Indonesia has introduced a new agrarian reform strategy to tackle social inequality in land ownership through land conflict resolutions and a land redistribution scheme which particularly prioritises indigenous peoples. New legal innovations have also been introduced to secure indigenous peoples' and local communities' rights to forests and farmlands (FPP 2016a, 2017).

However, such regulatory efforts have met with challenges and delays, especially as some AMS governments still considerably prioritise agribusiness investments. In turn, legal protection of local communities' land rights, as well as their right to remedy, remains weak and sometimes are undermined by competing investor-friendly laws and corporate interest (Ibid.). Gilson (2018: 53) argues that efforts by AMS governments are not yet sufficient or taken seriously enough to address the overarching and dire consequences of current land issues. He also argues that AMS' aspiration in furthering regional economic integration will likely continue to keep land-grabbing issues off ASEAN's agenda (Gilson 2018). Meanwhile, NHRCs and CSOs have been at the forefront of land rights advocacy, aiming to mainstream land rights as human rights in ASEAN (FPP 2016a, 2017; see also Hirsch and Scurrah 2015: 18, 22). A notable achievement was the 2011 Bali Declaration on Human Rights and Agribusiness in Southeast Asia (FPP 2011). These efforts will inevitably require AMS' political will to be fruitful.

As discussed earlier, there have been increasing efforts by AMS governments and relevant stakeholders to improve access to remedies for people affected by arbitrary land takings involving agribusiness companies. Some of the new grievance mechanisms; for instance, the inter-ministerial working group and IMG-introduced mediation in Cambodia, may help to fill the current gap in domestic access to remedies. In the meantime, given their respective challenges, it is too early to assess their long-term success. AMS governments have also been working together to prevent and combat corruption and bolster the rule of law, judicial systems and legal infrastructure as well as good governance in ASEAN (Mohan 2015: 140–142; Thomas 2015: 13–15). In recent years, some NHRCs have been working on a National Action Plan on Business and Human Rights. In 2017, the Indonesian NHRC launched a National Action Plan which creates normative standards for the State and businesses, among others, regarding remedies for victims (FIHRRST 2017). Malaysia also launched its National Action Plan in 2018 (Naidu 2018).

Conclusion

Alleged corporate land grabs or arbitrary land confiscations by AMS governments to make way for agribusiness plantations are rampant in ASEAN. There are various State-based and non-State-based grievance mechanisms to resolve business-related land conflicts in AMS. However, existing mechanisms have their own shortcomings and are not yet able to provide effective access to remedies for affected people. Their institutional and procedural weaknesses create various barriers to access to remedies. Victims of land grabs and related human rights abuses also face other barriers in accessing domestic remedies, including a lack of formally recognised rights to their land, awareness of the law and available redress options, legal assistance and resources.

New redress mechanisms have been introduced to resolve affected people's grievances. While some of these new mechanisms show the potential in filling the current lacuna in access to remedies in AMS, their long-term success is yet to be seen. In the meantime, affected people will have to continue to seek redress through other international avenues, such as the IFC's CAO, the OECD's national contact points or international human rights complaint mechanisms. Although remedies for business-related human rights violations, including land-grabbing, at the international level remain rare and limited, creative use of multiple forums and complaint mechanisms may improve affected people's chance of success. The recent conclusion of the Koh Kong sugarcane plantation case in Cambodia, following strenuous decade-long efforts using and exhausting all available domestic, regional and international forums (ERI and CLEC 2013: 9–12), provides a perfect example on this matter. Notably, the recent lawsuit filed on behalf of Cambodian farmers in the Thai court may potentially pave the way for extraterritorial corporate accountability and remedies for victims. If successful, transnational litigation will be another option for affected people to seek redress in ASEAN against companies coming from another AMS. The likely challenge for this option though is the general lack of independence, impartiality and effectiveness of most AMS' judicial system discussed above.

In short, while there has been some progress, access to remedies for victims of land-grabbing in the agribusiness industry in ASEAN, since the launch of the UNGP, remains generally limited. The lack of an effective forum for affected people to seek redress may exacerbate tensions and alleged social injustice in AMS and may even lead to social unrests (see e.g., 'No man's land' 2017). Given the growth of transnational business-related human rights abuses in ASEAN, concerted efforts by all AMS are needed to address the current problems, particularly in providing more effective access to remedies for victims. There is thus an urgent need for AMS, ASEAN and businesses to explore additional forum(s) that is accessible and effective for victims to seek redress.

References

Aguirre, D. 2017. 'Commentary: Businesses must prioritise access to remedy in states with weak rule of law', Cambridge Core, weblog post, 20 November 2017, viewed 20 June 2018, http://blog.journals.cambridge.org/2017/11/20/obligations-to-respect-and-protect-human-rights-are-meaningless-without-access-to-remedy-in-states-where-the-rule-of-law-is-weak-the-example-of-myanmar/.

Amado, Jose Daniel, Jackson Shaw Kern, and Martin Doe Rodriguez. 2018. *Arbitrating the Conduct of International Investors*. Cambridge: Cambridge University Press.

Asia Pacific Forum (APF). 2015. *Myanmar: Land grabbing tops list of rights violations*, viewed 20 June 2018, http://www.asiapacificforum.net/news/myanmar-land-grabbing-tops-list-rights-violations/.

Min, A.K. and Kuan, J. 2016. 'Human Rights Commission comes under fire over record', *Myanmar Times*, 3 February, viewed 20 June 2018, https://www.mmtimes.com/opinion/18786-human-rights-commission-comes-under-fire-over-record.html.

Balaton-Chrimes, S. and Macdonald, K. 2016. *Wilmar and Palm Oil Grievances: The Promise and Pitfalls of Problem Solving*, Non-Judicial Redress Mechanisms Report Series 8. Corporate Accountability Research. http://corporateaccountability.squarespace.com/s/NJM08_wilmar-tx4y.pdf.

Baird, Ian G. 2017. Resistance and Contingent Contestations to Large-Scale Land Concessions in Southern Laos and Northern Cambodia. *Land* 6 (1): 1–19.

Borras Jr, S.M., et al. 2016. *Study on Land grabbing and human rights: The involvement of European corporate and financial entities in land grabbing outside the European Union*, Policy Department, Directorate-General for External Policies. http://www.europarl.europa.eu/RegData/etudes/STUD/2016/578007/EXPO_STU(2016)578007_EN.pdf.

Bernard, Antoine (ed.). 2017. *Land of Sorrow: Human rights violations at Myanmar's Myotha Industrial Park*, International Federation for Human Rights (FIDH), Report. https://www.fidh.org/IMG/pdf/fidh_report_-_land_of_sorrow_-_human_rights_violations_at_myanmar_s_myotha_industrial_park.pdf.

Business & Human Rights Resource Centre (BHRRC). 2013. *Statement on behalf of a Group of Countries at the 24th Session of the Human Rights Council*. http://business-humanrights.org/sites/default/files/media/documents/statement-unhrc-legally-binding.pdf.

Cambodian Centre for Human Rights (CCHR). 2014. *The Failure of Land Dispute Resolution Mechanisms*, CCHR Briefing Note. https://cchrcambodia.org/admin/media/analysis/analysis/english/2014_07_28_CCHR_Briefing_Note_The_Failure%20of_Land_Dispute_Resolution_Mechanisms_(ENG).pdf.

———. 2013. *Cambodia: Land in Conflict: An Overview of the Land Situation*, Report. http://cchrcambodia.org/admin/media/report/report/english/CCHR%20Report%20%20Cambodia%20Land%20in%20Conflict%20An%20Overview%20of%20the%20Land%20Situation%20ENG.pdf.

Calderón-Meza, Juan Pablo, et al. 2016. An International Jurisdiction for Corporate Atrocity Crimes. *Harvard International Law Journal (Online Symposium)* 57: 1–6. https://harvardilj.org/wp-content/uploads/sites/15/Introduction_0615.pdf.

Calderón-Meza, Juan Pablo. 2016. Arbitration for Human Rights: Seeking Civil Redress for Corporate Atrocity Crimes. *Harvard International Law Journal*

(Online Symposium) 57: 60–65. http://www.harvardilj.org/wp-content/uploads/Calderon-Meza_0615.pdf.

Compliance Advisor Ombudsman (CAO). 2018. *Cambodia/Cambodia: VEIL II-01/Ratanakiri Province*, viewed 20 June 2018, http://www.cao-ombudsman.org/cases/case_detail.aspx?id=212dashboard/complaint-and-grievance-handling.

Carling, J., Halip, R. and Tessier, J. 2015. *Victims of development aggression: Indigenous Peoples in ASEAN*, Asia Indigenous Peoples Pacts (AIPP). https://business-humanrights.org/sites/default/files/documents/Victims%20of%20development%20aggression.pdf.

Chao, Sophie (ed.). 2013. *Agribusiness Large-Scale Land Acquisitions and Human Rights in Southeast Asia: Updates from Indonesia, Thailand, Philippines, Malaysia, Cambodia, Timor-Leste and Burma*, Forest Peoples Programme. http://www.forestpeoples.org/sites/fpp/files/publication/2013/08/lsla-studies.pdf.

Chau, T. 2018. 'Thilawa's complaint mechanism criticised as 'a process on paper'', *Myanmar Times*, 14 February, viewed 20 June 2018, https://www.mmtimes.com/news/thilawas-complaint-mechanism-criticised-process-paper.html.

Chung, Chang-ho. 2016. The Emerging Asian-Pacific Court of Human Rights in the Context of State and Non-State Liability. *Harvard International Law Journal (Online Symposium)* 57: 44–47. http://www.harvardilj.org/wp-content/uploads/Chung_0615.pdf.

Colchester, Marcus and Sophie Chao (eds). 2013. *Conflict or Consent: The oil palm sector at a crossroads*, Forest Peoples Programme (FPP), Sawit Watch and TUK INDONESIA. http://www.forestpeoples.org/sites/fpp/files/news/2013/10/Conflict%20or%20Consent_English_lowres.pdf.

Cronstedt, Claes, Jan Eijsbouts, and Robert C. Thompson. 2017. *International Business and Human Rights Arbitration*, Lawyers 4 Better Business (L4BB), Report http://www.l4bb.org/news/TribunalV6.pdf.

Dao, Nga. 2015. Rubber plantations in the Northwest: rethinking the concept of land grabs in Vietnam, *Journal of Peasant Studies* 42 (2): 347–369.

Dwyer, Michael B. 2015. The formalisation fix? Land titling, land concessions and the politics of spatial transparency in Cambodia. *Journal of Peasant Studies* 42 (5): 903–928.

EarthRights International (ERI). n.d. *Community-Driven Operational Grievance Mechanism (CD-OGM)*, viewed 20 June 2018, https://earthrights.org/what-we-do/land-rights/cdogm/.

EarthRights International (ERI) and Community Legal Education Centre (CLEC). 2013. *Business and Human Rights in ASEAN: The Implications of the Koh Kong Sugar Plantation and Factory Case in Cambodia for Due Diligence and Remedies*, Community Legal Education Centre, Case Study. http://www.

clec.org.kh/web/images/Resources/Res_Koh%20Kong%20ASEAN%20Case%20Study%202013%20-%20ENG1374035991.pdf.

Equitable Cambodia and Inclusive Development International (IDI). 2013. *Bittersweet Harvest: A Human Rights Impact Assessment of the European Union's Everything But Arms Initiative in Cambodia*, Inclusive Development International, Report. http://www.inclusivedevelopment.net/wp-content/uploads/2013/10/Bittersweet_Harvest_web-version.pdf.

Fitzpatrick, Daniel. 2015. 'The legal design of land grabs: Possession and the state in post-conflict Cambodia' in Carter, Connie and Andrew Harding (eds), *Land grabs in Asia: What Role for the Law?*, New York: Routledge.

Forest Peoples Programme (FPP). 2018. *Wilmar International implicated in police shooting of two farmers on oil palm estate*, FPP news article, 9 January, viewed 20 June 2018, http://www.forestpeoples.org/en/responsible-finance-private-sector-palm-oil-rspo/news-article/2018/wilmar-international-implicated.

———. 2017. *Pontianak Statement on Human Rights and Agribusiness in South East Asia*, Forest Peoples Programmes, Report. http://www.forestpeoples.org/sites/default/files/documents/PONTIANAK%20STATEMENT%20ON%20HUMAN%20RIGHTS%20AND%20AGRIBUSINESS%20IN%20SOUTHEAST%20ASIA%20final%20with%20recs.pdf.

———. 2016a. *Human Rights and Agribusiness in Southeast Asia', Report from the 6th Regional Conference on Human Rights and Agribusiness in Southeast Asia*, Kota Kinabalu, Malaysia, 3–4 November 2016, Forest People Programmes, Report. http://www.forestpeoples.org/sites/default/files/documents/Human%20Rights%20and%20Agribusiness%20Report%20WEB.pdf.

———. 2016b. *Wilmar fails to resolve conflicts with communities in West Kalimantan and West Sumatra*, FPP news article, 23 February, viewed 20 June 2018, http://www.forestpeoples.org/topics/palm-oil-rspo/news/2016/02/wilmar-fails-resolve-conflicts-communities-west-kalimantan-and-wes.

———. 2015. *5th Regional Meeting on Human Rights and Agribusiness in South East Asia*, Summary Report from the 5th Regional Meeting on Human Rights and Agribusiness in South East Asia. https://www.forestpeoples.org/sites/default/files/publication/2016/05/workshop-report-5th-human-rights-and-agribusiness-meeting-final-pdf.pdf.

———. 2013. 'Press Release – Sustainable Palm Oil: Marketing Ploy or True Commitment? New Research Questions Effectiveness of RSPO Standards', FPP Press Information for Immediate Release, 7 November, viewed 20 June 2018, https://www.forestpeoples.org/en/topics/palm-oil-rspo/news/2013/11/press-release-sustainable-palm-oil-marketing-ploy-or-true-commitme.

———. 2011. *Bali Declaration on Human Rights and Agribusiness in Southeast Asia*, https://www.forestpeoples.org/sites/default/files/publication/2011/12/final-bali-declaration-adopted-1-dec-2011.pdf.

Foundation for International Human Rights Reporting Standards (FIHRRST). 2017. Indonesia Launches National Action Plan on Business & Human Rights, viewed 20 June 2018, https://www.business-humanrights.org/sites/default/files/documents/Indonesia%27s%20NAP%20Launch.pdf.

Golden Agri-Resources (GAR). n.d. *Procedure for Grievance Handling*, viewed 20 June 2018, https://goldenagri.com.sg/sustainability-dashboard/complaint-and-grievance-handling.

Gillespie, John. 2017. Transforming Land-Taking Disputes in Socialist Asia: Engaging an Authoritarian State. *Law & Policy* 39 (3): 280–303.

———. 2014. Social Consensus and the Meta-Regulation of Land-Taking Disputes in Vietnam. *Journal of Vietnamese Studies* 9 (3): 91–124.

Gilson, Julie. 2018. ASEAN and Regional Responses to the Problem(s) of Land Grabbing. *Global Governance* 24 (1): 41–60.

Ginbar, Yuval. 2010. Human Rights in ASEAN—Setting Sail or Treading Water? *Human Rights Law Review* 10 (3): 504–518.

Global Witness. 2015. *Guns, Cronies and Crops: How Military, Political and Business Cronies Conspired to Grab Land in Myanmar*, Global Witness, Report. https://www.globalwitness.org/documents/17852/exec_summarygunscroniescrops.pdf.

———. 2014. 'Vietnam Rubber Group Says its Doors are Now Open to People Affected by Plantations in Cambodia and Laos', Global Witness Press Release, 20 August, viewed 20 June 2018, https://www.globalwitness.org/en/archive/vietnam-rubber-group-says-its-doors-are-now-open-people-affected-plantations-cambodia-and/.

———. 2013. *Rubber Barons: How Vietnamese Companies and International Financiers Are Driving A Land Grabbing Crisis in Cambodia and Laos*, Global Witness, Report. https://www.globalwitness.org/documents/10525/rubber_barons_lores_0_1.pdf.

Golay, Christophe (2015) 'Identifying and Monitoring Human Rights Violations Associated with Large-Scale Land Acquisitions: A Focus on United Nations Mechanisms and South-East Asia' in Gironde, Christophe, Christophe Golay and Peter Messerli (eds), *Large-Scale Land Acquisitions: Focus on South-East Asia*, Leiden/Boston: Brill Nijhoff, pp. 229–248.

Grimsditch, M. and Nick Henderson. 2009. *Untitled: Tenure Security and Inequality in the Cambodian Land Sector*, Bridges Across Borders Cambodia, Centre for Housing Rights and Evictions (COHRE) and Jesuit Refugee Service, Report. https://data.opendevelopmentmekong.net/dataset/14e507bd-99d7-40e4-8af1-c701e25b697d/resource/d6952d46-c5d2-4e9c-ab2d-e0ad55226db9/download/0feb821b-86da-4f31-84d8-4e89a2de6d66.pdf.

Hackett, Ciara and Luke Moffett. 2016. Mapping the public/private-law divide: a hybrid approach to corporate accountability. *International Journal of Law in Context* 12 (3): 312–336.

Hirsch, P. and Natalie Scurrah. 2015. *The Political Economy of Land Governance in the Mekong Region*, Mekong Region Land Governance, Report. http://www.mekonglandforum.org/sites/default/files/Political_Economy_of_Land_Governance_in_Region.pdf.

Hodal, Kate. 2014. 'European Union agrees to investigate Cambodian sugar industry', *The Guardian*, 11 December, viewed 20 June 2018, https://www.theguardian.com/world/2014/dec/10/european-union-cambodia-sugar-industry-human-rights.

Howe, Brendan M. and Seo Hyun Rachelle Park. 2015. Laos: The Dangers of Developmentalism?. *Southeast Asian Affairs* 1: 167–185.

Htet Naing Zaw. 2016. 'Govt Committee to settle all land grabs cases in six months', *The Irrawaddy*, 1 July, viewed 20 June 2018 https://www.irrawaddy.com/news/burma/govt-committee-to-settle-all-land-grab-cases-in-six-months.html.

Human Rights Now (HRN). 2012. *Human Rights Now, Fact Finding Report for Cambodian: In Cambodia, People are Deprived of Land*, Human Right Now, Report. http://hrn.or.jp/eng/activity/HRN%20Cambodia%20Report%20on%20Land%20Rights%202012.pdf.

Inclusive Development International (IDI). 2018a. 'Forcibly Displaced Cambodians File Historic Lawsuit against Asia's Largest Sugar Producer', Inclusive Development International News and Updates, 2 April, viewed 20 June 2018, https://www.inclusivedevelopment.net/forcibly-displaced-cambodians-file-historic-lawsuit-against-asias-largest-sugar-producer/.

———. 2018b. *Case Brief: Class Action Lawsuit by Cambodian Villagers Against Mirt Phol Sugar Corporation*, Inclusive Development International, Case Brief. https://www.inclusivedevelopment.net/wp-content/uploads/2018/03/Mitr-Phol-Class-Action-Case-Brief.pdf.

International Commission of Jurists (ICJ). 2018. *Achieving Justice for Gross Human Rights Violations in Myanmar*, ICJ Global Redress and Accountability Initiative, Baseline Study. https://www.icj.org/wp-content/uploads/2018/01/Myanmar-GRA-Baseline-Study-Publications-Reports-Thematic-reports-2018-ENG.pdf.

———. 2017. *Achieving Justice for Gross Human Rights Violations in Cambodia, ICJ Global Redress and Accountability Initiative*, International Commission of Jurists, Baseline Study. http://www.refworld.org/pdfid/5a212f144.pdf.

Jones, William J. 2014. Universalising Human Rights The ASEAN Way. *International Journal of Social Science* III (3): 72–89.

Johnson, Tomasz. 2015. 'Palm oil companies exploit Indonesia's people – and its corrupt political machine', *The Guardian*, 11 June, viewed 20 June 2018, https://www.theguardian.com/sustainable-business/2015/jun/11/palm-oil-industry-indonesia-corruption-communities-forests.

Kaeb, Caroline. 2016. The Shifting Sands of Corporate Liability under International Law. *The George Washington International Law Review* 49: 351–403.

Kaufmann, Christine, et al. (eds). 2013. *Business and Human Rights in ASEAN: A Baseline Study*, Human Rights Resource Centre, e-book. http://hrrca.org/wp-content/uploads/2015/09/Business-and-Human-Rights-in-ASEAN-Baseline-Study-ebook.pdf.

Kerkvliet, Benedict J. Tria. 2014. Protests over land in Vietnam: Rightful resistance ad more. *Journal of Vietnamese Studies* 9 (3): 19–54.

Kenney-Lazar, Miles. 2012. Plantation rubber, land grabbing and social-property transformation in southern Laos. *Journal of Peasant Studies* 39 (3–4): 1017–1037.

Koshy, Shaila. 2016. 'Baby Steps towards an ASEAN court' Human Rights in ASEAN (Online Platform) (online) 13–17 July 2016, https://humanrightsinasean.info/article/baby-steps-towards-asean-court.html.

Land Information Working Group (LIWG). 2018. *NA members push for compliant land allocation*, viewed 20 June 2018, http://www.laolandinfo.org/2018/04/24/na-members-push-for-compliant-land-allocation/.

———. 2017a. *Land should benefit everyone: PM*, viewed 20 June 2018, http://www.laolandinfo.org/2017/12/25/land-should-benefit-everyone-pm/.

———. 2017b. *LIWG Newsletter*, Land Information Working Group, Quarterly Vol May–September, Issue 1. http://www.laolandinfo.org/wp-content/uploads/2017/05/LIWG-Newsletter-May-Sep-2017_English-version.pdf.

———. 2014. *Supporting Rationale for LIWG Recommendations: Establishing an independent grievance mechanism*, Land Information Working Group, Report. http://www.laolandissues.org/wp-content/uploads/2014/05/Grievance-Mechanisms-%E2%80%93-Rationale-for-Laos-and-Cases-from-Other-Countries.-LIWG-2014.pdf.

Lim, Delphia and Geetanjali Mukherjee. 2015. 'Business and human rights challenges in ASEAN: the role and modalities of State', in Mohan, Mahdev and Cynthia Morel (eds.), *Business and Human Rights in Southeast Asia: Risk and the Regulatory Turn*, 1st edn, New York: Routledge, pp. 30–56.

Middleton, Carl and Ashley Pritchard. 2013. *Corporate Accountability in ASEAN: A Human Rights-Based Approach*, Asian Forum for Human Rights and Development (FORUM-ASIA), e-book. http://www.forum-asia.org/uploads/publications/2013/September/Corporate-Accountability-ASEAN-FINAL.pdf.

Mohan, Mahdev. 2015. 'Human rights risks amidst the 'gold-rush': Cambodia, Laos, Myanmar and Vietnam', in Mohan, Mahdev and Cynthia Morel (eds), *Business and Human Rights in Southeast Asia: Risk and the Regulatory Turn*, 1st edn, New York: Routledge, pp. 133–160.

Naidu, Sumisha. 2018, 'PM Najib launches national human rights plans for a 'kinder Malaysia', *Channel News Asia*, 1 March, viewed 20 June 2018, https://www.channelnewsasia.com/news/asia/najib-launches-national-human-rights-plan-for-kinder-malaysia-10002574.

NAMATI. 2017. *Evidence is not sufficient to secure land rights in Myanmar; Impartial and transparent procedures are critical*, NAMATI, Report. https://namati.org/wp-content/uploads/2017/01/4.Evidence_Land-Rights_-Myanmar-2017-Final.pdf.

Neef, Andreas. 2016. *Land Rights Matter Anchors to Reduce Land Grabbing, Dispossession and Displacement: A Comparative Study of Land Rights Systems in Southeast Asia and the Potential of National and International Legal Frameworks and Guidelines*, Brot für die Welt, Study, Analysis 60. https://www.brot-fuer-die-welt.de/fileadmin/mediapool/2_Downloads/Fachinformationen/Analyse/Analysis_60_Land-Policy-Study.pdf.

NGO Forum on Cambodia. 2016a. *Statistical Analysis of Land Disputes in Cambodia, 2016*, NGOF Publication (Khmer Version), Report. http://ngoforum.org.kh/files/bedbb8c5746e44dc456c976f6a60e350-Layout-Land-dispute-report-2016-Kh.pdf.

———. 2016b. *Statistical Analysis of Land Disputes in Cambodia, 2015*, NGOF Publication (Khmer Version), Report. http://ngoforum.org.kh/files/e1f20a9889d8ae9144413f14d7b2053e-Layout-Land-dispute-report-2015-Eng.pdf.

'No man's land: Property disputes are Vietnam's biggest political problem'. 2017. *The Economist*, 15 June, viewed 20 June 2018, https://www.economist.com/asia/2017/06/15/property-disputes-are-vietnams-biggest-political-problem.

Office of the UN High Commissioner for Human Rights (OHCHR). 2018a. 'Open-ended intergovernmental working group on transnational corporations and other business enterprises with respect to human rights', https://www.ohchr.org/EN/HRBodies/HRC/WGTransCorp/Pages/IGWGOnTNC.aspx.

———. 2018b. *OHCHR Accountability and Remedy Project: Improving accountability and access to remedy in cases of business involvement in human rights.* http://www.ohchr.org/EN/Issues/Business/Pages/OHCHRstudyondomesticlawremedies.aspx.

———. 2018c. *Improving accountability and access to remedy for victims of business-related human rights abuse through State-based non-judicial mechanism: Report of the United Nations High Commissioner for Human Rights.* UN Doc A/HRC/38/20, OHCHR. https://documents-dds-ny.un.org/doc/UNDOC/GEN/G18/132/70/PDF/G1813270.pdf?OpenElement.

———. 2018d. *Improving accountability and access to remedy for victims of business-related human rights abuse through State-based non-judicial mechanism: explanatory notes to final report. Report of the United Nations High Commissioner for*

Human Rights. UN Doc A/HRC/38/20/Add.1*, OHCHR. https://documents-dds-ny.un.org/doc/UNDOC/GEN/G18/166/37/PDF/G1816637.pdf?OpenElement.

———. 2018e. *OHCHR Accountability and Remedy Project III: Enhancing effectiveness of non-State-based grievance mechanisms in cases of business-related human rights abuse*. https://www.ohchr.org/EN/Issues/Business/Pages/ARP_III.aspx.

———. 2016. *Improving accountability and access to remedy for victims of business-related human rights abuses: Report of the United Nations High Commissioner for Human Rights*. UN Doc A/HRC/32/19, OHCHR. https://documents-dds-ny.un.org/doc/UNDOC/GEN/G16/093/78/PDF/G1609378.pdf?OpenElement.

———. 2011. *Guiding Principles on Business and Human Rights: Implementing the United Nations "Protect, Respect and Remedy" Framework*, OHCHR, Report. https://www.ohchr.org/Documents/Publications/GuidingPrinciplesBusinessHR_EN.pdf.

Pech, Sotheary. 2018a. 'Koh Kong villagers return to Land Ministry', *Khmer Times*, 18 May, viewed 20 June 2018, https://www.khmertimeskh.com/50491050/koh-kong-villagers-return-to-land-ministry/.

———. 2018b. 'Locals call for an end to land dispute', *Khmer Times*, 22 January, viewed 20 June 2018, https://www.khmertimeskh.com/50103497/locals-call-for-an-end-to-land-dispute/.

Persch-Orth, Meri and Esther Mwangi. 2016. *Company-community conflict in Indonesia's industrial plantation sector*, CIFOR infobrief, No. 143. http://www.cifor.org/publications/pdf_files/infobrief/6141-infobrief.pdf.

Phan, Hao Duy. 2009. A Blueprint for Southeast Asian Court of Human Rights. *Asian-Pacific Law & Policy Journal* 10 (2): 384–433.

Pietropaoli, Irene. 2015. *Are human rights being side-lined to make way for ASEAN economic integration?*, Business & Human Rights Resource Centre, viewed 20 June 2018, https://business-humanrights.org/en/are-human-rights-being-side-lined-to-make-way-for-asean-economic-integration.

Pietropaoli, Irene and Bobbie Sta. Maria. 2015. *Briefing: Development for all, or a privileged few?: Business & human rights in Southeast Asia*, Business & Human Rights Resource Centre, Briefing report. https://www.business-humanrights.org/sites/default/files/Southeast%20Asia%20Briefing%2016%20April%202015.pdf.

Poch, Sophorn. 2018. 'Alternative Land Conflict Transformation: A Cambodia Innovation', paper prepared for presentation at the "2018 World Bank Conference on Land and Poverty" at the World Bank, Washington DC, 19–23 March 2018, viewed 20 June 2018, https://www.conftool.com/landandpoverty2018/index.php/09-13-Poch-298_paper.pdf?page=downloadPaper&filename=09-13-Poch-298_paper.pdf&form_id=298&form_version=final.

Ruggie, John. 2008. *United Nations Human Rights Council Report of the Special Representative of the Secretary-General on the Issue of Human Rights and Transnational Corporations and Other Business Enterprises: Protect, Respect and Remedy: A framework for Business and Human Rights*, A/HRC/8/5 (7 April 2008), Report. https://documents-dds-ny.un.org/doc/UNDOC/GEN/G08/128/61/PDF/G0812861.pdf?OpenElement.

Scheffer, David. 2016. Corporate Liability under the Rome Statute. *Harvard International Law Journal (Online Symposium)* 57: 35–39. http://www.harvardilj.org/wp-content/uploads/Scheffer_0615.pdf.

Scurrah, Natalia and Philip Hirsch. 2015. *Dispute resolution and access to justice: Extended synopsis*, RCSD Chiang Mai University, Conference Paper. https://data.opendevelopmentmekong.net/dataset/ee129952-7ea0-4ee7-ac67-6b37efcbc32d/resource/21f3c7d5-a671-426c-930c-584e9cd57d6e/download/extended-synopsis-08-dispute-resolution-and-access-to-justice.pdf.

Soth, Koemsoeun. 2018a. 'Koh Kong villagers bitter over longstanding land dispute', *The Phnom Penh Post*, 3 May, viewed 20 June 2018, https://www.phnompenhpost.com/national/koh-kong-villagers-bitter-over-longstanding-land-dispute.

———. 2018b. 'Preah Vihear evictees demand land years after village razed' *The Phnom Penh Post*, 01 May, viewed 20 June 2018, https://www.phnompenhpost.com/national/preah-vihear-evictees-demand-land-years-after-village-razed.

———. 2018c. 'Koh Kong land dispute resolved, ministry says', *The Phnom Penh Post*, 22 March, viewed 20 June 2018, https://www.phnompenhpost.com/national/koh-kong-land-dispute-solved-ministry-says-0.

Steinitz, Maya. 2014. The Case for an International Court of Civil Justice. *Stanford Law Review Online* 67: 75–83. https://www.stanfordlawreview.org/online/the-case-for-an-international-court-of-civil-justice/.

Thio, Li-ann. 1999. Implementing Human Rights in ASEAN Countries: Promises to Keep and Miles to Go before I sleep. *Yale Human Rights and Development Law Journal* 2 (1): 1–86.

Thomas, Thomas. 2015. 'Wither corporate social responsibility and the UN Guiding Principles on business and human rights in ASEAN?', in Mohan, Mahdev and Cynthia Morel (eds), *Business and Human Rights in Southeast Asia: Risk and The Regulatory Turn*, 1st edn, New York: Routledge, pp. 13–29.

Thuon, Ratha. 2018. Holding corporations from middle countries accountable for human rights violations: a case study from the Vietnamese company investment in Cambodia. *Globalisations* 15 (1): 152–167.

Transnational Institute (TNI). 2018. *"A Declaration of War on Us": The 2018 VFV Law Amendment and its Impact on Ethnic Nationalities*. https://www.tni.org/en/article/a-declaration-of-war-on-us.

United Nations Development Programme (UNDP). 2011a. *People's Perspective on Access to Justice Survey in Four Provinces of Lao PDR*, UNDP, Report. www.la.undp.org/content/dam/laopdr/docs/Reports%20and%20publications/A2J%20Final_English%20&%20Lao.pdf?download.

———. 2011b. *Customary Law and Practice in Lao PDR*, UNDP, Report. http://www.la.undp.org/content/dam/laopdr/docs/Reports%20and%20publications/Customary_Law_Laos2011_english_master1.pdf.

Wetzel, Julia Ruth-Maria. 2016. *Human Rights in Transnational Business: Translating Human Rights Obligation into Compliance*. Switzerland: Springer.

PART III

New Frontiers in BHR Studies

CHAPTER 10

As Smart Worlds Collide: Citizen Agency and Human Rights in the Smart City

Jonathan Woodier and Andreas Zingerle

Introduction

While governments have a duty to protect fundamental human rights, public-private partnership in developing smart cities may be defeating this duty. Countries around the world are embracing the "smart city" concept for local urban development as the management and sustainability of urban areas becomes one of the most critical challenges society faces today. And yet, life in the smart city is likely to provide the UN Guiding Principles on Business and Human Rights with its biggest test to date as Big Data, Artificial Intelligence (AI) and the Internet of Things (IoT) gather the citizens of these new urban environments in an electronic embrace setting them head-to-head with the state and the "Silicons".

By 2050, it is estimated that almost 70 per cent of the world's populations will be in cities. Three million people migrate to cities every week

J. Woodier (✉)
London, UK
e-mail: james@asiacentre.co.th

A. Zingerle
Bergen, Norway
e-mail: mail@andreaszingerle.com

J. Gomez, R. Ramcharan (eds.), *Business and Human Rights in Asia*,
https://doi.org/10.1007/978-981-15-7273-9_10

and urban areas are already responsible for two-thirds of all energy use, three-quarters of all energy-related greenhouse gas emissions, and four-fifths of all economic output. These shares will obviously increase as the urban development swells (Daadler 2018).

Governments, both national and local, are searching for solutions to the effective ordering of their increasingly urban populations. With those living in cities in the developing world expected to double between 2000 and 2030, smart cities are being heralded as the most sustainable option for metropolitan development: made more efficient, cleaner, and safer by the integration of technology, increasing data generation, and centralising that data to provide better services such as transport, health care, and education.

The amount of data being collected is increasing exponentially as IoT, the interconnection via the Internet of computing devices embedded in everyday objects enabling them to send and receive data, becomes firmly established. The centralization of this data collection contributes to the creation of a constantly surveilled space in which the whereabouts and activities of citizens are monitored and relayed to the central "brain".

In this way, smart city initiatives potentially facilitate human rights abuses, particularly in countries with poor human rights standards and where data protection laws do not exist or are not enforced. If the "brain"—whatever agencies or companies it may comprise—is unaccountable or opaque, the potential for abusive uses of collected data increases. Beyond the utopian vision promoted by smart city companies and local governments, the development of smart cities has thrown up concrete challenges to the realization of privacy and human rights, from increased policing and surveillance to issues of exclusion and the reinforcement of social imbalances (Privacy International 2017: 15).

Thus AI and Big Data are helping to realise a Deleuzian surveillance state. Decoding the visions of on going smart city initiatives in East Asia and around the world can make an important contribution to highlighting the challenges of smart city life, and, begin to throw a light upon the social, political, and economic shapes that the digital world will engender as capital gathers around the few and relationships between the state, the "Silicons" and the citizen threaten to breakdown and reform, led by technological change.

While there is a growing amount of literature examining smart city issues, the number specifically addressing human rights and, in particular, the UN Guiding Principles on Business and Human Rights and how these impact the relationship between the State, the Corporates and the Citizen, is limited. That is beginning to change as surveillance-enabled smart environments, the improvement in AI and its use in analysing Big Data, and the use of facial recognition technology become largely implemented with the 4th industrial revolution begin to concern both academic researchers, civil society and activists.

To mention a few examples, concerns were recently raised by researchers from the Centre for Risk Studies at Cambridge Judge Business School about the impact on the economies of the world's largest cities of a nine percent increase in cyber attacks in 2018 (Centre for Risk Studies 2018), and The Design Friction design studio has been experimenting with participatory projects using three mitigation tactics playfulness, participativeness, and weirdness to question the directions of decision making in today's cities. They describe smart cities as a "playground to observe and discuss socio-technological controversies" (Kerspern 2018).

Finally, at the "Sharing Cities Summit 2018" in Barcelona, city representatives from around the globe had the opportunity to discuss new policies and propose actions regarding the platform economy. In a shared declaration signed by more that 40 cities committed to address the "new models of the platform economy based on collaboration and sharing, and foster an atmosphere of vibrancy, innovation and economic prosperity for citizens and cities by creating opportunities for individuals and communities to interact, support and benefit from mutual engagements in shared interests." Further they agreed to "protect citizens digital rights and ethical digital standards", and "protect basic human rights". These digital standards include the rights of privacy, security, information self-determination and neutrality, giving citizens a choice about what happens to their digital identity, who uses their data online, and for what purpose (Share Barcelona 2018).

This chapter, then, will examine the emergence of this new arena of conflict and confusion and the solutions proposed by governments and corporations by looking at "smart city" projects in the Republic of Korea (ROK). In a comparative study of three projects in the ROK, the chapter will take a critical look at the standards and practices of governments and corporations in securing a networked world. Through information collected from interviews with smart city (urban) planners, corporate, state and community, the chapter will consider the questions of the development of the smart city model and the issues it raises. These include how are smart city technologies implemented and who controls them and their data?

The chapter will examine, in the Korean context, how citizens are involved in the process, if at all, and who fights their corner, protecting their rights against the powerful interests of the state and big business. By doing so, it will begin to consider important cultural nuances, and whether citizens of the digital polis are increasingly inclined to accept the digital erosion of their basic rights. We believe this will play an important part in beginning to understand the consequences smart city citizens may face in the near future, the importance of informal socio-economic activities, citizen agency, and the emerging inadequacy of the normative principles of human rights in an increasingly illiberal world.

The Rise of Dataism, the New Techno Elite and the Smart City

Cities around the world, from Barcelona to Beijing and Singapore to San Francisco, are bandying around smart city terminology and seeking to make use of Big Data and AI, to direct traffic, control lighting and ensure the efficient disposal of waste. A 2018 report identified 355 smart city projects in 221 cities around the world, suggesting they are projects that "integrate data and insights across multiple operations and service sectors (Navigant Research 2018). Whether described as U-City (ubiquitous (computing) city), Eco-city, or Smart City, the number of projects continues to increase substantially, both in number and level of ambition.

Smartification is big business. From large multinationals to small start-ups, the corporate world wants to tap into the multi-billion dollar municipal budgets and long-term government contracts earmarked for 'smart city' development. The global smart cities market, which comprises of interrelated domains that impact urban living, is forecast to reach US$1.2 trillion by 2019. These domains include industry automation, smart grid, security, education, home and building, health care, transport, and water and waste (Chua 2018).

Led by companies like IBM, Cisco, Siemens, Dassault Systemes working with Singapore, and Alibaba in China and Malaysia, the global smart city market is moving into a period of increasing maturity as more cities embrace innovation to streamline and enhance city services and operations. As a result, smart street lighting, smart parking systems, mobility solutions, air quality monitoring, and smart waste are also becoming common deployments.

Western liberals stumble in the face of the power of big tech and its offer of the dream of efficiency, economic growth and employment. Citizens, seduced by the promise of ease and low costs, are embracing technological change. With the expansion of 'IoT', the promises of a bright, connected future with improved living standards, optimizing efficiency, sustainable development, Eco-friendliness and personal security in a 4th generation of smart cities, where "Imagination Becomes Reality" (IFEZ 2016) have grown to fever pitch.

In the new smart city, "Big Brother" is watching: In 2017, more than 127 million video surveillance cameras will be sold via professional channels. These comprise some 98 million network surveillance cameras, 28 million high-definition CCTV cameras, 4,000,000 body-worn cameras shipped to law enforcement agencies globally (Woodhouse 2017).

While Big Data is not new, the convergence of mobile telephony, always on computing and high speed Internet access means there has been an explosion in the amount. The trickle has become a torrent. Governments, companies and crooks are sifting through these terabytes with greater ease and expertise. For many, this is about scrambling to monetize their platforms, for others it is about surveillance security and control, and for some it is merely perfidy. AI, meanwhile, makes ubiquitous surveillance worthwhile, because every bit of data is potentially valuable and yet, few laws govern how data are collected and used.

Human Rights in the Era of Smart Cities

In this environment, human rights are looking increasingly frail. Globalization has changed the world we live in. It presents new and complex challenges for the protection of human rights. Economic players, especially multinational companies that operate across national borders, have gained unprecedented power and influence across the world. These companies have an increasing impact on people's lives and the communities in which they operate.

Amnesty International, for example, outlines what it describes as 'countless instances when corporations exploit weak and poorly enforced domestic regulation with devastating effect on people and communities'. The organization suggests there are few effective mechanisms at national or international level to prevent corporate human rights abuses or to hold companies to account: 'States have a responsibility to protect human rights. However, many are failing to do this, especially when it comes to company operations—whether because of lack of capacity, dependence on the company as an investor or outright corruption.'

As Tamy Guberek and Romesh Silva outline in "Human Rights and Technology", while new technology offers human rights activists with new opportunities, in the digital world there are mounting concerns around who wields power and control, and therefore the potential to abuse rights. In a world of globalized surveillance, there is a growing need 'to ensure the safety and security of activists, human rights defenders, and everyday citizens' (Guberek and Silva 2014: 1).

Even the arena for this conflict, the smart city, is notoriously hard to define. A World Bank urban planning strategy paper issued in July 2010, announced that it was rethinking its approach to urbanism, identifying it as a defining phenomenon of the twenty-first century. With the importance of urbanization as a powerful force in support of economic growth and poverty reduction, and the fact the developing world is where this demographic transformation is taking place, the Bank emphasized important questions about the process of managing urbanization and delivery mechanisms for urban development assistance (The World Bank 2010).

The European Commission defines smart cities as a place where: 'digital technologies translate into better public services for citizens, better use of resources and less impact on the environment' (European Commission 2013). The British Department for Business Innovation and Skills, meanwhile, describes smart city solutions as 'applying digital technologies to address social, environmental and economic goals' (BIS 2013).

While the Korean government's definition is similar the essence in Korea and across East Asia, is different. A recent study sponsored by chip maker Intel, highlighted the issue, emphasizing that North American and West European cities were more advanced in terms of transparency as well as their openness in adopting processes that rely on inter-city best practices and learnings. This means that information regarding smart city projects and cities' overall vision is far more readily available; meanwhile, these cities actively seek expertise from a wide range of actors, including third party entities and citizens themselves. Cities in East Asia and China on the other hand, are 'more opaque' in terms of their approach (Juniper Research 2018).

The manipulation of the U-City concept, however, proved useful as an attractive solution at a time of global crisis to create a "U-Eco-City in a box". This was especially true for the developing countries mindful of the climate change agenda and related financial-aid conditions, but looking to build new developments. It was an idea South Korea decided to own with a focus not only on the development of smart cities in Korea, but the idea of exporting the smart city as a "flat pack" option, with Korean companies doing the assembly. The K-city has become an important part of the Korean government's export drive and in synch with Korea's desire to be seen as the world's most connected and "smart" country.

The Korean Context, Songdo, Sejong Busan: A Brief History of Ubiquitous Korea

The Korean government initiated several projects to promote IT use in Korea. The first project started in 1984, the National Basic Information System (NIS) which generated a supply-push to the industry. This was followed in 1994, by the second Korean National Information Infrastructure (NII) project aimed at building a governmental and public information network and to develop core software technology. Through these initiatives the government wanted to ensure its competitiveness, still both projects faced financial setbacks (Shin 2009). From 1999–2001, the third NII project "Cyber Korea 21" focused on fostering a knowledge-based economy through quality of life improvements for the general public, establishing an e-commerce system in traditional industries (steel, shipbuilding, etc.), and an electronic document distribution system for administrative bodies.

Since the IT839 strategy was initiated in 2004, government, industry and policy makers have focused on ICT-based, ubiquitous computing environments such as connected homes and ubiquitous cities (u-cities), linking virtually everything to a nationwide ubiquitous grid through wireless network and radio frequency identification (RFID) technology. The stated goal is to create smart cities and a ubiquitous society, always connected through the IoT to ensure a more secure, humane and environmental lifestyle (MIC 2006). These plans have been more about the technological design implementation (Shin 2007), and less about organizational, policy and management decisions in deploying a u-city and the likely fundamental changes of social and cultural milieu (Kim et al. 2009).

In 2006, the non-profit organization "Korea U-city Forum" was formed to foster the u-city proliferation project as a Korea's future economic growth strategy. Membership is dominated by the powerful high-tech *chaebol* industries (KT, SKT, Samsung Data Systems), government agencies (NCA, MIC and MCT), and city developers. In a u-Korea masterplan infrastructure standards have been defined and administrative and procedural framework designed to make Korea the world's first ubiquitous nation (Jeong and King 1996). For this the forum was heralding a futuristic society and u-city services for societal and citizens' needs. Further goals included better communication between the government and the private sector as well as establishing ubiquitous Korea (U-Korea) as a "test bed" for world-class domestic and international companies. The forum produced detailed plans for the implementation of RFID and ubiquitous sensor networks but notably completely neglected discussion on possible social issues and cultural problems (Larson and Park 2014).

In 2008, a major step towards a u-society was done with the "Act on Ubiquitous City Construction" (MCT 2006). This was the first specific legislation to be passed in any country to enable the smart city. The act defines a u-city as 'a city in which ubiquitous based services are offered at any time and in any place in urban spaces by realizing high-tech IT, construction, and traffic application technologies to enhance urban life quality and city competitiveness.'

Since 2008, the Korean government has invested heavily on smart city development. As the country has tried to position itself as a leading smart economy, national expenditure by the central government on smart city research and development has totalled at least USD120 million. The policy has formed the latest element in a thirty-year housing policy aimed at reducing the historical housing shortage and improving the quality of dwellings (OECD 2018).

Since the turn of the century, each administration has unveiled its "smart city" policies. Given the current President Moon Jae-in's emphasis on job creation, it was not long after his election that his administration was talking about its K-city projects. During his presidential campaign, Moon promised to expand smart cities into a future growth engine in response to the Fourth Industrial Revolution, and in the autumn of 2017, the government said it would move ahead with a 'Smart City New Deal' project which would provide financing for cities chosen by a contest to test bed new smart city technologies (Herh 2017).

In January 2018, the Korean government again underlined its commitment to creating a ubiquitous nation situated in smart cities, releasing an 'innovative growth' report, unveiling new policies to promote technological development around 13 sectors clustered into four main groups: Intelligent Infrastructure, including big data, AI, and 5G and the Internet of Things, Smart Transportation which includes drones and self-driving vehicles, Combined Services, which includes the smart city, and Industrial Foundation, which includes intelligent semi-conductors, advanced materials, innovative medicine, and new and renewable energy.

Korea's first official smart city, The Songdo IBD, was announced in 2002, as part of former President Lee Myung-bak's effort to promote green and low-carbon growth as an avenue for future development after 60 years of reliance on export-oriented manufacturing. Still promoted as a model of Korean smart city development, closer investigation indicates being smart can be more about hype than reality.

Songdo as Demo City

Songdo is part of the Incheon Free Economic Zone (IFEZ). Situated close to Incheon International Airport, the intention was to create a new hub for the North-East Asian regional economy to compete with established international financial centres in the region, such as Singapore and Hong Kong (Mullins 2017: 6).

Songdo was designed and built by U.S. developers, Gale International. It was heralded as the first truly smart city, a car-free world, with 40 per cent green space and dozens of kilometres of cycling routes. Technology is ubiquitous. It was Korea's opportunity to showcase its "smart city in a box" export drive. Songdo even promised to get rid of dustbin men. Rubbish is pneumatically "sucked out" of houses and recycled to generate electricity.

The city is managed by the Incheon Free Economic Zone authority (IFEZA), a government authority but privately-owned and funded—Gale International owns 60 percent of the project, Korea's steel company POSCO owns 30 percent, and Morgan Stanley real Estate owns 9 percent. What neither the Korean government nor these private companies reckoned with was the global financial crisis which coincided with the initial opening in 2008. As damaged western companies retreated from Asia, Songdo was built but nobody came.

The owners went back to the drawing board and it was decided to try to market the new city to Korean companies and Korean residents as a salve to ease the congestion in the capital Seoul—the dominant urban centre in the country. American smart city company Cisco became a key provider of smart solutions in Songdo. In 2011, alongside Gale, Posco and Korean technology giant LG, Cisco created u.Life Solutions, to deliver smart services to businesses and residents in Songdo. In addition, Cisco products and technologies were integrated into new construction projects in Songdo and it became a global showcase for the company's Smart+Connected Communities technology solutions (CISCO 2011).

A smart city dream built within 25 miles of Seoul. It was to be the antithesis of the suffocating, overpopulated capital: a new way of living for more than 300,000 residents, spread out over 600 hectares of reclaimed land from the Yellow Sea. But the reality is somewhat different. While official figures are hard to come by, reports suggest that more than a decade on from its inception the city is less than a quarter full, with just 70,000 residents. It's an odd mixture of wasteland intermingled with random large-scale development. People aren't coming and neither are businesses—fewer than 50 big brands have bothered (White 2018).

Because it is expensive to live there and public transport is generally inconvenient—a two-hour connection to central Seoul—many of the Koreans who work in the few local companies that moved some of their operations to Songdo, commute by car from Seoul. This has clogged the roads forcing a rethink and redevelopment which is widening the roads and cutting room for those cycle paths. The rubbish system also has teething problems. Only Songdo residents get a key to the smart trash bins, the commuters just dump their rubbish by the side of the road, causing unsightly mounds of trash. Promoted as the answer to the ills of modern-day living in Seoul, the development is 'overdue, overpriced and under populated…[with a] a Chernobyl-like emptiness' (White 2018).

What is important in the context of this study is that the top-down driven focus on technology meant the city's social dimensions were ignored, and the 'inherent inflexibility of a closed-system approach meant [it] was not sufficiently resilient to shocks…[unable] to cope with the complexity and dissonance that occurs in relation to the "glocal" challenges of today' (Mullins 2017: 4).

Sejong the New Capital

Songdo's top-down design is very representative of the development approach being taken in Korea. The Special Autonomous City of Sejong, billed as Korea's new administrative centre, began as a 2002 campaign pledge from future president Roh Moo-hyun, who wanted to win voters in a critical swing region and promised to relocate the capital entirely. It still represents a controversial idea to redistribute power, authority and urban development away from the dominance of Seoul metropolitan area, one of the largest in the world with more than 25 million people, more than half the country's population and half of its businesses.

When the project was officially opened in 2012, under a new, right-wing administration, then President Lee Myung Bak did not attend the ceremony and court action hampered the original plan to move all the country's administration to the new city. To this day, however, despite continuing political wrangling, the intention remains to build an alternative centre to Seoul, with ongoing plans to relocate almost 40 ministries and agencies to the city, as well as building apartments for a population of 500,000 by 2030, on what was farm land (Harlan 2012).

Sejong, in central Chungcheong Province, has become another test bed for the Korean government's smart city projects. The latest was identified in late 2017. A new 274.1 million-square-meter, greenfield development selected by the new Moon administration to build an IoT ready city from the ground up, so from smart transport to a social credit system (Green Bean), the new development would be an ideal platform for future technology.

The new administration's 'Presidential Committee on the Fourth Industrial Revolution' announced more details in early 2018, naming selected districts in Sejong and the southern port city of Busan as places to apply innovative technologies, including autonomous driving, AI, smart energy management and virtual reality, in order to make them world-renowned smart cities by 2023. The committee designated the district named Yeondong-myeon in Sejong, to be developed as a smart city focusing on energy and transportation (Song 2018).

Sejong itself, when it was first designed, with its decentralized urban structure and ring-shaped development area was heralded as a symbol of the ideology of democracy and balanced national development. But despite the government providing various incentives such as preferential rights for house purchases for government officials and employees of state-owned research institutes slated to move to Sejong City, many people still prefer to live in Seoul and, if forced to work in Sejong, commute.

As a result of the lack of a residential population, many problems remain including:

> a lack of infrastructure (e.g., schools, stores, and cultural facilities); some inefficiency arising from the separation of some administrative functions from organizations based in Seoul; the latent opposition of residents in the capital to moving central administrative agencies; and the recurring controversy over the issue of relocating each new administrative agency. (Kwon 2015)

In 2017, the population of Sejong was reported to have reached the 250,000 mark, with 40 central government agencies and 15 state-run research institutes based in the city (Korean Economic Daily 2012). It is now marketed as "the city of children and women", the perfect place to raise a family (Lee 2017), and was feted recently for having the highest birth rate in Korea, of 1.67 children per family, more than double that of Seoul (KBS 2018).

Busan U+IoT Convergence Test Project (Smart Citizens Inclusive)

Busan, the other city on the Presidential Committee's list, is the second largest city in South Korea with a population of 3.6 million. Bounded by sea on one side and hills on the other, the city is being hampered in its growth by lack of space and is struggling with congestion problems. In 2015, it became the location for the Global Smart City Test Bed project, an IoT-based project organized by Korean Ministry of Science, ICT, and Future Planning, Busan Metropolitan Government and Korean utility giant, SK Telecom.

The purpose of the project was to respond to various urban problems (environment, energy saving, traffic) by using the latest ICT and environmentally-friendly technologies. The smart city test bed would share and analyze data created from sensors and CCTVs installed in various urban facilities through the Internet, and provide new information technologies in various fields including energy, traffic, and building management, for the purpose of improving quality of life in the city.

The project was built around an IoT-based smart city platform. This was an open platform through which all data created from sensors within the smart city can be collected and shared, to provide urban services focused on citizens' experience, to improve the city's competitiveness and, as the promotional materials explained, support globalization and global competitiveness by cooperating with other cities in South Korea and other smart cities around the world.

Building on a total investment of USD 320 million, what was initially known as Busan Green "u-City" planned to combine ICT infrastructure, technology, and services into housing (home automation), economic, transportation, tourism, safety and security, environmental, and other city infrastructures and systems to create an intelligent management system that delivers better urban services to increase economic growth and improve quality of life: 'Green u-City, on the other hand, takes into account green-growth initiatives not only for achieving intelligent city management, but also for realizing social inclusion and environmental sustainability' (ESCI-KSP 2016).

This appears to be one of the first smart city projects in Korea that actively engaged the community in the planning of the urban space. Living labs encouraged citizens to come to give their opinions, along with subject experts, public officials and representatives from the private sector. Indeed the project included surveying Busan's citizens to ask which smart services they wanted.

Test bed completed, the local government decided it would not continue to the next stage of introducing the new smart technologies around the city. The costs of continuing the project, installing and maintain the sensors, in particular, were deemed too burdensome on the city budget. The results of the focus group study have not been made public, and it is still uncertain whether any of their suggestions will be included in the new Presidential Committee's "Eco Delta" smart city project.

The new project—a greenfield development, this time—comprises a 219.4 million-square-meter area near Busan's Gimhae. Eco Delta is to be developed with a focus on global logistics, to maintain its port city image, and the development will be overseen by six government branches, including the Ministry of Land, Infrastructure and Transport, Ministry of Strategy and Finance and the Ministry of Science and ICT.

Like the new Sejong project, the Presidential Committee says Eco Delta is to be "human-centered". Smart homes will be provided with everything from emergency warnings to information regarding the weather and fine dust, and intelligent transport systems to reduce commuting times, in line with President Moon belief that smart cities should allow people to experience the fourth industrial revolution, an economic mantra of the Moon government (Song 2018).

Comparing the new programme to previous state-run development projects where decisions were unilaterally made by the government and led by public institutions, the committee vowed to lead the upcoming projects based on "open expandability" that will encourage the private sector to take part in realizing smart services. It also urges the participation of the public which from the example of Busan's Living Labs, but even if we are to accept input from the public will be influential, there are few civic groups in this arena to organize citizen participation into meaningful interest groups leaving these developments in the hands of the state and big business.

Who Fights Their Corner?

South Korea is not without its local and civil society actors. The growth of civil society has benefitted from developments such as the Asian financial crisis of 1997–1998, increasing regional inequalities, declining level of trust in the central government and after the impact of democratization. The holding of local elections and increasing local autonomy under the strong central government has also strengthened these groups, and there has been a diversification, professionalization, and institutionalization of civil society activities (Bae and Kim 2012: 279).

Indeed, Korea remains a beacon of democratic process in the region and, in 2017, managed to impeach and replace a president without anybody being killed. The country, however, was ranked 51st in the world by Transparency International in its recent Corruption Perceptions Index—behind Japan at 20th and the US at 16th and near the bottom among members of the OECD, a club of mostly rich nations (Transparency International 2018). This underlines, the fact that that despite the democratic progress in the country, South Korea remains locked in a culturally corrupt, techno-Confucian, top-down governance process, with a relatively compliant population, hardwired to conformity and with a focus on the family rather than on community. Local voices from below have been largely 'rejected or ignored because decentralization literally meant sharing power with local and civil society and thus shrinkage of the central government's power' (Bae and Kim 2012: 279).

The OECD notes that, in the face of housing affordability challenges, Korea's smart city policy is still promoted as being a part of a housing policy aimed at creating a more inclusive society. Korea is linking housing and urban regeneration strategies to respond to the complex challenges of social inclusion, job creation, housing and economic revitalization, and hopes smart city development will be the vehicle for inclusive growth (OECD 2018).

There is little obvious evidence that the state's top down governance will change in the near future, and while some Big Tech have been active in protecting user's privacy against state intervention, at least one smart city company does not see it as its business to watch the watchers. In a recent interview, when asked about two smart city projects the company was involved in in China, and questioned about selling gear that helps the government collect more data that could be used for government surveillance, Cisco's CEO Chuck Robbins' answer: '"The data are theirs," he says flatly. "I can't control what policies people have or what they do. They own it, we don't"' (Waters and Thornhill 2018).

Conclusion: Big Brother Watch

In the year that marks the 70th anniversary of the Universal Declaration of Human Rights, the UN has issued a clear warning that civil society and the people who defend it around the region, are under attack (Gilmour 2018). In the East Asia's smart city, these rights are looking increasingly flimsy in the face of the illiberal state and global corporations which, by their very nature (quarterly reporting, publicly-listed entities), are focused on shareholder value not citizens' rights. There is little to be found in the top-down Korean state that offers anything but a pessimistic view for the urban digital future, proving only the emerging inadequacy of the normative principles of human rights.

Korea is setting itself up as a showroom for smart city technology, inviting best practice from corporates around the world as it looks for solutions not only to urban problems and the dominance of Seoul, but also to national economic development. K-city exports are another broadside from the k-wave, cultural *hallyu* world, and the country remains a leader in the field with its ambitious and nation-wide initiatives (Lee et al. 2008).

There are suggestions smart cities should be a driver of change in urban planning participation processes, which provides an opportunity for establishing a true e-democracy (Rotondo 2012). Korea's top down development approach, however, not only threatens to increase social polarisation and urban segregation, but the lack of public participation which could help make these cities more resilient and regenerate local economies from the bottom up, threatens to leave them as creative wastelands. In the developing country context these sorts of projects are even more likely to be subject to political influence and corruption (Yigitcanlar and Lee 2013: 111).

In these electronic ghettos, commoditized life reaches its apotheosis. Here every moment is connected. For corporates it is a sales dream of constant customer touch points and data streams just waiting to be monetized. For the state it is a unique opportunity for surveillance and control, and human rights look set to be brushed aside by both the state and the Silicons. In the smart city, access is everything. As Deleuze points out, modern control societies are all about the password (Galič et al. 2016).

Citizens in a post 9/11 world have willingly begun to surrender their rights in exchange for a promise of safety and security in an increasingly illiberal world. We hold out little hope that governments, ever more bent on control, will champion human rights and hold big business to account. Who will champion our privacy in IoT-monitored smart city spaces in an urban future that increasingly look like life in Singapore and China. In these smart cities, the state controls and business complies.

These issues involved a qualitative judgment on the power of the state, its nature and the decisions it takes. The only solution is the rule of law, multi-agency safeguarding, effective judiciary prepared to effect adequate sanction. In addition, a strong civil society and an independent media are needed to ensure power is held to account. In Korea, many of these institutions are still not robust enough and, with the growing confidence of illiberal states, there is a very clear threat to the UN Guiding Principles on Business and Human Rights and to government accountability as public-partnerships are forged at the expense of citizen rights.

References

Amnesty International. *Corporations.* https://www.amnesty.org/en/what-we-do/corporate-accountability/.

Bae Yoo-il, and Kim Sun-hyuk. 2012. Civil society and local activism in South Korea's local democratization. *Democratization* 20 (2): 260–286. http://ink.library.smu.edu.sg/soss_research/105.

Centre for Risk Studies. 2018. GDP@Risk. *Global Risk Index 2019.* Cambridge Judge Business School. https://www.jbs.cam.ac.uk/faculty-research/centres/risk/publications/multi-threat/global-risk-index-2019/.

Chua Kong Ho. 2018. Alibaba's next moon shot is to make cities adapt to their human inhabitants, technology seer says. *South China Morning Post* 17 (12). http://www.scmp.com/tech/innovation/article/2123856/alibabas-tech-seer-sees-making-cities-adapt-their-inhabitants-next.

Cisco. 2011. Cisco and New Songdo International City Join Forces to Create One of the Most Technologically Advanced Smart Connected Communities. *Press Release* 6 (8). https://newsroom.cisco.com/press-release-content?articleId=426592.

Daadler, Ivo. 2018. The battle for liberal democracy will be waged in cities. *Ft.com* 6 (7). https://www.ft.com/content/f6422018-68a5-11e8-b6eb-4acfcfb08c11?ftcamp=crm/email/_2018___06___20180606__/emailalerts/Keyword_alert/product.

Department for Business. 2013. Innovation and Skills, The Smart City Market: Opportunities for the UK. *BIS Research Paper No. 136* (10). http://bluegreenuk.com/references/government_institutional/bis-research-paper-smart-city-market-opportunties-uk.pdf.

ESCI-KSP. 2016. Busan u-City and Haeundae Smart City Test-bed. *Smart Grids* 29 (11). https://esci-ksp.org/project/busan-u-city-and-haeundae-smart-city-test-bed/.

European Commission. 2013. Smart Cities. *Digital Single Market Policy* 14 (10). https://ec.europa.eu/digital-single-market/smart-cities.

Galič, M., Tjerk Timan and Bert-Jaap Koops. 2016. *Bentham, Deleuze and Beyond: An Overview of Surveillance Theories from the Panopticon to Participation* 13 (5). https://link.springer.com/content/pdf/10.1007/s13347-016-0219-1.pdf.

Gilmour, Andrew. 2018. Imprisoned, threatened, silenced: human rights workers across Asia are in danger. *The Guardian* 18 (5). https://www.theguardian.com/commentisfree/2018/may/18/imprisoned-threatened-silenced-human-rights-workers-across-asia-are-in-danger.

Guberek, T. and Romesh Silva. 2014. Human Rights and Technology: Mapping the Landscape to Support Grantmaking. *Prima*, (9). https://www.fordfoundation.org/media/2541/prima-hr-tech-report.pdf.

Harlan, Chico. 2012. With New Sejong City, South Korean Government aims to rebalance power. *Washington Post* 17 (9). https://www.washingtonpost.com/world/asia_pacific/with-new-sejong-city-south-korean-government-aims-to-rebalance-power/2012/08/17/e8f6dc60-e2bd-11e1-a25e-15067bb31849_story.html?noredirect=on&utm_term=.6082886701f8.

Herh, Michael. 2017. Korean Gov't to Accelerate Construction of Big Data-Based Smart City. *Business Korea*, 31 (10). http://www.businesskorea.co.kr/news/articleView.html?idxno=19682.

Jeong, K.H. and John L. King. 1996. National information infrastructure initiatives in Korea: Vision and policy issues. *Information Infrastructure and Policy* 5: 119–134.

Juniper Research. 2018. Smart Cities – What's in it for Citizens? *Intel Newsroom* 11 (3). https://newsroom.intel.com/wp-content/uploads/sites/11/2018/03/smart-cities-whats-in-it-for-citizens.pdf.

KBS. 2018. Sejong City's Birthrate Highest in S. Korea at 1.67. 4 (3). http://world.kbs.co.kr/english/news/news_Dm_detail.htm?No=134393.

Kerspern, Bastien. 2018. Critical and Playful mitigation: Tackling smart city controversies with fictions and games. L. Kronman, & A. Zingerle (Eds.). *The Internet of other people's things*. KairUs publication.

Kim, Yeon-mee, Kim Hyng-soo, Moon Soo-young and Bae So-yoen. 2009. Ubiquitous eco-city planning in Korea. A project for the realization of ecological city planning and ubiquitous network society. *Real Corp Proceedings* 22–25 (4). https://www.corp.at/archive/CORP2009_174.pdf.

Korean Economic Daily. 2012. Sejong City Populations Surpasses 250,000 in 56 months 22 (2). http://english.hankyung.com/economy/2017/02/22/1151201/sejong-city-population-surpasses-250000-in-56-months.

Kwon Young-sang. 2015. Sejong Si (City): are TOD and TND models effective in planning Korea's new capital? *Cities* (42): 242–257.

Larson, J.F. and Park Jae-min. 2014. From developmental to network state: Government restructuring and ICT-led innovation in Korea. *Telecommunications Policy* 38 (4): 344–359.

Lee Choon-hee. 2017. Sustainable Development Strategies of the city of Sejong. *Asia Pacific Cities Summit*, Daejeon, ROK. http://online.apcsummit2017.org/pre_file/PS0301.pdf.

Lee, Sang-Heon, Tan Yigitcanlar, Han Jung-hoon and Leem Youn-taik. 2008. Ubiquitous urban infrastructure: Infrastructure planning and development in Korea. *Innovation: Management, Policy and Practice* 10 (2/3): 282–292.

Lee Young-geun. 2016. *IFEZ Journal 71* (09/10) Public Relations Division, Incheon Free Economic Zone Authority Sep./Oct.

MIC. 2006. *u-Korea Master Plan*. Korean Ministry of Information and Communication (5).

MCT. 2006. *Ubiquitous city and infrastructure planning*. Ministry of Construction and Transportation.

Mullins, Paul D. 2017. The Ubiquitous-Eco-City of Songdo: An Urban Systems Perspective on South Korea's Green City Approach. *Urban Planning* 2 (2): 4–12.

Navigant Research. 2018. Smart City Tracker 1Q18: Global Smart City Projects by World Region. *Market Segment, Technology, and Application*. https://www.navigantresearch.com/research/smart-city-tracker-1q18.

OECD. 2018. *Housing Dynamics in Korea: Building inclusive and smart cities*. OECD Publishing. https://doi.org/10.1787/9789264298880-en.

Privacy International. 2017. *Smart Cities: Utopian Vision, Dystopian Reality, Privacy International* (10). https://privacyinternational.org/report/638/smart-cities-utopian-vision-dystopian-reality.

Rotondo, Francesco. 2012. The u-city-paradigm. *Future Internet* 4 (1): 563–574.

Share Barcelona. 2018. Common Declaration of principles and commitments for Sharing Cities. *Sharing Cities Summit*. http://www.share.barcelona/declaration/.

Shin Dong-hee. 2007. A critique of Korean National Information Strategy: Case of national information infrastructures. *Government Information Quarterly* 24 (3): 624–645.

Shin Dong-hee. 2009. Ubiquitous city: Urban technologies, urban infrastructure and urban informatics. *Journal of Information Science* 35 (5): 515–526.

Song Su-hyun. 2018. S. Korea to turn Sejong, Busan into safe, smart cities by 2023. *Korea Herald* 29 (1). http://www.koreaherald.com/view.php?ud=20180129000793

The World Bank. 2010. *Finance, Economics, and Urban Department, Sustainable Development Network, Systems of Cities: Harnessing Urbanisation for Growth and Poverty Alleviation* (8) http://siteresources.worldbank.org/INTURBANDEVELOPMENT/Resources/336387-1269651121606/FullStrategy.pdf.

Transparency International. 2018. *Corruption Perceptions Index 2017* 21 (2). https://www.transparency.org/news/feature/corruption_perceptions_index_2017.

White, Chris. 2018. South Korea's 'Smart City' Songdo: Not Quite Smart Enough. *SCMP.com* 25 (3). http://www.scmp.com/week-asia/business/article/2137838/south-koreas-smart-city-songdo-not-quite-smart-enough.

Waters, R. and John Thornhill. 2018. Cisco's Chuck Robbins: delivering on a back-to-basics promise. *FT.com* 11 (7). https://www.ft.com/content/7431b4f8-600d-11e8-ad91-e01af256df68?ftcamp=crm/email/_2018___06___20180610__/emailalerts/Keyword_alert/product.

Woodhouse, Josh. 2017. Tape and disk storage present viable long-term video surveillance storage options. *IHSMarkit.com* 20 (7). https://ihsmarkit.com/research-analysis/tape-and-disk-storage-present-viable-long-term-video-surveillance-storage.html.

Yigitcanlar, T. and Lee Sang-ho. 2013. Korean ubiquitous-eco-city: A smart-sustainable urban form or a branding hoax? *Technological Forecasting & Social Change* 30 (9). https://www.sciencedirect.com/science/article/pii/S0040162513002199.

CHAPTER 11

Towards an Empirical Understanding of Ethical Consumption in Southeast Asia

Daniel Polomski, Emily Klukas, and Matthew Mullen

Introduction

There is no consensus and a limited empirical basis for understanding the potential role of consumers as vehicles of change in Southeast Asia. Is ethical consumption a silver bullet? Is it a myth? This study is a search for apt questions and methodologies. A series of semi-structured interviews with eight key informants around the region, as well as a literature review, highlighted the need to move beyond theory and pursue an empirical understanding of ethical consumption in Southeast Asia. To this end, we discuss the limits of trying to understand ethical consumption independent of dynamics like state regulations, industry standards or the role of civil society. Conversely, there is the risk of a business and human rights lens that fails to adequately capture how consumers fit into the business ecosystem. An apt research agenda, thus, pursues empirical data-points through an

D. Polomski (✉) • E. Klukas
Bangkok, Thailand
e-mail: james@asiacentre.co.th

M. Mullen
Lincoln, NE, USA

J. Gomez, R. Ramcharan (eds.), *Business and Human Rights in Asia*,
https://doi.org/10.1007/978-981-15-7273-9_11

ecological systems lens which places ethical consumption within a field of interconnecting state, market and civil forces. Such an approach could lead to a more complete discourse around headlining issues like the slave trade and human trafficking in the region.

Throughout 2014 and 2015 the *Guardian* ran a series of articles and videos under the headlines 'Supermarket Slave Trade' and 'Slavery in Thai fishing industry', sparking consumer boycotts and demonstrations principally in Europe and North America. Consumer networks rallied governments and companies to demand an overhaul of the Thai Seafood Sector. The threat of sanctions, yellow and red-cards, and the withdrawal of contracts compelled commitments to reform, the effectiveness of which remains unclear. Viewing ethical consumption—or values-driven purchasing—through these series of events raises a range of pertinent questions about ethical consumption in general. Why did consumers decide to target this issue at that moment over any number of other injustices? How did consumers decide where to channel their discontent? Do these kinds of consumer backlashes actually tackle the root cause of the problem and lead to sustainable improvements for target beneficiaries? These meta-questions certainly deserve attention. But the Thai Seafood case lends itself to even more fundamental questions about ethical consumption in Southeast Asia.

Media outlets effectively captured a scene of consumers in Europe and North America who were outraged and unwilling to tolerate or contribute to the injustices underway in the Thai Seafood Sector. Did they overlook the response of consumers in Thailand and Southeast Asia more broadly? Was the regional movement somehow less familiar or recognizable? Is ethical consumption even 'a thing' in Southeast Asia? If so, what is unique about ethical consumption in Southeast Asia? Or were consumers in Southeast Asia less willing or able to mount a movement against these kinds of injustices in the region? Perhaps there is limited awareness or means that prevent consumers from mounting a response. Perhaps ethical consumption has yet to gain momentum in Southeast Asia. Or is there something more fundamental at play around the intersection of authoritarianism, capitalism and cultural violence?

These are questions of crucial importance to business and human rights in Southeast Asia as both states and business entities are staked to the economy (and ultimately the consumer), to one degree or another. Consumers have power in regard to sales. While many people connect ethical consumption to Western countries, the existence of Halal, Kosher and Vegetarian food offerings represent a long-held consumer behavior tied to ethical consideration across many cultures. Why are companies in Australia producing Halal products? Because a lot of people buy them and a lot of people *won't* buy non-Halal. Consumers in this instance are going beyond price, quality and material concerns making purchasing decisions based on values—social, environmental and moral concerns.

Our contention is that we need to understand how consumers fit into the business ecosystem. Focusing on any one level, stakeholder, or dynamic leaves far too many variables and viewpoints unaccounted for. For instance, one could point to the Protect, Respect, Remedy framework and position the state as the key unit to catalyze ethical consumption, but this assumes a certain legitimacy and authority in markets and consumption that may be illusionary in Southeast Asia. Alternatively, using an ecological systems lens attempts to account for the collective interactions between personality, culture, capabilities, community, institutions, legislation, legitimacy, markets, the media, civil society, regional bodies and international bodies.

Methodological Approach

As this study is meant to serve as a starting point for a collaborative series of precise, empirical research aimed to influence strategy and action, the study was designed as a qualitative study using a simplified version of Bengtsson's work as a starting point (Bengtsson 2016). The study team took an informal approach and conducted online interviews with experts in the region. Eight people were contacted via email with a standard series of questions regarding ethical consumption in Southeast Asia. The key informants provided responses representing Indonesia, Singapore, Thailand, Vietnam, and in the case of Véronique Salze-Lozac'h a wider angle on Southeast Asia. For a complete list of those who contributed to this process, please see the acknowledgements section. We did not require everyone to complete all questions, rather accepted comments in any format, including one skype discussion.

The following sections summarize our approach and initial findings based on these interviews and literature review. We then present a proposed research agenda to filling the empirical gaps in knowledge, based on ecological systems theory, needed to build a strategy that incorporates ethical consumption into the reality of state and business practices and responsibilities, hence identifying key questions for future research. This study is meant to be a catalyst for collaborative conversation and research to understand if and how ethical consumption has a role in the business-state ecosystem realities in ASEAN.

Ethical Consumption: An Ecological Lens

Respondent 4 (R.4) provides a useful working frame of ethical consumption:

> *Depending on the 'ethic' of the buyer, ethical consumption is the act of buying a product or service that is environmentally friendly, that is free of animal cruelty, respectful of human rights (no child labor, good labor conditions in the production and distribution line, etc.) and with a fair retribution of all actors in the value chain.*

Ethical consumption may manifest at the level of the individual consumer, but one can see in R.4's quote an entire ecosystem in motion. Bronfenbrenner's social ecological model offers perhaps the most practicable view to illustrate this (see Fig. 11.1). One can begin by looking at the individual. Pending that they have the awareness and means, which is a premise to investigate rather than presume, each individual has the power to choose what they consume and can thus directly impact sales if there is diversity in the marketplace and an adequate level of information. In a sense, there are ethics involved in every transaction. Even when consumers do not intend to 'be ethical' they have an impact on peoples' lives and the environment. One of the core questions at the individual level is who or what determines the legitimacy of a certain ethic. Is 'ethical' consumption in the eye of the beholder? At a purely individual level, this may be the case. But other forces in the ecosystem provide varying measures of what constitutes an ethical act.

Moving out from the individual, the focus moves to the microsystem. These are the people and institutions that most directly influence a person. At this level, one can begin to explore how household dynamics and belief systems may impact ethical consumption. The mesosystem focuses more on community influences than the individual or immediate influences. At the mesosystem, one can see ethical consumption as something that is at least partially the product of local customs, cultures, identities and signaling.

In the microsystem and mesosystem, the individual is an active agent with direct influence over that particular ecological level. When moving to

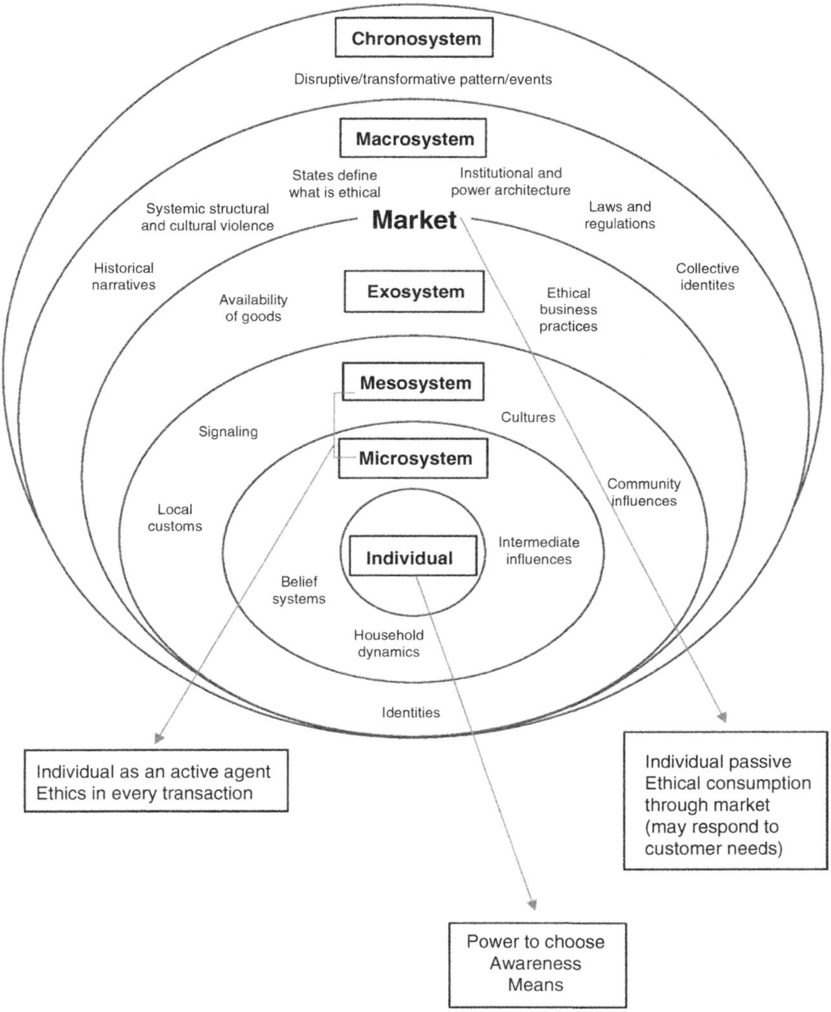

Fig. 11.1 Applying Bronfenbrenner's ecological systems theory to ethical consumption in Southeast

the exosystem, the individual is in more of a passive position. For ethical consumption, one could interpret the exosystem as the market. How available are ethically made goods and resources? After all, as a key informant captures below, save for a blanket boycott scenario like vegetarianism, ethical consumption requires ethical production. In this sense, ethical consumption can be seen as a phenomenon that occurs through rather than to markets. Put another way, ethical consumption can be seen as inextricably linked to ethical business practices.

The market could also be seen as part macrosystem, which refers to the institutional and power architecture that overlays an ecosystem. Markets may respond to consumers, but states legislate what is ethical and acceptable in societies as a whole. Whether this reflects reality or not is another question. Indeed, one hypothesis could be that ethical consumption rarely has a human rights orientation in Southeast Asia because governments in the region do not offer an enabling environment. Nonetheless, viewing ethical consumption as part of macrosystems, the focus goes to laws, regulations, narratives of history and collective identity, and systemic structural and cultural violence. Here, ethical consumption could be seen as something that taps into a defined or relatively defined system of ethics. Finally, the chronosystem refers to patterns or events that may shift the entire environment. A new set of global norms or a new trend may transform the way in which individuals and collectives understand and practice ethical consumption. Thinking in terms of chronosystem, it is possible to see ethical consumption as fluid, something that is constantly redefined as circumstances change.

An ecological lens of ethical consumption provides a useful way of mapping the phenomenon that is ethical consumption. However, there remains ambiguity as to whether it is possible to demarcate what makes consumption ethical. One could argue that ethical consumption is endlessly individual and subjective. However, if we consider an ecological systems lens, we can see many regulatory and normative structures that inform or qualify consumption as ethical or otherwise. A good example of this is the UN Guiding Principles on Business and Human Rights, which provide one definitive framework against which to measure.

The Literature on Ethical Consumption

The UN's Sustainable Development Goals (SDGs) are a universal call to action to guide the fast-paced change of the world onto a more prosperous and sustainable path. Along this path, international frameworks mostly focus their attention on the duties and responsibilities of states and businesses, as we describe above. However, SDG 12 on responsible consumption and protection touches upon ethical consumption, broadening the focus to include the individual and acknowledging the agenda-setting potential of consumers through ethical consumption. The SDGs demarcate ethical consumption as a worthy pursuit with mainstream potential.

Searching for a historical understanding of ethical consumption, one sees an act or practice that has contributed in one way or another to notable shifts. Consumers took a stand against slavery through the purchase anti-slavery sugar and other products. The 'White Label' movement took shape in protest to sweatshops. Gandhi led a boycott under the tag of 'buy Indian' to confront British imperialism and colonialism more broadly. More recently, consumers have taken stands against predatory multinationals, free-trade agreements, blood-diamonds, environmental harm, human trafficking and exploitation in a general sense. For instance, in 2003 Thai consumers boycotted Nestlé for making genetically modified products (Racela 2012). Whether taking a stand for 'fair-trade,' 'responsible business,' or another imperative or against harmful, predatory production, ethical consumption "...is a convenient catch-all for a range of tendencies within contemporary consumer culture today" (Lewis and Potter 2011: 4). While ethical consumption is generally a discourse that evokes altruism, it is not without cynics and critical questions.

In a chapter entitled, *What's wrong with ethical consumption?*' Jo Littler (2011) offers a useful summation of popular cynical views of ethical consumption:

> ...ethical consumption is ultimately ineffective because it is merely used by a minority as a panacea for middle-class guilt; that it is an individualistic form of politics, a means through which neoliberal governments encourage consumers to become 'responsibilised' amidst the atrophying of wider social safety nets; that it is produced primarily through the whitewashing and profit-seeking actions of corporations and as such can have little radical purchase; and that it is, in itself, a fractured field of often dissociated and contradictory practices, or simply too large a category to be meaningful.

Such critiques are formidable and deserve reflection. The scope of this study does not allow for engagement with the range of rebuttals to ethical consumption. Suffice it to say that a study of ethical consumption in Southeast Asia should account for both support and cynicism towards ethical consumption.

Moving away from history and politics and considering consumer attitudes and purchasing behavior: Does ethical consumption work? Academics agree that there is a link between a company's ethics and consumer behavior with ample evidence showing how either favorable or unfavorable impressions of a company impact people's attitudes around the company's products (Brunk 2017). According to Brunk, there is mixed evidence regarding whether these perceptions translate into consumer purchasing behaviors with some studies showing a connection and others not. In particular, research suggests differences between consumers' intentions to consume ethically, and their actual purchasing behavior—an "attitude-behavior gap" (Bray et al. 2011; Irwin 2015; Eckhardt et al. 2010). In addition, while survey results propose that a large group of people are interested in ethical consumption, the marketplace for ethical consumption is limited to a niche group (Eckhardt et al. 2010). As these studies suggest, it is critical to pursue empirical data-points to better understand when and why rhetoric translates to practice and what effect that action may have.

Ethical Consumption and the Business and Human Rights Discourse

With marketing departments of companies from various business sectors increasingly recognizing consumers' ethical decision-making processes, tailoring campaigns and whole product lines accordingly, one would expect academics to pick up on this, providing research on the connection of ethical consumption and business and human rights. However, this appears not to be the case, which seems to reflect the strong institutional focus on the states' and businesses' duty to protect and respect human rights as championed for by the UN Protect, Respect, and Remedy framework and the UNGPs as the guidance benchmark in the field of business and human rights. Focusing on the state and businesses as principal duty bearers, the UNGPs in particular (in contrast to the SDGs) and the business and human rights discourse in general tend to avoid questions around responsibilities at the individual level and lack effort in connecting SDG

12 with the business and human rights discourse. It appears that such gap is apparent in the body of academic literature as well.

Whereas academia so far seems to fall short in connecting ethical consumption with the business and human rights discourse, privately-led initiatives and solutions are more active. Such innovative projects make use of opportunities brought forward through the digital revolution. *Bluenumber*, spearheaded by former member of the UN Working Group on Business and Human Rights Puvan Selvanathan, offers governments and businesses with assistance for policy and procurement decisions and passing on traceability to the consumer by providing a global platform that links people to supply chains. *Good on You*, whose executives refer to SDG 12 as an inspiration, provides an app that offers trusted ethical ratings for brands and their impact on people to consumers. Both examples recognize the importance of the individual consumer and ethical decision-making processes for the field of business and human rights. A recognition that appears to not yet having had an impact on academia.

However, it is noteworthy that NGOs and businesses relate the two concepts with each. The *Ethical Trading Initiative* and *Ethical Consumer* are two examples where civil society organizations either conduct research into supply chains and providing a database of practices based on an ethical rating system, helping consumers to make informed decisions (Ethical Consumer) or partner with trade unions and businesses to increase respect for workers' rights through mutual efforts (Ethical Trading Initiative).

Together with innovative tech-initiative, these organizations appear to do the pioneer work on advancing the business and human rights discourse towards an inclusion of the individual consumer by recognizing the importance of individual decision-making.

Ethical Consumption in Southeast Asia: Knowns and Unknowns

In the Southeast Asian context, literature paints a patchy, somewhat contradictory picture of the state of ethical consumption in the region. On one hand, several surveys suggest a healthy amount of ethical consumption in the region. In a Nielsen survey of 30,000 consumers in 60 countries, Southeast Asian consumers were the most willing to pay more for sustainable products compared to all other regions. Within the Southeast Asian region, 80 per cent of consumers said they "preferred to buy from companies who are committed towards creating a positive social and environmental impact," compared to Asia Pacific (76 per cent), Middle East/

Africa (75 per cent) and Latin America (71 per cent), Europe (51 per cent) and North America (44 per cent) (Nielson 2015).

On the other hand, state-level research describes a more moderate interest in the space. For instance, R.3 mentions a study by the NTUC Fairprice Co-operative in Singapore having conducted a customer survey that found that while they were in favour of organic and ethically produced products, customers were not prepared to pay more for them. Reflecting further on our discussion above regarding the varying opinion of what is "ethical," one survey looking across countries found that in Indonesia, creating jobs and supporting the economy was the most important thing a company can do to be seen as socially responsible (Guibeleguiet 2014).

Another reality touched on by Panya and Sirisai (2003) is the diversity in consumer attitude and behavior both regionally and socio-economically within states. The authors suggest that the general public in Thailand "lack a sense of personal efficacy and responsibility feeling that environmental action is outside the individuals' responsibility and that it belongs to the urban-based elite and environmentalist experts." Arttachariya (2012) seems to build on this sentiment exploring in-depth the positive relationship between "green attitudes" and green consumer behavior among Bangkok graduate students.

Several authors examined ethical consumption within cultural and religious contexts including an exploratory study of moral philosophy, materialism and consumer ethics in Indonesia (Lu and Lu 2010) and an ethnographic study of the impact of Buddhism on consumer attitudes (Srisaracam 2015). Additionally, Abdulrazak and Quoquab (2018) explored consumers' motivations for sustainable consumption finding that within the Southeast Asian region, sustainable consumption has particular strong links to communal practices.

"The Unknowns" are vast, and one can argue that "we don't know what we don't know." Thus, a narrow window of the unknowns includes a limited understanding around ethical consumption in regard to non-environmental issues—such as labor. Interviewees described an ethical consumption as involving labor practices, human rights, health and safety, fair price, animal welfare, as well as environmental sustainability. Overall, most literature examines the topic in the light of green consumption and blurs the notion of "buying organic" with environmental sustainable. This leaves researchers and practitioners with many questions about what issues gain prominence from ethical consumers and why.

Initial Findings: Contrasting Views on Ethical Consumption in the Region

An analysis of the key informant interviews shed light on the contrasting views on ethical consumption in the region. These insights are highly valuable in so far as they provide a starting point to fill the gaps in our understanding. Importantly, throughout the interviews, aspects of various ecological systems emerged as touchpoints for a deeper understanding of the landscape of business and human rights. Themes that emerged center around the presence of ethical consumption in Southeast Asia, a possible regional uniqueness of the concept, the identification of key drivers and possible factors serving as catalysts to advancing the concept, and overall perceived (real?) challenges around ethical consumption. Through these themes two common issues became apparent. First, the key informants occasionally held very contrasting views on ethical consumption. Second, there were limited use of empirical data points regarding the themes. These two findings inform our contention that a research agenda for ethical consumption in the region should utilize an ecological systems lens and pursue a deeper empirical basis. This section will also build on the initial findings and identify key questions for further research.

Is Ethical Consumption 'a Thing' in the Region?

A fundamental question for the overall research agenda is whether ethical consumption is 'a thing' in Southeast Asia. Key informants provided differing vantage points spanning from the perception that ethical consumption has not yet arrive in the region to the idea that more traditional forms of ethical consumption are practiced by particular societal groups.

R.3 asserts that the awareness around ethical consumption would not be very high and that "the main reason why this has not taken root in [Southeast Asia] is because of 'growth and profits at all cost' mentality... a mentality that would be supported by governments that also follow the mindset of 'GDP growth at all cost.'" Similarly, R.2 notes that "ethical consumption is a thing in SEA [Southeast Asia]." He nevertheless acknowledges that "certain people in the middle class [...] have awareness of human rights and [the] environment." The importance of the middle class for ethical consumption is also pointed out by R.4 who finds that "in Southeast Asia, ethical consumption may be expanding among the new generations, with a growing purchasing power, however, it remains marginal." While, regardless of their different conceptions of ethical consumption, most key informants seemed to mutually agree that ethical consumption remains a marginal phenomenon; R.6 adds an interesting angle on regional forms of ethical consumption:

> [The] concept [ethical consumption] is not too alien for Southeast Asian people. At least for Muslims. Halal labelling has been going on for ages. This being the case, the idea that people may want to know what it is they are consuming (on ethical as well as physical grounds) is quite common.

Such notion is supported by R.2 who suggests that indigenous groups "might be more incline[d] to ethical consumption as part of their way of life, however they may not call them ethical consumption." All of this lends to the take-away that to understand ethical consumption in the region one has to look at the traditions, attitudes, beliefs and institutions that shape it.

Who or What Are the Key Drivers?

Using an ecological systems lens, as well as the discussion of ethical consumption in Southeast Asia and its regional particularities into account, it has become clear that we cannot focus on a singular actor in our analysis of the phenomenon. Whereas a focus on, for example, the state as the unit of analysis could provide valuable insights into the current interest of states, such singular focus would fall short in terms of a holistic analysis of the overall ecological system regarding ethical consumption as it relates to business and human rights and the interplay of its key drivers. As this study seeks to initiate conversation around a research agenda that deals with the phenomenon holistically, key informants where asked to discuss these key drivers. There are again no clear empirical data points presented and while there seemed to be a consensus for the role of the young middle class, key informants were divided over which stakeholder is to be considered as key driver.

R.8 finds the key driver of ethical consumption within the exosystem. She looks on ethical business practices with a focus on labor rights: "Good labor practices of the producer are the most important agenda [item] that businesses MUST have." For R.8, the key driver of the business and human rights agenda, including ethical consumption, should be the businesses. As has already been mentioned, one can perceive ethical consumption to be happening through the market rather than to the market and as businesses are an essential part of the market, they are in the driver seat for providing the conditions to advance human rights through facilitating ethical consumption.

Informed consumers in turn are also key drivers that influence how businesses behave. R.3 points out that some international standards "were driven by consumer demand for ethical production." R.1 also identifies the consumer as an important actor: "It is true that ethical consumption should come from consumers first to demand for change at the production side."

R.3, R.4. and R.7 offered interesting perspectives on different tools as key drivers that might contribute to an increase in ethical consumption—regional stock exchanges and social media. R.3 holds that "stock exchanges are influencing listed companies to have non-financial disclosures." Such non-financial disclosures of corporate social responsibility, sustainability and business and human rights efforts, which are mandatory under some national stock exchanges, are becoming increasingly common among Southeast Asian listed companies. Although such practices are bridging the exo- and macrosystems by providing institutional, as well as ethical business frameworks, those practices alone will not suffice to mainstream ethical consumption in the region due to an apparent attitude-behavior gap. At the same time R.4 points out that "social media is a very powerful means of communication on products [...]." It is hard to single out one key driver of ethical consumption; rather, one must look at the interplay of different systems in order to facilitate a holistic analysis of the phenomenon.

Is There Something Unique About Ethical Consumption in South East Asia?

The key informant interviews did not only bring forward a wide array of perceptions on the presence of ethical consumption, but also shed light on some supposedly unique features of ethical consumption in the region. Again, it seems that there are limited empirical data points and different informants defined uniqueness in such singularities that it is hard to say whether ethical consumption in Southeast Asia must be conceptualized differently from other world regions.

What seems a unique perspective on ethical consumption, not in a way that it doesn't happen in for example Europe or the United States as well, is the idea of consuming organically produced food. This notion has been brought forward by key informant R.3, who recalled the above-mentioned study by NTUC Fairprice Co-operative and pointed out that consumers "were in favour of organic and ethically produced products." This was also supported by R.1, who notes that:

> change in organic agriculture, in reducing plastic use, in recycling habit etc. [and in] some other movements [such as] fair trade (agriculture), fair wear (in garment and textile) [has] been raised into action because [it] is more obvious for consumers to know how these products are produced in SEA and they can put pressure on MNCs [multinational corporations] or TNCs [transnational corporations] over their supply chain.

Again, what we find here, are various ecological systems at play. On the exo-level we find goods that are produced on the global market by ethical (organic or good labor practices) made available for purchase to the individual, which is being influenced not only by intermediate contacts such as family and friends through the microsystem, but also subject to local customs and wider community influences that are conveyed by the mesosystem. But possibly more prevalent in Southeast Asia than to other regions is the so-called "attitude-behavior gap" that has been briefly mentioned before. For instance, R.3 stressed the conclusion of the NTUC Fairprice Co-operative survey that customers "were not prepared to pay more for them [organically produced goods]" and adds that "the mood is still for cheap products regardless of how they are produced." It is a possibility that although Southeast Asian customers principally are in favor of ethical consumption, as found in the Neilson survey described above, behavior does not appear match such ethical concerns (although we are lacking empirical purchasing data needed to fully make this claim).

Another interesting feature of ethical consumption in Southeast Asia described by the key informants is the lack of governments, businesses and individuals alike to push for an increase in ethical production/consumption. Many of the informants contest a regional focus on economic capital and development through economic growth. However, R.7 finds, at least for the cases of Thailand and Vietnam, the business model of Social Enterprises as being related to ethical consumption and actively promoted by the state. "In terms of [ethical] business practices, Social Enterprises (SE) which hold two missions: (1) Social; and (2) Economic, are proposed." He argues that "laws that will facilitate the growth of SE have been drafted in many countries in ASEAN, for example, Thailand and

Vietnam." Hence one might find some form of uniqueness in such model, which, if R.7's assumption would prove to be true, it would underscore our ecological argument that ethical consumption happens through rather than to the market. The individual's awareness on issues related to ethical consumption and its means (read for example: purchasing power) depend heavily on the micro- and mesosystems (e.g. family, community, culture) and, as has been pointed out above, the apparent attitude-behavior gap among individual customers does not set a favorable frame for the overall success of Social Enterprise to spark a change that could ultimately affect the chronosystem and create disruptive change of business practices, government behavior and individual consumption patterns.

What Conditions Are Necessary to Catalyze Ethical Consumption in Southeast Asia?

The ecological systems lens provides us with inter-related perspectives to approach such question; the key informants speak to the question of necessary conditions by offering differing perspectives and many possibilities. R.2 argues in favor of a both a stronger state and the promotion of traditional lifestyles of Southeast Asian peoples. Although "the role of state should be as a regulator for the business and consumers", he does not have high hope that the state could be an agent of change. Complementing this sentiment, he suggests shifting attention away from the macrosystem and its institutional and power architecture, towards traditional lifestyles, local customs and institutions of the meso- and microsystems. Such shift from a sphere in which the individual is passive (the state level) towards a realm in which the individual acts as an active agent (local communities, daily life, the workplace), is remarkable in so far, as it mirrors the current move towards stakeholder engagement in human rights due diligence processes.

This shift seems to be grounded in the disconnect between the market and the wider society. R.7 deciphers this disconnect and provides an ecological-focused explanation of the phenomenon described by his colleague.

> Though societies are market driven, however, in reality, societies are not existing by materials alone but are also socially driven [...] a consumerist model that is ethical and sustainable is possible. To develop this model, you have to think about social and economic (SO+EC) [sides of things].

For R.8, this first step of bringing the social and economic together, and thus bearing the possibility of crafting a new macro- or even chrono-system, is making sure that workers' rights are protected: "Once the workers have good working conditions, they could produce good products and then the company could take care of things outside the company."

R.3 suggests that "education, awareness building is needed to drive ethical consumption." An increased level of information on business practices of big business on parts of both the consumer and the state seems to be mandatory, as R.1 finds that:

> Big companies have more space and market monopoly even over the governments. It's difficult to monitor what these big companies produce and how they operate. Therefore, consumers [have] hardly access to or demand ethical business from these big players.

The point made here has serious implications for the ecological system of ethical consumption. The market as part of the meso- and exosystem does not only have an impact on the individual, but also on the macrosystem level of the state. It is exactly this train of thought that leads us to argue that ethical consumption does not happen to but through the market. In order to drive ethical consumption, education and awareness building must focus on different ecological systems of ethical consumption. R.8 uses the example of labor rights to stress the negative consequence of the cultural view that "we" are not included as "laborers," and thus we don't connect with the issue of human rights.

I could say that here in Thailand people do not know their basic rights, the examples, of trade union rights here in Thailand [...], office workers, engineers, teachers, nurses, or other professionals, they don't recognize themselves as laborers (labor in their views are people who use their energy to work; construction workers, drivers, etc.). That's because their educational background [has] shaped their attitude to be like that.

Given the variety of necessary conditions to catalyze ethical consumption offered by the key informants, we find these to be another strong case in favor of the ecological systems lens to understanding and mobilizing ethical consumption as a tool for protecting human rights in the realm of business.

Challenges Abound

Having already identified certain key drivers, we will shift our focus towards some challenges in ethical consumption. The key informants pointed out four main themes—the state as a regulator, the relationship of basic needs and purchasing power, a lack of information and diversities in worldviews around ethical behavior.

Since Thomas Hobbes' *Leviathan*, it goes without question that the state has a responsibility to its citizens. In terms of ethical consumption, however, there is no clear set of rules as to what a state must guarantee. In this context, R.3 argues that: Ethical production for ethical consumption works for the benefit of citizens. [The] state has an important role to play in creating the operating environment for businesses with good laws that are well enforced. Also, a culture of integrity under the rule of law will make a big difference.

Although the state has an important role to play in terms of the rule of law, R.3's colleagues do not find states in Southeast Asia to be in the driver's seat of ethical consumption. This is highly problematic, as the state, being part of the macrosystem, provides the institutional framework and power architecture in which all the other systems operate. When states fail to pick up signals sent to them by other systems and actors, be it the market, CSOs, or individuals, it can lead to missed opportunities for growth and can create a warped direction of progress.

Another challenge presented by several of the key informants are the differing levels in purchasing power and a perceived prioritization of cheap products among Southeast Asians. According to R.2, "ethical consumption has not taken shape in Southeast Asia because most people, especially urban society, [have] more concern for their basic needs." R.3 takes this one step further: "The mood is still for cheap products regardless of how they are produced. This mindset has to change and will only change if it is shown to affect the consumer as an employee." This challenge, too, touches upon various levels of the ecological systems. On the individual level the economic means to opt for ethically produced goods need to be matched with an awareness on the issue.

Coming back to the need for awareness around ethical consumption on the individual level, a third challenge is access to information. R.4 impressively highlights the many dimensions of this crucial aspect:

> The challenges are the level of information of consumers, the transparency of the value chain, the capacity of consumers to access and understand true, verifiable and verified, reliable information. Another challenge is when the product is not clearly identified (by its label or brand) and where there is no "traceability" to ensure that the product is ethical. Control is another challenge, that varies from one sector to another, from one country to another. Clear, transparent, reliable information and accountability and control on the other side are key to ethical consumption.

R.1 goes on to note that:

> *The challenges are: (i) …not all consumers are at the same awareness on their consumption behavior for sustainability of production so they prefer to pay less or buy cheap products; (ii) the consumers [have a] lack of monitoring information on the field… (iii) big players often …rely on CSR, not on consumers' ethical wish.*

Possibly of highest importance is the aspect of diversities in worldviews around ethical behavior and consumption, as R.4 continues to argue,

> *[The] boundaries [of ethical consumption] are the boundaries of the buyer and what he/she considers as ethical. It can also be the boundaries of what is considered as socially acceptable that may differ from one society to another and within various group of a society, depending on their beliefs, convictions, commitments.*

R.4's argument confronts us with important questions—can ethical consumption be used against what we, as a field, consider human rights? We can find a huge diversity of worldviews on the individual level, which is, through household dynamics, belief systems and local customs, at an interplay with the micro- and mesosystems. On the levels of the exo- and macrosystems, worldviews in forms of legislation and international frameworks are at play that in turn influence the levels in which the individual acts as an active agent. To drive ethical consumption forward It is necessary to approach these challenges at all levels. Given the limited empirical data points on ethical consumption in Southeast Asia, research that spans the different systems is necessary. In the following we will therefore suggest a preliminary research agenda.

Conclusion: where should Researchers Focus?

Bringing in ethics into consumerism; i.e. the identification of issues behind the product is something which can take hold. It's just how it is put forward and 'sold'.—*R.6*

Considering the above preliminary findings, it is clear that there is a need for further empirical evidence to understand how consumers fit within the business ecosystem as a mechanism for advancing human rights in Southeast Asia. Furthermore, an empirical approach using an ecological systems lens may shed light on key points of leverage for state duty in protecting human rights. Policies designed to influence purchasing are already used widely in various sectors, such as excise taxes for tobacco (punishment-based) or tax credits for purchasing eco-friendly cars (reward-based). An empirical understanding of consumer attitudes within the business ecosystem in Southeast Asia may help states be more efficient and effective in policy development, tailored to the local context.

However, it is not necessary for ethical consumption as a strategy in the region to follow the path of the West. Rather, through a mix of empirical research that tests locally-relevant hypotheses and strategies within the reality of the ecosystems of the regions, a unique approach may arise to facilitate and support ethical consumption, ultimately advancing human rights holistically. Based on our initial findings via the literature review and key informant interviews, several important questions come to the surface.

Microsystem

- What "ethics" do people care about? What are the "big problems" people are concerned about? How does this impact behavior? (i.e. will they pay more for an item? Will they buy more of an item? Will they shop more often or longer? Will they buy more types of products from the same company? Will they recommend friends and family? What other actions?)
- How does key groups' definition of "ethics" and "big problems" differ? i.e. middle class, millennials, government.
- Which of the above behaviors are influential to business decision-makers in light of human rights practices? (i.e. if consumers are not willing to pay more, but are willing to shop more often, buy other

products and recommend the company to friends, is that persuasive in order to revise business practices in regards to labor rights?

MESOSYSTEM

- What aspects of culture and values are beneficial in developing ethical consumption in the region? (i.e. religion, connection to family and community)
- How can social media play a role in ethical consumption in the region?
- What are the mechanisms for ethical consumption to interact with civil society activism?
- How do people learn about whether a business has ethical practices?
- How can we secure a standard on information about production? Do we have it with the UNGPs and related reporting frameworks? If so, how can we mainstream knowledge around the UNGPs among consumers in order to make them push for implementation?

Exosystem and Macrosystem

- What is the governments' awareness of ethical consumption as a mechanism for advancing human rights in the business ecosystem?
- Where, within the realities of each government's framework and functioning, can ethical consumption benefit the overall goal for growth and development? What are the leverage points?
- What role can governments play to increase incentives to consume ethically, especially in the middle class?
- Is there something like an information gap on business behavior in terms of ethical production between businesses and consumers? If so, how do we close this gap?
- Given the focus on information and trackability, what are innovative means of mainstreaming ethical consumption through automation/digitization/IoT/new technology, such as the Blue Number Initiative?
- How can consumers leverage their purchasing preferences with the government to create a human rights agenda that is responsive to local priorities?

"You cannot have ethical consumerism without ethical production", as R.3 puts it. He further states: "the palm oil and paper products companies went out to show that they are responsible. There was also pressure on banks as they financed these companies and their activities. The government stepped in with standards for 'responsible lending' and for banks to release ESG [Environmental and Social Governance] reports. Pressure works." What motivates ethical consumption in Southeast Asia? What are the impacts and limitations of ethical consumption in the region? These questions are too big to look at from one dimension and too important to guess at.

References

Abdulrazak, Sham, and Quoquab, Farzana. 2018. Exploring Consumers' Motivations for Sustainable Consumption: A Self-Deterministic Approach. *Journal of International Consumer Marketing* 30(1): 14–28.

Arttachariya, Patricia. 2012. Environmentalism and Green Purchasing Behavior: A Study on Graduate Students in Bangkok, Thailand. *Bangkok University Academic Review* 11(2): 1–11.

Bengtsson, Mariette. 2016. How to Plan and Perform a Qualitative Study Using Content Analysis. *NursingPlus Open* 2: 8–14.

Bray, Jeffery, Johns, Nick, and Kilburn, David. 2011. An Exploratory Study Into the Factors Impeding Ethical Consumption. *Journal of Business Ethics* 98(4): 597–608.

Brunk, Katja. 2017. Shedding Light on the Ethical Consumer Debate: Evidence From a Qualitative Investigation of Body Shop Consumers. In The Customer is NOT Always Right? Marketing Orientations in a Dynamic Business World: 292–300. Springer, Cham.

Eckhardt, Giana, Belk, Russell, and Devinney, Timothy. 2010. Why Don't Consumers Consume Ethically?. Journal of Consumer Behaviour 9(6): 426–436.

Guibeleguiet, C. 2014. Redefining Sustainability in Asia. http://www.kering.com/en/magazine/redefining-sustainability-asia.

Irwin, J. 2015. Ethical Consumerism Isn't Dead, It Just Needs Better Marketing. https://hbr.org/2015/01/ethical-consumerism-isnt-dead-it-just-needs-better-marketing.

Lewis, Tania, and Potter, Emily. 2011. Introducing Ethical Consumption. In Ethical Consumption: A Critical Introduction: 3–23. Routledge in association with GSE Research.

Littler, Jo. 2011. What's Wrong with Ethical Consumption? In Ethical Consumption: A Critical Introduction: 27–39. Routledge in association with GSE Research.

Lu, Long-Chuan, and Chia-Ju Lu. 2010. Moral Philosophy, Materialism, and Consumer Ethics: An Exploratory Study in Indonesia. Journal of Business Ethics 94(2): 193–210.

Nielson. 2015. Sustainability Continues to Gain Momentum Among Singaporeans and Southeast Asian Consumers. http://www.nielsen.com/sg/en/press-room/2015/sustainability-continues-to-gain-momentum-among-singaporeans-and-southeast-asian-consumers.html.

Panya, Opart, and Sirisai, Solot. 2003. Environmental Consciousness in Thailand: Contesting Maps of Eco-Conscious Minds. Japanese Journal of Southeast Asian Studies 41(1): 59–75.

Racela, Olimpia. 2012. Perceptions of Business Ethics in Thailand: Consumers' Willingness to Act. International Journal of Business Research 12(5): 1–12.

Srisaracam, Nattida. 2015. The Role of Self on Ethical Consumption in a Religious Culture. PhD dissertation. Bradford: University of Bradford.

CHAPTER 12

Designing a Human Rights Management Systems Standard: A Practical Approach to Business Enterprise Human Rights in Asia

Robert Sadleir

Introduction

The intent of this chapter falls under the United Nations' *Guiding Principles on Business & Human Rights*, particularly pillar one:

> States must protect against human rights abuse within their territory and/or jurisdiction by third parties, including business enterprises. This requires taking appropriate steps to prevent, investigate, punish and redress such abuse through effective policies, legislation, regulations and adjudication.[1] (OHCHR 2012)

A challenge for those seeking to protect against human rights abuses in a globalised, liberal, capitalist world is that State governments are not best placed to protect them. Corporations can arbitrage international

[1] OHCHR. 2012. Guiding Principles on Business and Human Rights: Implementing the United Nations "Protect, Respect and Remedy" Framework.

R. Sadleir (✉)
Geneva, Switzerland
e-mail: james@asiacentre.co.th

J. Gomez, R. Ramcharan (eds.), *Business and Human Rights in Asia*,
https://doi.org/10.1007/978-981-15-7273-9_12

boundaries to seek competitive advantage. Governments are bureaucratic, slow to respond, and can be subject to regulatory capture by business as nations seek economic growth and development. State-directed capitalism which is found throughout Asia suggests corporations and the State can be too closely aligned in their interests to engage in meaningful human rights protection. Moreover, in Asian societies there is the emphasis on the collective as opposed to the individual. As well human rights have increasingly become a vehicle to remedy a broad range of wrongs from social problems and social welfare; as a consequence human rights policy in general has become too unwieldy for governments to engage effectively from the perspective of human rights *law*.

Assuming this context for the purposes of this chapter, the aim here is twofold: first, to suggest how we can apply management systems standards, and the process of standardisation, to develop a prevention tool for human rights abuse by establishing a human rights management system within a business enterprise, thereby reducing reliance on the State and government institutions to enforce human rights. Second, seek to ensure corporations employ these systems effectively by adhering to their standards and ensuring they allocate the appropriate amount of resources within an organisation to prevent and curtail human rights abuses. The chapter suggests this can be achieved by introducing the measurement of the Value of Statistical Human Life (VHL) as a tool to enhance accountability. It means a business enterprise needs to ask: How do companies value a human life? How valuable is an employee or a stakeholder? What values, indicators and metrics should a company use to value a human life for human rights purposes. By measuring VHL we can determine whether the amount of resources spent on preventing human rights abuses is proportionate to what a corporation values and its assets.

Designing a human rights management system within corporations is a new topic hitherto unexplored. It is noteworthy that policy makers in the UK developed a guide titled "Good Business Implementing the UN Guiding Principles on Business and Human Rights" in September 2013 As of 2013, Company directors of UK companies had to include human rights matters in their annual reports in line with the Government's guidelines. (HMG 2013) The EU has considered a Proposed Directive aimed at enhancing the transparency of large companies on social and environmental matters (amending Directives 78/660/EEC and 83/3four9/EEC). the Proposed Directive had sought to at require: a description of the policy pursued by the company in relation to these matters; the results of these policies; and, iii. the risks related to these matters and how the company manages those risks. Scholarly works on HRMS have yet to be written. This chapter seeks to fill that gap.

The chapter will proceed by first outlining the challenges to developing a regulatory and framework in Asia before secondly looking at solutions that can arise from applying the use of technical standards and standardisation approaches to human rights The solution lies in developing an ISO technical standards approach to human rights as Asian firms are already familiar with ISO applications in quality assurance and systems management. To allocate resources proportionately within a company to ensure a human rights management system can develop firms could examine value of statistical life approaches.

Brief Overview of the Asian Regulatory Environment

To understand why standardisation is a viable method for business enterprises to approach human rights we need to step back and look at approaches in the Asia region to integrating the capitalist system as an engine of growth for economic development. Initially, when the economies of Asia sought pathways to development they were wary of the *laissez-faire* economics of *entrepôt* states like Hong Kong. Instead from the 1970s onwards, economic development was the result of directed State capitalism, a partnership between government and corporations in strategic industries. The approaches in Asia may have been different: partnerships with family conglomerates in *zaibatsus* in Japan or the *chaebols* in South Korea; in Indonesia, Vietnam and Burma this partnership also included the military. China espoused corporatism by encouraging state enterprises to model themselves on western enterprises; the effects were similar in all countries: politics and business became entwined. The *measure of effective policy* for technocrats in Asia over the last half century has been *political stability and economic growth.*

Thus, in Asia the challenge to regulate human rights by the State is compounded by directed state capitalism and the notion of 'regulatory capture' where those bodies regulating industries become sympathetic to the businesses they are supposed to be regulating. One should add this is not just an issue in Asia alone, but a problem arising from capitalism in general. Modern capitalism, itself, "is a complex game," according to Joseph Stiglitz, the former IMF and World Bank economist:

> those who win at it have to have more than a little smarts. But those who win at it often possess less admirable characteristics as well: the ability to skirt the law, or shape the law in their own favour; the willingness to take advantage of other, even the poor and to play *unfair* when necessary.[2] (Stiglitz 2013)

And as *The Economist* points out:

> With the West in a funk and emerging markets flourishing, [Asian economies] no longer see state-directed firms as a way-station on the road to liberal capitalism; rather, they see it as a sustainable model. They think they have redesigned capitalism to make it work better.[3] (The Economist 2012)

In short, state capitalism is here for the long haul and those seeking mechanisms to improve human rights must find solutions within this environment. It should also be noted at this point that as technocrats design policy to enhance their governance system from an economic perspective, one of the challenges that both corporations and governments have is investing resources (money, time, people), is they are unable to allocate resources to human rights because it is difficult at a national level or corporate level to *measure* the return of investment (contribution to national wealth) in human rights and because they cannot measure the net benefit of human rights. In short, there are few frameworks to build the *business* case for human rights. Therefore, one of the challenges is: how can you adapt to the process, mindset or culture for policy development and implementation within government, their parliaments, and the wider community including most importantly businesses.

Asian Values

The second check on effective measure to prevent human rights abuse in the context of Asia is '*Asia values*'. In Asia, the debate on human rights has been obscured by notions of 'Asia Values' a blend of authoritarian and family values and a greater emphasis on collective social welfare as opposed to individual rights. This topic is well-known and was propounded by Lee Kuan Yew and Mahathir Mohamad, leaders of Singapore and Malaysia in

[2] Stiglitz Joseph (2013) *The Price of Inequality* Penguin Books, London p. 46.

[3] 'The rise of state capitalism:' (2012) https://www.economist.com/node/21543160.

the 1990s,[4] as the second generation of tiger economies came to the fore. The discussion is framed by both the notion of Asian values and the 'Rights vs Security' debate which holds that since Asian nations are less economically developed compared to Western nations, it is not realistic to expect them to uphold all of the rights listed in the *Universal Declaration of Human Rights*. China and Pakistan, for example, have argued they may sacrifice political and civil freedoms to provide economic security for their people and maintain stability in their society as they develop. To be fair to Asia, balancing the collective well-being over the notion of individual human rights, is also challenged in the West by ambiguity.

Ambiguity of Standards

The third impediment to human rights is that it is hamstrung by ambiguity. Human rights means different things to different people: particularly among those people who are not directly engaged in human rights issues or well versed in legalities. Sometimes we use a proxy term so that people may grasp the concept—the word "dignity." Yet:

> Dignity is sometimes invoked as another way of justifying human rights. The problem is that dignity is extremely indeterminate and historically complex concept, often used as a placeholder in morality. (Moeckli et al. 2014)

Other approaches speak of human rights in terms of self-evident "standards of behaviour." But as Kenneth Roth, head of *Human Rights Watch* points out, "the great challenge facing human rights groups is often less concerned with arguing the law's finer points or applying them to the facts of the case than with convincing the public that violations are wrong" (Moeckli et al. 2014).

Ambiguity is also present even in the use of the term: 'standards'. The challenge, with using the word: 'standard', is that it also means different things. According to *The Oxford Dictionary*, a standard may be defined as:

(A) a required or agreed level of quality or attainment;
(B) something used as a measure, norm, or model in comparative evaluations;
(C) principles of conduct.[5]

[4] Prime Minister Mahathir has recently returned to power in Malaysia.
[5] https://en.oxforddictionaries.com/definition/standard.

Understanding standards in the human rights context using definition "A" or "C" means building consensus and this can be a slow, frustrating and a costly exercise particularly in the context of business enterprise and human rights. Moreover, it encourages a passive acceptance of circumstance or indifference, as the solution is perceived to be in the hands of technical experts, bureaucrats, politicians and lawyers. The question is how can we improve human rights standards in a pro-active manner? One, in which business can develop standards aligned with their organisational culture, management structure, corporate values, shareholders and other stakeholders, but reinforced by internal company systems and rules?

A mechanism for enforcement is important to encourage better behaviour. For Kenneth Roth, "shame is a powerful motivator." (Moeckli et al. 2014) Yet within the context of the corporate world I would disagree. It may be effective at a personal level but not at a corporate level. Perhaps, a better approach is to encourage the design of management systems within companies to be more responsive to human rights, and changing corporate culture within rather than relying on governments to be the driver of change. At any rate, globalisation means corporations can arbitrage national boundaries and regulatory obligations. We can speak of brand damage, loss of reputation, providing some form of censor; yet the 24-hour news cycle, opinion poll driven policy and the silos created by internet tribes means corporate abuses are quickly forgotten, smoothed over, or were never a priority. Furthermore, corporations have resources to slow legal proceedings or can use sharp business practice to reduce the damages of any conviction. Recall *Union Carbide*, in Bhopal. If you recollect, in December 1984, the *Union Carbide* chemical plant in Bhopal released at least 30 tons of a highly toxic gas. 600,000 people were exposed to the deadly gas cloud; 15,000 died over the years; 40,000 were maimed and the surrounding area contaminated with toxins *Union Carbide*'s headquarters transferred liability by claiming sabotage and sold its stake in the Indian subsidiary. In 1989, *Union Carbide* did settle with the Indian government for USD$470m. The court in India delivered its judgment in 2010, 26 years after the incident, holding seven senior employees responsible for the world's worst industrial tragedy—a hollow justice. (The Atlantic 2014)

Therefore, the pathway lies in definition "B"—the means to build a standard where accountability can occur through measurement, norms, or models in comparative evaluations. All these characteristics are found in the process of standardisation. In doing so the solution to reconciling ambiguity in standards and perspectives, and ensuring business enterprises' accountability on human rights in a state capitalist system in Asia, lies in the process of standardisation through the mechanics of systems management. Thus, the focus of my chapter is designing a self regulatory approach grounded in the practice of businesses that can prevent human rights abuse by developing a management systems process using International Standards Organisation (ISO) guidelines.

International Standards (ISO) and Management System

An international standard "provide requirements, specifications, guidelines or characteristics that can be used consistently to ensure that materials, products, processes and services are fit for their purpose." Standards are well regarded tools in the commercial sector to enhance systems and improve quality of services and production and manage assets. Standards act as a framework to design organisational behaviour without government regulation. Perhaps the most popular standard and most well-known is ISO 9001: Quality Assurance. There are over one million companies and organizations in over 170 countries certified to ISO 9001 and many more who choose to self-certify. In Asia, as the private sector has grown, ISO 9001 has also become an important marketing tool to enhance the value of a brand and improve pricing. (UNIDO 2012). The following chart highlights the take up of ISO 9001 in China (See Chart 12.1).[6]

Currently, around 350 000 companies in China across all business sectors from primary industries such as mining and agriculture to the services sector are certified against ISO 9001 (UNIDO 2012).

Most businesses in Asia[7] have become increasingly familiar with ISO 9001 (See Chart 12.2). As the market economy grew since the standard and the practices it encouraged provided guidance for companies and organisations who wanted to ensure that their products and services con-

[6] This chart only shows companies who are formally certified to ISO 9001. Many firms choose to self-certify and are not included in this chart. The stabilisation of Japanese companies may reflect a preference for developing bespoke standards for companies as companies mature; and/ or the preference for self-certification; or the choice to switch to other types of standards as a company matures.

[7] UNIDO (2012) ISO 9001—Its relevance and impact in Asian Developing Economies: A survey covering quality management system development, certification, accreditation and economic benefits.

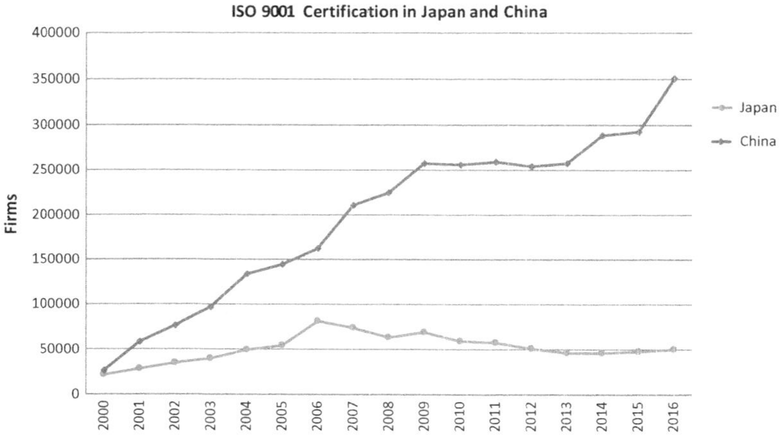

Chart 12.1 ISO 9001 Certification in Japan and China. (Compiled from UNIDO [2012] ISO 9001—Its relevance and impact in Asian Developing Economies)

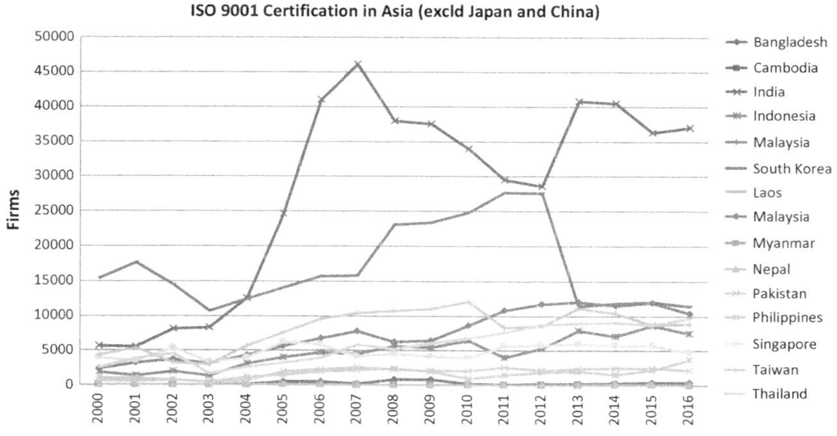

Chart 12.2 ISO 9001 Certification in Asia's smaller. (Compiled from: UNIDO [2012] ISO 9001—Its relevance and impact in Asian Developing Economies)

sistently met customer's requirements, and that quality consistently improved. This enabled the creation of extensive and dynamic supply webs throughout Asia supporting intra regional and international trade on a vast scale. Businesses adopting and adhering to ISO 9001 have greater opportunities to create wealth through such networks; businesses operating without ISO 9001 certification are less likely to be integrated directly into such networks.

From a human rights perspective, the significance of ISO 9001 in Asia is not a quality assurance system *per se* but that ISO 9001, once embedded in the management and organisational structure of a company, over time influences the system and changes the culture of a company: from creating a customer complaints system, and sensitivity to external stakeholders, that managers are accountable for implementing, and managing, as well as introducing the concept of continuous improvement within a firm.

A standard, in short, is an internal mechanism or platform to change a company from within. Not from without which is often a human rights activist approach to change. Standards channel employee and management behaviour and are enforced by internal incentive mechanisms such as Key Performance Indicators (KPIs), promotions, and internal company processes, rules and regulations. ISO 9001 Quality Assurance is traditionally considered the introductory standard for most companies and as firms develop and mature they incorporate management system standards to improve performance. And management systems standards influence management behaviour as they evolve. The ISO defines a management system as:

> the way in which an organization manages the inter-related parts of its business in order to achieve its objectives. These objectives can relate to a number of different topics, including product or service quality, operational efficiency, environmental performance, health and safety in the workplace and many more. (ISO 2014)[8]

The attraction of a systems management approach is manifold:

- Firstly, the complexity of the system is determined by each organisation's specific context. For some organisations, especially smaller ones, it may simply mean depending upon strong leadership from

[8] *Management system standards 2018 What is a management system?* https://www.iso.org/management-system-standards.html.

the business owner, providing clear guidelines to each employee and how these expectations contribute to the organisation's overall objectives, without the need for extensive documentation. More complex businesses operating, for example, in highly regulated sectors such as the chemical industry, may need comprehensive documentation and controls to meet their legal obligations and organisational objectives. (ISO 2014)

- Management system standards assist firms improve their performance by identifying repeatable steps that organisations consciously implement to realise their goals and objectives, and to create an organisational culture engaged in a continuous cycle of self-evaluation, correction and improvement of operations and processes through heightened employee awareness and management leadership and commitment. (ISO 2014)
- A management system once it comes into existence has to perform. Thus, performance management often in the form of KPIs encourages the delivery of results over time. Indeed, this is the beauty of management systems for they create an environment where those who are unfamiliar with a concept are obliged to understand and deliver against it, in order to receive benefits whether pecuniary, career promotion, or other. So firms do not have to change behaviour due to altruism alone but due to pragmatic organisational reasons and drivers.
- A management system can be embryonic, but over time as resources (however small) are allocated to it, it creates an ecosystem of its own within an organisation which develops robustness to influence a corporate culture and modify corporate behaviour. An analogy may be risk management in the financial sector, which may have been viewed with scepticism initially by the front office of an investment bank who are incentivised to take greater risk for greater reward, but gained traction during the financial crisis as banks sought to protect their capital.
- Systems management is about capacity building, encouraging enterprises to implement their own reforms rather than relying upon regulation, and seeing human rights as a component of an effective and successful business enterprise.
- Systems can be integrated into IT platforms allowing the barriers to reporting human rights abuses being reduced and processed more quickly; and human rights can be integrated to the broader ecology

of systems and data collection. Moreover, once data is introduced into the system there is a data foot print that is difficult to remove or cover-up.

In short, any business enterprise can employ a management system whether it be a sole proprietor, a small to medium enterprise, a large corporation or a multi-national corporation. Once the management system is embedded in a corporation it can be scaled up as a firm grows. Indeed, there is much to be said for a human rights management system being embedded in a company when it is small because it becomes ingrained in the firm's culture from the outset—it becomes part of the corporate DNA. Whereas when such systems are bolted on at a later stage, the culture of the organisation has to adapt and change to accommodate the new system. Such circumstances can lead to resistance and the necessity for assertive and sustained change management practices. In the short term, a new management system simply raises awareness and through the organigram is disseminated across the corporation. It may be viewed with scepticism at first, but over time it creates a *raison d'etre*. A similar internal wariness to new systems occurred with *Occupational Health and Safety* or *Environment Management* systems. Yet today most companies would employ a management system in these areas. Within corporations there are employees and managers who champion these causes. The evolution of firms' attitude towards Climate Change and environmental management could be a pathway for human rights engagement by business enterprise.

When considering current ISO management standards there are a number which could be employed to frame a *Business Enterprise Human Rights Management Systems* standard. The solution lies in developing an ISO standards approach to human rights.

A Human Rights Management System Standard

ISO has developed a range of tools, one of which is management system standards. A *Human Rights Management System (HRMS)* could be designed using components of existing management system and quality assurance standards (See Table 12.1): These include:

- The International Standard (ISO) on Quality Assurance—ISO:9001
- Environmental Management—ISO:14001

Table 12.1 Possible components for a business enterprise human rights management system

Standard	*ISO:9001 Quality Assurance*	*ISO:14001 Environmental Management*	*ISO:31001 Risk Management*	*ISO:28001 Supply security chain*	*ISO:45001 Occupational Health & Safety*
Key Principles	Customer focus	Compliance statutory/ regulatory requirements	Develop a risk management strategy	Assess threats in their supply chain	Improve employee safety
	Leadership	Employee Engagement	Identify and mitigate risks	Facilitate global trade	Reduce workplace risks
	Engagement of people	Confidence of stakeholders	Protect assets	Reassures stakeholders of firm's commitment to the safety of individuals and security of goods and services	Reduced absenteeism and staff turnover, leading to increased productivity
	Process	Strategic business aims alignment	Cost Benefit Analysis		Creation of a health and safety culture
	Improvement	competitive and financial advantage	Decision making to effectively allocate resources	Benchmarks firms security management practices with international best practice	Employees take an active role in their own OH&S
	Evidence-based decision making	Environmental performance of suppliers by integrating them into the firm's business system	Improving an organisation's governance		Reinforced leadership commitment to proactively improve OH&S performance
	Relationship building (Complaints systems)				Enhanced reputation

Sources: Compiled from existing ISO Standards

- Risk Management—ISO:31001
- Supply Security Chain—ISO:28001
- Occupational Health & Safety-ISO:45001

Each of these standards have principles or characteristics which drawn together can become the ingredients of a nascent HRMS: *Quality Assurance* brings the notion of creating a customer complaints system and the notion of using feedback for continuous improvement; *Environmental Management* highlights the importance of incorporating a management structure within a company to deal with environmental issues and ensuring this management team review environmental processes regularly; *Risk Management* that any decision must truly analysis the cost and benefit of each action and the importance of stakeholder engagement as well as identifying and treating risk events appropriately; *Supply Chain Management* reminds a firm that it does not act in isolation but must also consider its whole business ecosystem of suppliers and treat risks along the supply chain. *Occupational Health and Safety* highlights not just protecting worker; and prevention but collecting data and setting targets to reduce work place absences and change culture.

An example of a highly effective management system is the United States' Federal Aviation Administration (FAA) approach to commercial aviation. The FAA system has used the target of zero fatal accidents to design safety engineering and management systems for commercial passenger aviation. In 2018, each day over 43,000 flights carrying 2.6 million passengers were handled by the FAA (FAA 2018). Yet since 2009 (as of June 30, 2018) there has only been one commercial passenger fatality in the US. Why has this system been so successful?

Obviously, regulatory enforcement is important as airlines fear losing a license to operate but this is not the whole picture when considering the extremely low fatality rate. A key component is the statistical value of a human life (VHL) which in the US is high (≈USD 10m). Thus, a typical commuter plane in the US, e.g. a Boeing 737 carrying 120 passengers, needs to have a safety management system and security management system designed to protect an asset (people) worth USD$1.2bn excluding the aircraft. That means safety is designed with much greater redundancy i.e. protection, to ensure the likelihood of accidents is reduced. In short, the FAA errs on the side of caution. Moreover, the complete ecosystem feeding commercial aviation in the US needs high safety and security processes from the supply chain of high quality of spare parts to high quality maintenance and security systems to ensure the system is not compromised. Another thing that is interesting about the aviation model is that once people are seated in the aircraft and during the flight all passengers' lives are valued equally for the duration of the flight and that welfare is John Rawls "Good" principle where the proper maximand is the welfare of the worst-off individual (Sen 2017, 193).

Value of Statistical Human Life[9]

VHL is an important measurement in a world where determining net benefit is a cornerstone of public policy. The intent of organisations and institutions that use this concept is to optimise the allocation of resources and improve the quality of lives of citizens, stop lives being needlessly lost, and enhance sustainability. It raises the question from a human rights perspective: could we strengthen human rights protection by incorporating VHL as a component of the HRMS for business enterprise? Such a question is perhaps not completely aligned with human right advocacy where the justification of human rights are self-explanatory—there is an irreducible value that is not in need of further justification (Moeckli et al. 2014). Yet, it may be a practicable solution for human rights in Asia.

Afterall, the FAA model illustrates that if a human is valued highly enough then a robust protection system can be created. Would VHL enhance the enforcement of human rights? The likelihood is, "yes" as at the very least it allows managers a mechanism to determine the optimal allocation of resources for human rights; and facilitate decision-making through measuring impact. Key factors for managing a project in business. Applying a VHL model would also raise questions about the appropriate methodology companies would use to measure the value of human life and such decisions would raise questions within a corporation about the ethos of the company. Should the value of a human life be based solely on human capital measures; or on the quality of life and or "well-being." What indicators and metrics should be used to measure the VHL?

In essence, in a HRMS—as described above—the VHL would be a key component to determine the cost-benefit of human rights measures. It

[9]There are different methodologies to measure the Value of Statistical Human Life. The most common are: Human Capital Method, Prevention of Mortality, Compensation, Willingness to Pay or Accept Risk etc. Determining the appropriate methodology is context specific.

suggests that if methodologies for VHL determined the value of a human life to be higher, investment on protecting human rights would be greater not just within the company but also in measures taken in understanding how sub-contractors, suppliers and other stakeholders treat their workers. From a human rights activist point of view it would give those who wish to improve human rights an additional approach to improving human rights: developing a methodology to measure the VHL in a human rights context.

VHL also would also provide greater transparency as bench marking of VHL across companies by external consultants or human rights activists would give greater insight into the broader culture of an organisation. Just as quality assurance under ISO 9001 has been used as a marketing tool in business, a HRMS backstopped by VHL could make firms more marketable and competitive. This may generate a virtuous circle: as one human rights delegate at the recent *38th Session of the Human Rights Council* in Geneva, Switzerland commented: "When you have the money, you fight for your rights. When you are poor, you fight for your money" (Aishwarya 2018).

Measuring the Impact of Human Rights Using VHL

Public policy good practice has—as its cornerstone—the measurement of impact. Developing and designing good human rights practice is hampered by the inability to measure the net benefit of human rights. Allocating resources to human rights at the corporate or government level is challenging because it is difficult to measure the return of investment in good human rights practice when additionally one is unable to measure the cost of human rights abuses. Determining the VHL is one way this can be realised through firstly attributing a value to human life and then modelling a cost to human rights abuse at a national level and also a corporate level. See the following table:

In essence, Table 12.2 determines the VHL in USD$ (2004) in selected countries in Asia. It then looks at how violence reduces this value in percentage terms. It multiplies the loss from violence by national population to get an overview of the cost of violence at a national level. Overall the table shows that the scale costs to violence are in the billions and trillions of dollars. Recognising such large costs of violence should further incentivise both governments and business enterprises in Asia to invest resources in human rights because the cost of violence makes an economy less wealthy and consumers less able to participate in the economy by purchasing goods or services or contribute to government services by paying taxes.

Table 12.2 Cost of human rights abuses based on VHL

Country	*Value of a human life (21), USD 2004*	*Violence cost (22) (%)*	*Cost violence per capita*	*Population (2018)*	*National annual cost (USD mn)*
China	562,225	3.5	$19,678	1,415,045,928	27,845,097
India	147,403	8.6	$12,677	1,354,051,854	17,164,852
Thailand	222,056	7.1	$15,766	69,183,173	1,090,740
Malaysia	722,022	4.3	$31,047	32,042,458	994,820
Indonesia	92,433	2.0	$1849	266,794,980	493,213
Bangladesh	71,066	3.8	$2701	166,368,149	449,279
Philippines	41,330	8.4	$3472	106,512,074	369,780
Vietnam	53,063	7.0	$3714	96,491,146	358,408
Singapore	924,420	4.6	$42,523	5,791,901	246,291
Myanmar	51,245	8.5	$4356	53,855,735	234,586
Cambodia	18,864	7.3	$1377	16,245,729	22,372
Laos	4617	6.5	$300	6,961,210	2089

Sources: Compiled from various sources: Institute for Economics and Peace (2018) *The Economic Value* of *Peace 2016*; McMahon Kate and Said Dahdah; (undated) *The True Cost of Road Crashes: Valuing Life and the cost of serious injury IRA*; OECD (2012) The Value of Statistical Life: A Meta-Analysis

This table is for illustrative purposes and the data needs to be refined particularly in the GDP cost for violence and the total cost to a country annually. But the basic premise remains: violence reduces the value of a human life and is a cost to society; Kate McMahon, Said Dahdah; (no date) *The True Cost of Road Crashes: Valuing Life and the cost of serious injury IRAP*; The Institute for Economics and Peace (IEP) (2018) *The Economic Value* of *Peace* 2016 Sydney

Conclusion

We need to develop different approaches to human rights protection, or look for different approaches to reinforce the principles. Justice arising from human rights law takes a long time to "trickle down" from state actors to vulnerable people whose lives are blighted by conflict, unfair and unsafe work practices, human trafficking, and the slow dehumanisation and desensitisation of incremental bureaucratic social justice systems of governments.

This chapter suggests that standards incorporated into management systems and the process of standardisation can be applied to human rights, to develop more robust prevention mechanisms for business enterprises in Asia to strengthen business's role as a human rights actor. Such an approach reduces reliance on the State and government institutions to enforce human rights. Secondly, to ensure corporations employ these systems effectively by not only adhering to their standards but ensuring they allocate the appropriate amount of resources within an organisation to prevent and address human rights abuses, I argue the Value of Statistical Human Life can be applied as a measurement to enhance accountability. For if the value is too low change is less likely to occur. Moreover, VHL can be used to benchmark business enterprises commitment to human rights.

The creation of a *Human Rights Management System Standard* for business enterprises would blend the qualities of ISO standards such as: *ISO 9001:Quality Assurance* with its customer feedback and complaint system; the contextual sensitivity of *ISO 31001: Risk Management Standard* which seeks proportionate allocation of resources; *ISO 28001: Sustainable Supply Chain* to ensure suppliers and other stakeholders are engaged in the process; and *ISO 45001: Occupational Health and Safety* for its system of data collection and use of targets to reduce workplace injuries. Human rights technical experts can add further insight into the design. The approach makes sense in Asia as Asian businesses are already familiar with the standardisation process through ISO 9001—the ubiquitous quality assurance standard. It also makes sense when we understand the cost of human rights abuse to Asia's national economies.

I hope in considering this chapter, the reader may reflect upon how he/she systematically values their own life, and how together we can improve the quality and dignity of all lives both at a personal level, and in the context of the workplace.

References

Federal Aviation Authority (2018) "Air Traffic by Numbers," Accessed on 1 October 2018. https://www.faa.gov/air_traffic/by_the_numbers/

Federal Aviation Authority (FAA) 2018. https://www.faa.gov/air_traffic/by_the_numbers/.

Her Majestys' Government (HMG). 2013. "Good Business Implementing the UN Guiding Principles on Business and Human Rights" in September.

International Standards Organisation (ISO) 2014. Developing Standards: Deliverables. Accessed 1 October 2018 https://www.theatlantic.com/photo/2014/12/bhopal-the-worlds-worst-industrial-disaster-30-years-later/100864/

———. 2018. https://www.iso.org/deliverables-all.html#IS.

———. 2018. https://www.iso.org/management-system-standards.html.

———. 2018. https://www.iso.org/standards.html.

McMahon Kate and Dahdah Said. undated. *The True Cost of Road Crashes: Valuing Life and the cost of serious injury: IRAP.*

Moeckli, Daniel, Shah Sangeeta and Sivakumaran Sandesh. eds. 2014. *International Human Rights Law.* Oxford: Oxford University Press. p. 34.

OECD. 2012. *The Value of Statistical Life: A Meta-Analysis.* Working Party on National Environmental Policies *OECD.*

OHCHR. 2012. *Guiding Principles on Business and Human Rights: Implementing the United Nations "Protect, Respect and Remedy" Framework.* Geneva: Publishing Services United Nations.

Oxford Dictionary 2018. https://en.oxforddictionaries.com/definition/standard.

Raghu Aishwarya. 2018. Intern, Maldives Permanent Mission to the UN. 38th Human Right Session Geneva, *Advancing Access to Justice for All:* 25th June 2018.

Sen Amartya. 2017. *Collective Choice and Social Welfare.* London: Penguin Random House. p. 193.

Stiglitz, Joseph. 2013. *The Price of Inequality.* London: Penguin Books. p. 46.

———. 2012. 'The rise of state capitalism:' https://www.economist.com/node/21543160.

The Atlantic 2014. "Bhopal: The World's Worst Industrial Disaster, 30 Years Later," 24 December.

———. 2018. https://www.theatlantic.com/photo/2014/12/bhopal-the-worlds-worst-industrial-disaster-30-years-later/100864/.

The Institute for Economics and Peace. 2018. *The Economic Value* of *Peace 2016*: Sydney IEP.

UNIDO. 2012. *ISO 9001—Its relevance and impact in Asian Developing Economies: A survey covering quality management system development, certification, accreditation and economic benefits.* Vienna: UNIDO.

CHAPTER 13

Conclusion: Duty of the State to Protect—New Issues in the Post-COVID-19 Era

James Gomez and Robin Ramcharan

The duty of the State to protect human rights and regulate the behaviour of business organizations was the focal point of discussions at Asia Centre's International Conference on Business and Human Rights: Holding Governments Accountable (BHR Conference), held on 12 and 13 July 2018 in Bangkok. The focus on the duty of the State was deemed important as Asian countries increasingly considered the development of national action plans (NAPs) on BHR. Experts from around the world analysed the multifaceted linkages between business operations and international human rights norms but circled back to point to the duty of the State to protect. They highlighted policy and legislative challenges affecting the capacity of states to uphold such norms as stipulated in Pillar One of the UN Guiding Principles (UNGPs) on Business and Human Rights.

A number of key points emerge from the preceding chapters. (1) States need to uphold their duty to protect and to be accountable for any failure to do so, especially amidst a difficult rights situation in Asia; (2) Governments' duty to protect a key aspect of the UNGPs; (3) Governments

J. Gomez (✉) • R. Ramcharan
Asia Centre, Bangkok, Thailand
e-mail: james@asiacentre.org; robin@asiacentre.org

J. Gomez, R. Ramcharan (eds.), *Business and Human Rights in Asia*,
https://doi.org/10.1007/978-981-15-7273-9_13

have serious challenges in relation to holding business organisations accountable to human rights standards—ranging from lack of political will, to lack of domestic legislation and policies, to poor implementation of laws and policies and to balancing competing goals of national growth and development versus protecting rights; (4) The UN through the UNGPs continues its role as norm entrepreneur and has been instrumental in coaxing states to move towards the adoption of NAPS that adhere to international human rights norms; (5) Multiple avenues may be pursued by states, especially where the UNGPs and BHR agenda have not taken hold yet, as attested to by chapters on minimum wage policy in Myanmar and on legal reforms in Indonesia; (6) A core challenge of ensuring sovereignty over natural resources versus respecting the rights of indigenous peoples; (7) The challenge for States to uphold rights in an era when smart cities involve public and private partnerships that affect the full scope of a person or a community's life; (8) The regulation of companies in an era when consumers, who want security and material comforts supplied by the products and services of business organisations, also demand 'ethical behaviour' by such companies whose primary duty is to their shareholders; and (9) Failing a vigorous government role in ensuring corporate accountability, an HRMS as an integral part of a company's strategy, planning, operations and control, built on a valuation of human life, may be the way forward.

As Asia Centre pursues its exploration of BHR in Asia, a number of contemporary issues are noteworthy. First, the UN's norm entrepreneurship on BHR (Droubi 2016) has led the UN-HRC to start the process of negotiating a Treaty on Transnational Corporations and human rights. BHR advocate Hertanti Rachmi of Indonesia for Global governance hailed this as a "step closer to justice". (Rachmi, quoted in Transnational Institute 2018) It is instructive to highlight some of the issues raised in the HRC report on the first session of the intergovernmental working group on transnational corporations and other business enterprises with respect to human rights (UN Human Rights Council 2016)

- 23. A number of delegations noted that the Guiding Principles on Business and Human Rights did not get to the core of the discussion on maximum protection of human rights and access to remedies, and that a complementary international instrument was needed in order to strengthen national capabilities to ensure human rights protection in the domestic sphere. It was also highlighted by one delegation that transnational corporations and other business enterprises must conform to the values and principles of the United Nations. Several delegations reaffirmed that the principles of universality, indivisibility, participation, accountability and transparency should be applied. One delegation noted that many advances had been made in the area of business and human rights and that a new instrument would be a logical extension of that work. Another delegation considered that the priority was the implementation of the Guiding Principles rather than the development of a new international instrument

- 38. The panellist noted that a legally binding instrument may help to advance and strengthen human rights and to reaffirm the call for States to implement national action plans to address business and human rights. He also noted that, in its resolution 26/22, the Human Rights Council had invited the OHCHR to explore legal options for victims of human rights abuses, and that this had led to an accountability and remedy project.
- 40. One panellist explained that there were ways in which States and intergovernmental organizations could change the rules of the game by having policies that deter and refuse companies with bad human rights records. (p.9)

Second, the protection of indigenous peoples deserves greater attention, especially as mining and deforestation for commercial gain impacts their very survival. In this regard Storey has noted in this book the challenge of achieving a balance between the sovereign 'right to development' and indigenous peoples' rights, including their right to prior informed consent. In the most advanced NAP development process in Southeast Asia, Thailand's NAP, the absence of any provisions on indigenous peoples has been noted as well as the lack of consultation with affected communities. (Manushya 2019) The same scrutiny must be applied to the forthcoming Indonesian NAP, which was due to be announced in December 2019. (National Actions on Business and Human Rights 2019)

Third, the idea that corporations have human rights and that they can profit from it has arisen. (Khoury and Whyte 2017a, b; Emberland 2006). The contours of this discussion are as follows:

- There is a highly controversial principle in human rights law that allows corporations and other "legal persons" to apply for the same protections as real persons at human rights courts.

- But corporations cannot be held accountable for human rights violations. So, while corporations can be protected by human rights law, they can at the same time enjoy impunity for committing human rights violations.
- In its final version, Article 1 of Protocol 1 [of the European Convention] reads: "Every natural or *legal* person is entitled to the peaceful enjoyment of his possessions" (italics added). The inclusion of "legal persons" in Protocol 1 has had a significant impact on the concept of rights in Europe and proved to be a watershed for the endorsement of the principle that corporations can be entitled to human rights protections.

Judicial precedent has accompanied this development. Marius Emberland has written in his book *The Human Rights of Companies*, of 3307 judgments delivered in the European Court of Human Rights between 1998–2003, 126 (or 3.8%) originated in applications filed by companies or other persons pursuing corporate interests. (Emberland 2006). He notes further, that:

> Both the Inter-American and European jurisdictions consider shareholders' interests to be pre-eminent—either upheld directly as individual shareholders' rights, or vicariously as "corporate rights". This raises an unsolvable contradiction—shareholders are rights-holders without having any corresponding responsibility for the potential human rights violations committed by the company in which they have invested. (Ibid.)

In other words, in human rights law, as Canadian law professor Harry Glasbeek observes: "[Shareholders] have no responsibility for what is done, to whom or to what injury is done. They are legally immune and socially irresponsible." A similar situation may exist in the United States where Adam Winkler of the Huffington Post reported that "corporations Are People, And They Have More Rights Than You". (Winkler 2014; see also Torres-Spelliscy 2019)

This situation is reminiscent of the early stages of the development of a UN Code of Conduct for Transnational Corporations in the 1970s, when the Global North group of rich countries sought protections against losses by their corporations in their demand for a "treatment standard". This "treatment standard" was to give their transnational corporations (TNCs) the right to protection from discriminatory or other potentially damaging treatment by host states.

A fundamental assumption—that corporations have a “right” to development and therefore a “right” to profit—can be found in the debate going on today at the UN Human Rights Council. As it develops its new treaty standard on business and human rights, the UN Human Rights Council should address some profound contradictions. Is it acceptable to human persons that corporations can use human rights courts to pursue decisions that ultimately enhance the profitability of business rather than human dignity, freedom or equality? What is the point of human rights law if not to protect humans? (Emberland 2006)

Fourth, BHR advocates must pay attention to the issue of a parallel legal regime that allows corporations to escape attention. (Hamby 2016) This refers to investor-state dispute settlement, or ISDS. Such a legal system is already found in a vast network of treaties that set the rules for international trade and investment. Hamby notes that this is a powerful and secretive regime that is kept from public scrutiny. The most “deeply hidden” aspects are the threats, uttered in private meetings or ominous letters, that invoke those courts [ISDs]. The threats are so powerful they often eliminate the need to actually bring a lawsuit. Just the knowledge that it could happen is enough.” (Hamby 2016: 5)

Sixth, the business case for access to justice is being considered. The OECD has asked, is there a business case to be made for ensuring better human rights adherence by corporations? (OECD C.2019) It noted that “...its costs can be conservatively estimated in a range going from 0.5 to 3% of GDP in most countries” surveyed by the OECD. Its suggestion is to move towards alignment with SDG 16 in that regard, it noted.

- In September 2015, the General Assembly of the United Nations adopted, as part of the 2030 Agenda for Sustainable Development, a goal referring to universal access to justice.
- Sustainable Development Goal 16: Promote peaceful and inclusive societies for sustainable development, provide access to justice for all and build effective, accountable and inclusive institutions at all levels.
- One of the four targets under SDG 16 is devoted to “promot(ing) the rule of law at the national and international levels and ensur(ing) equal access to justice for all” (Target 16.3).

- Ensuring that every individual has the practical capacity and means to enforce his or her rights is therefore a fundamental duty for all States and has intrinsic value. (p.5)

Seventh, an ongoing discussion concerns the need to pay attention to governments holding shareholders responsible. Glasbeek has noted that the major shareholders must be personally responsible for the misdeeds of the corporation. Only then will there pressure be generated to change the conduct of the corporation. He notes, in the case of Canada, that few or none of the significant instances of wrongdoing—from tobacco to asbestos to negligently manufactured cars, tires, poisonous chemicals, etc.—have led to a single shareholder being held criminally responsible. Moreover, they are seldom made to account fiscally for the profits they made at the expense of broken bodies, spoiled environments, bankrupted communities, etc. No shareholder had been asked to return monies made as a result of asbestos or tobacco poisonings. At worst, he notes, shareholders may lose part of their investment as share values become depressed. However, absent are consequences as stigmatization, incarceration, punitive treatment for profiteering from stolen goods. (Glasbeek 2005)

Finally, the impact of the COVID-19 crisis on the implementation of UNGPs in Asia needs to be analysed. The World Health Organisation (WHO) has called upon governments and businesses to take action to protect the health of workers. (WHO 2020) In this regard, the International Federation for Human Rights (FIDH) lamented in April 2020, a number of abuses: employers in the mining sector forcing their employees to work as the crisis raged, the inability of garment workers to take sick leave, continued crowded work conditions and violations of labour laws. These global trends were also present across Asia (FIDH 2020) The UN Human Rights High Commissioner called upon states to halt rises in inequality by taking measures to prevent greater unemployment (United Nations 2020). In regard to the latter, the International Labour Organisation (ILO) has estimated that up to 25 million people could lose their jobs worldwide. Unemployment and underemployment will lead to large income losses. Working poverty is expected to rise. (ILO 2020). Oxfam has warned that the crisis could push over half a billion into poverty and called on governments to prevent this potential outcome by, inter alia, ensuring that "bailouts of big corporations should be conditional on measures to uphold the interests of workers, farmers and taxpayers and to build a sustainable future." (Oxfam 2020)

Governments are naturally called upon to mitigate the harmful effects of the COVID-19 crisis by assisting business entities to undertake human rights due diligence. The International Federation has commented on government actions thus far:

> a model based on self-regulation, voluntary commitments or soft law instruments is simply not robust enough to protect fundamental rights. The time has come for governments to accelerate the implementation of binding domestic and international norms, which would turn human rights due diligence into a set of legal obligations, while ensuring liability for corporate abuses in third countries. (FIDH 2020)

These are strands of the BHR discussion that Asia Centre will explore in relation to BHR in Asia through its Human Rights Programme and advocacy initiatives. This programme includes investigations of the regional human rights architecture, such as Asia Centre's work on The Universal Periodic Review of Southeast Asia: Civil Society Perspectives (Gomez and Ramcharan 2018) and National Human Rights Institutions in Southeast Asia: Selected Case Studies (Gomez and Ramcharan 2020) and ongoing work on the ASEAN Intergovernmental Commission on Human Rights and civil society. The Centre is currently engaged in a four-year exploration of freedom of expression in the context of governmental responses to the dramatic increase of fake news, disinformation and related hate speech, that have limited fundamental freedoms. The programme also examines topical rights issues such as the impact of geopolitics on human rights standards in Southeast Asia, freedom of religion or belief, and the impact of COVID-19 on democracy and human rights. BHR issues are expected to be very much part of these discussions.

References

Droubi, Sufyan (2016) "Transnational Corporations and International Human Rights Law," Notre Dame Journal of International & Comparative Law: Vol. 6: Iss. 1, Article 9. Available at: http://scholarship.law.nd.edu/ndjicl/vol6/iss1/9.

Emberland, Marius (2006) *The Human Rights of Companies: Exploring the Structure of ECHR Protection*. Oxford: Oxford University Press.

FIDH (2020), Don't wash your hands of human rights obligations—Corporate due diligence in times of COVID-19 and lessons for the future, 17 April.

Available: https://www.fidh.org/en/issues/globalisation-human-rights/don-t-wash-your-hands-of-human-rights-obligations-corporate-due.

Glasbeek, Harry (2005) War on Shareholders," *Canadian Dimension*, Vol. 39, No. VOLUME 39, NUMBER 5: September/October 2005. https://canadiandimension.com/articles/view/war-on-shareholders-harry-glasbeek.

Hamby, David (2016) The Secret Threat That Makes Corporations More Powerful Than Countries https://www.buzzfeednews.com/article/chrishamby/the-billion-dollar-ultimatum.

Gomez, James and Ramcharan, Robin (2018) The Universal Periodic Review of Southeast Asia: Civil Society Perspectives.

Gomez, James and Ramcharan, Robin (2020) National Human Rights Institutions in Southeast Asia: Selected Case Studies. Palgrave Macmillan.

ILO (2020). Almost 25 million jobs could be lost worldwide as a result of COVID-19, says ILO, Press Release, 18 March. Available: https://www.ilo.org/global/about-the-ilo/newsroom/news/WCMS_738742/lang%2D%2Den/index.htm.

Khoury, Stefanie and Whyte, David (2017a), How human rights law has been used to guarantee corporations a 'right to profit', The Conversation, 16 March.

Khoury, Stefanie and Whyte, David (2017b) *Corporate Human Rights Violations: Global Prospects for Legal Action*, New York and Oxon: Routledge.

Manusha and ThaiBHR Network (2019) Summary Of Joint Comments On The Final Draft National Action Plan On Business And Human Rights In Thailand (NAP-BHR). 27 June https://docs.wixstatic.com/ugd/a0db76_0a0709e4800e4691abc8eed264bb61af.pdf.

National Action Plans on Business and Human Rights (2019) Indonesia. https://globalnaps.org/country/indonesia/.

Oxfam (2020) Dignity not destitution: An 'Economic Rescue Plan For All' to tackle the Coronavirus crisis and rebuild a more equal world. 9 April. Available: https://oxfamilibrary.openrepository.com/bitstream/handle/10546/620976/mb-dignity%20not%20destitution-an-economic-rescue-plan-for-all-090420-en.pdf.

Transnational Institute (2018) A step closer to justice for those affected by transnational corporations' activities," 16 March. https://www.tni.org/en/article/a-step-closer-to-justice-for-those-affected-by-transnational-corporations-activities.

OECD (C.2019) (Building a Business Case for Access to Justice: An OECD White Paper in collaboration with the World Justice Project. Preliminary Draft.

UN Human Rights Council (2016) Report on the first session of the open-ended intergovernmental working group on transnational corporations and other business enterprises with respect to human rights, with the mandate of elaborating an international legally binding instrument, A/HRC/31/50, 5 February 2016. http://igj.or.id/wp-content/uploads/2016/12/Report-First-session-A.HRC_.31.50_E.pdf.

Torres-Spelliscy, Ciara (2019) "Does "We the People" Include Corporations?" American Bar Association. Accessed 1 September. https://www.americanbar.org/groups/crsj/publications/human_rights_magazine_home/we-the-people/we-the-people-corporations/.

United Nations (2020) Protecting Human Rights Amid COVID-19, Department of Global Communications. Available: https://www.un.org/en/un-coronavirus-communications-team/protecting-human-rights-amid-covid-19-crisis.

Winkler, Adam (2014) "Corporations Are People, And They Have More Rights Than You," Huffington Post, 30 August. Available: https://www.huffpost.com/entry/corporations-are-people-a_b_5543833.

WHO (2020), ICC-WHO Joint Statement: An unprecedented private sector call to action to tackle COVID-19, 16 March. Available: https://www.who.int/news-room/detail/16-03-2020-icc-who-joint-statement-an-unprecedented-private-sector-call-to-action-to-tackle-covid-19.

Index[1]

[1] Note: Page numbers followed by 'n' refer to notes.

J. Gomez, R. Ramcharan (eds.), *Business and Human Rights in Asia*,
https://doi.org/10.1007/978-981-15-7273-9

The manufacturer's authorised representative in the EU is Springer Nature Customer Service Centre GmbH, Europaplatz 3, 69115 Heidelberg, Germany. If you have any concerns regarding our products, please contact ProductSafety@springernature.com

Printed and bound by CPI Group (UK) Ltd, Croydon, CR0 4YY
30/09/2026
02225457-0013